7 -

D1562740

BRIEF AND TO THE POINT

BRIEF
AND TO THE POINT

Suggestions for Preachers

by

ARTHUR E. DALTON

Foreword by
THE REV. WILLIAM BARCLAY, D.D.
The University of Glasgow

JAMES CLARKE & CO. LTD.
Cambridge & London

First published 1961
SECOND IMPRESSION 1970
THIRD IMPRESSION 1973

To my Wife

ISBN 0 227 67419 7

Foreword

As soon as I saw Mr. Dalton's book I knew that it would be of the very greatest use in far more than one field.

It is obviously of great use to the preacher. It does not tell him what to preach in the sense of writing his sermon for him, but it does give him sparks to set his own thought alight, and it does give him seeds out of which he can make the harvest of many a sermon. I have not the slightest doubt that to the preacher this will be a most useful book.

The book will also be of extreme use to the teacher. It will tell the teacher time and time again what he ought to concentrate on in any passage which he is trying to teach either to adults or to children. This book will provide the teacher again and again with the structure or skeleton of many a lesson.

But this book has a still wider use. It will be useful to the preacher and it will be useful to the teacher, but it will be of at least equal use to the private student of the Bible. Again and again when faced with a passage of Scripture the private student of the Bible hardly knows what to do with it. This book will tell him what to look for. It will tell him what any passage says to him. It will tell him what any passage wishes him to do. This book will have very great value for the private student in telling him both the meaning, the significance and the relevance of the Word of God.

I could wish that this book could get into the hands of every preacher, every teacher and every student of the Bible. It will do very great work in elucidating the meaning of Scripture and in making study easier and more profitable.

WILLIAM BARCLAY

Preface

This is not a book about preaching but it is intended for preachers, both ministerial and lay. It is submitted to my younger brethren more particularly in the hope they will welcome these suggestions and find them serviceable as an encouragement to the regular and systematic presentation of the Word of God.

It has not been my intention, in preparing these studies, to be so bold as to attempt to do another man's thinking for him. I have merely tried to suggest starting points for the preparation of messages growing out of the Scriptures and I trust this consideration will be remembered.

When this work was begun a few years ago, it was very far from my mind to undertake the study of the whole Bible along these lines but the Publishers, to whom I am very much indebted, showed great interest and prompted its completion.

It remains for me to add that I have received many courtesies and constant encouragement from the Rev. William Barclay, D.D. of the University of Glasgow, and to him my warmest thanks are due.

A.E.D.

Contents

OLD TESTAMENT

Genesis

1: 1
1. God is Personal.
2. God has a Purpose.
3. God has a Pattern.

1: 3–5
1. When God speaks there is Illumination
2. When God looks there is Inspiration.
3. When God divides there is Instruction.

1: 6–8
1. Compassion in Creation. (*v. 6*).
2. Comfort in Crisis (*v. 7*).
3. Country of our Confidence (*v. 8*).

1: 9–12
1. A Pattern is decided upon (*v. 9*).
2. A Programme is drawn up (*v. 10*).
3. Provision is dedicated (*v. 11–12*).

1: 17–18
1. Divine Establishment.
2. Divine Enlightenment.
3. Divine Enterprise.

1: 20–31
1. When God calls He provides.
2. When God creates He has a Purpose.
3. When God considers He is pleased.

1: 26a, 27
1. Man made according to Divine Pattern.
2. Man made for Divine Partnership.
3. Man made for Divine Privilege.

2: 15–16 3:6. 7: 15
1. Mankind receives its orders —Responsibility.
2. Man is called to obedience —Righteousness.
3. Man commits his first offence —Rebellion.
4. Man ordained to overcome sin —Reconciliation.

3: 22–24
1. The Self-Importance of man.
2. The Severity of God.
3. The Service man must render.
4. The Secret man must respect.

4: 5, 6, 10, 15
1. A Jealous disposition (*v. 5*).
2. A Joyless countenance (*v. 6*).
3. A Judgement declared (*v. 10*).
4. Justice proclaimed (*v. 15*).

4: 16
GOD OVERRULES THE WRATH OF MAN TO HIS PRAISE.
1. Cain—banished from Fellowship with God.
   Built a city for his Family.
   Became Forerunner of Invention.

4: 26 (end)
1. Our Worship has an ancient Record.
2. Our Worship is our Response to God's Revelation.
3. Our Worship is an acknowledgement of God's Redemption.

1

6: 5–8
1. An assurance that God cares.
2. An affliction that God shares.
3. An attitude that God dares.
4. An action that God declares.

6: 14, 18, 21, 22
1. God provides for man's Salvation (v. 14).
2. God proclaims his plan for man's Salvation (v. 18).
3. God pronounces preparations for man's Salvation (v. 21).
4. God's purpose prospers in faithful Noah (v. 22).

7: 1
1. A family divinely accepted.
2. A family divinely appointed.
3. A family divinely approved.

7: 16 (end)
'and the Lord shut him in'
1. There's a reason for it.
2. There's Redemption in it.
3. There are Resources for it.

8: 1, 15; 9: 1
1. Divine Remembrance (v. 1).
2. Divine Requirement (v. 15).
3. Divine Reward (v. 1).

8: 22
1. A Promise made.
2. The Provision referred to.
3. The Power implied.

9: 14–15
1. Some sorrows are of God's appointment (v. 14a).
2. Some sorrows are common to us all (v. 14b).
3. Some sorrows are big with Mercy (v. 15).

10: 32
1. A common Origin—Birth.
2. A common Order—Humanity.
3. A common Obedience—Reverence.

11: 4–8
1. The Spirit of the Pioneer and the Spirit of Pride (v. 4a).
2. The Praise of God or the Praise of Men (v. 4b).
3. The Providence of God and the Poverty of Man (v. 8).

12: 1, 2, 4, 7–9
1. The Order (v. 1).
2. The Opportunity (v. 2–3).
3. The Obedience (v. 4).
4. The Offering (v. 7).

13: 5. 6. 11, 14, 15
1. Prosperity brings its Problems.
2. Choice reveals Character.
3. Renunciation receives its Reward.

14: 18–20
1. The sudden appearance of M.
2. The sympathetic approach of M.
3. The sacred appointment of M.
4. The symbolic action of M.

15: 5–6
1. The Challenge to A's Faith.
2. The Contrast concerning the Future.
3. The Character of A's Faith.

15: 17
THREE SOURCES OF ILLUMINATION.
1. Sun—everywhere sometimes.
2. Man made—limited in usefulness.
3. Supernatural—everywhere always.

17: 1b
1. The Declaration—*'I am'*.
2. The Demand—*'Walk'*.
3. The Destination—*'be thou'*.

17: 2–3
1. The Promise is made.
2. The Prayer is offered.
3. The Privilege is known.

18: 2–8

1. Heartfelt sincerity with which he welcomed them.
2. Humility with which he addressed them.
3. Hospitality he extended to them.

18: 23, 25, 32 (end)

1. The enterprise of Abraham—'*drew near and said*'.
2. The Enquiry of Abraham—'*wilt thou*'.
3. The Enlightened Conviction of Abraham (Enlightenment)—'*Shall not the Lord*'.
4. The Encouragement of Abraham—'*I will not destroy*'.

20: 9–11, 14–15

1. The Accusation—'*What*'.
2. The Admonition—'*Then*'.
3. The Answer—'*because I thought*'.
4. The Amendment—'*and Abimelech*'.

21: 1

1. The Invisible at work—'*the Lord*'.
2. The Incredible happens—'*visited Sarah*'.
3. The Inheritance is assured—'*did unto Sarah*' etc.

21: 11–12

1. The struggle of the Pioneer—'*very grievous*'.
2. The Solution is prepared—'*Let it not be*'.
3. The succession is Promised—'*for in Isaac*'.

21: 17d

1. A voice that cries.
2. A Victim of circumstances.
3. A Victory is confirmed.

21: 19

1. Vision is granted—'*God opened*'.
2. Provision is found—'*a well of water*'.
3. Preservation is ensured—'*gave the lad*'.

22: 1–17

1. The call addressed to Abraham.
2. The Courage revealed by A.
3. The Compassion shown by A.
4. The Consolation of A.

26: 18–19

1. First things first.
2. First things founded in the Past.
3. First things fouled in the Past.
4. First things faithful to the Past.
5. First things following out of the Past.

27: 8, 20–21, 22–41

1. Determination of a troubled Mother (*See v. 26–35*)
2. Dismay of a Tired Father (*v. 20–21*).
3. Dishonesty of a Timid Son (*v. 22*).
4. Distress of a Tempted Brother (*v. 41*).

28: 15

1. Divine Partnership is announced.
2. Divine Protection is asserted.
3. Divine Promise is made.
4. Divine Purpose is declared.

28: 12

1. Was Conscience at work?
2. Was Character asserting itself?
3. Was there Comfort in the dream?

28: 16–18

1. The Awakening from Darkness.
2. The Awe-inspiring discovery.
3. The Action following decision.

28: 20; Job 13: 15; John 12: 32

1. '*If God ... I will give*'—Jacob's Bargain.
2. '*Though He slay me*'—Job's Boldness.
3. '*And, I, if I be lifted up*'—Jesus' Blessing.

29: 17, 30, 31, 35b; 30: 22

1. The Contrast in Appearance. (*v. 17*).
2. The Conflict in Affections. (*v. 30*).
3. The Consolation in Afflictions (*v. 31, 35b*).
4. The Compassion that Amazes (*v. 30, 32*).

31: 24, 42; 32: 1

1. Dishonesty makes for Disharmony.
2. Disappointment makes for Distress.
3. Diligence makes for Discovery.

32: 26, 29

1. Salvation is not earned (v. 26b).
2. Salvation does not depend upon knowledge (v. 29).
3. Salvation is God's free Gift (v. 29b).

25: 29; 27: 23; 33: 4

1. Esau—cheated of his Birthright.
2.   cheated of his Blessing.
3.   charitable toward his Brother.

35: 8 (24: 59)

'But Deborah died'

1. Unknown but not unimportant.
2. Unsung but not uninspiring.
3. Unhonoured but not without honour.

37: 2

JOSEPH—'The man God uses'.

1. As a son he is spoilt—unpopular.
2. As a worker he is a tale-bearer —detested.
3. As a brother he is proud—unwelcome.
4. As a man he is completely different.

37: 33–35

1. Recognition of cherished possession —SIN.
2. Remorse for cherished person—SELF.
3. Refusal of Children's profferred help —SALVATION.

39: 1, 2, 9

JOSEPH.

1. A bad beginning—Spoilt.
2. A bad bargain—Sold.
3. A big blessing—Successful.
4. A bold Burden-Bearer—Steadfast.

37: 28; 39: 20; 41: 52

JOSEPH.

1. Born to Favour but Banished.
2. Brilliant Favourite but Banished again.
3. Bold and Fearless but Benevolent.

37: 2; 39: 8; 41: 52

JOSEPH.

1. Young and on Trial.
2. Young and Tempted.
3. Young but Triumphant.

41: 29, 34–35, 56

JOSEPH.

1. He had prophesied (v. 29).
2. He had prepared (v. 34–5).
3. He now provided (v. 56).

42: 35

1. Salvation is Free.
2. Salvation is Full.
3. Salvation is for all.

43: 1, 2, 8–10, 14

1. Emergency—Famine.
2. Enterprise—Fatherly Concern.
3. Enthusiasm—Family Compact.
4. Endowment—Father's Prayer.

43: 16, 18, 23, 30

1. Identification (v. 16).
2. Invitation (v. 16).
3. Imagination (v. 18).
4. Inspiration (v. 23).
5. Insufficiency (v. 30).

45: 3b, 4, 5

1. Conscience accuses them.
2. Challenge awakens them.
3. Comfort awaits them.
4. Conclusion assures them.

45: 9, 10, 11

1. Providence is acknowledged.
2. Poverty is threatening.
3. Provision is promised.

45: 1a

1. God overrules men's Intentions.
2. God oversees men's Integrity.
3. God overcomes men's Inefficiency.

45: 20

1. Rely not on our own Possessions.
2. Rely not on our own Powers.
3. Rely on God's bounteous Provision

45: 26b, 27b, 28

1. It is hard to believe in God.
2. It is harder not to believe in God.
3. It is hardest of all to have no one in whom to believe.

46: 2, 3

1. Encounter (*v. 2*).
2. Enabling (*v. 3a*).
3. Encouragement (*v. 3b*).
4. Enterprise (*v. 3c*).

47: 18, 19

1. Honesty towards God.
2. Helplessness before God.
3. Hopefulness in God.

47: 11-12

1. The Place allotted them.
2. The Provision made for them.
3. The Principle applied to them.

47: 15

1. When Poverty was at the door.
2. When Priority was bread for the poor.
3. When Plenty was there, inside the door.

47: 25

1. A Grateful Acknowledgement— SAVED.
2. A Graceful Request—SATISFIED.
3. A Generous Promise—SERVICE.

48: 15-16

1. God, Source of Faith in the Past.
2. God, Source of Faithfulness in the Present.
3. God, Source of Fruitfulness in the Future.

49: 26

1. Separate by Distance.
2. Separate by Destiny.
3. Separate by Divine Decision.

50: 15-21

1. Force of Circumstances—Departure.
2. Fear of Consequences—Dismay.
3. Faults are Confessed—Duty.
4. Frailty is Confessed—Dignity.
5. Forgiveness is Claimed—Declaration.

Exodus

1: 5–7
1. A Family with a Mission.
2. A Faith with a Message.
3. Fellow-labourers with a Master.

1: 8–14
1. A New Deal.
2. A New Devilry.
3. A New Diligence.

1: 15–22
1. The Order issued.
2. The Obedience given.
3. The Obedience refused.
4. The Outcome.

2: 1–10
1. Chosen of God.
2. Cherished by Mother.
3. Covenant entered into.
4. Care bestowed.

2: 11–14
1. The Unknown Spectator.
2. The Unwelcome Spectator.
3. The Unsuspecting Spectator.

2: 16–22
1. The Runaway.
2. The Romance.
3. The Reason.

2: 23–25
1. The Training of the People.
2. The Trustworthiness of God.
3. The Thoughtfulness of God.

3: 1–6
1. The Discipline.
2. The Discovery.
3. The Description.
4. The Declaration.
5. The Desolation.

3: 7–10
1. A Declaration of Concern.
2. A Declaration of Campaign.
3. A Declaration of Commission.

3: 11–12
1. His Dismay.
2. His Distinction.
3. His Dedication.

3: 13–15
1. His Uncertainty about his Authority.
2. The Unveiling of his Authority
3. The Universal nature of his Authority.

3: 16
1. The Lord of all Ages.
2. The Lord of all Activities.
3. The Lord of all Authority.

3: 19–21
1. The Promise.
2. The Protection.
3. The Provision.

4: 1–5, 10, 14
1. Uncertain of his own Authority.
2. Uncertain of God's ability.
3. Unwilling to co-operate with God.
4. Unexpectedly, he co-operates with his Brother.

4: 17
1. A Symbol of Authority.
2. A Symbol of Obedience.
3. A Symbol of Ability.

4: 21–23
1. The Direction given.
2. The Discipline imposed.
3. The Dedication declared.

4: 24–26
1. A Time of Testing.
2. A Tribute to Tradition.
3. A Truth to Testify.

4: 27–31
1. An order given.
2. An Obedience given.
3. An Operation begun.
4. An Offering is made.

5: 1–3
1. The Command.
2. The Curiosity.
3. The Conviction.

5: 6–9, 22, 23
1. The Will of God is frustrated.
2. Their Witness to God—a seeming failure.
3. The Work of God, a failure, too?

6: 1–6
1. The Enlightening Word of God.
2. The Encouraging Word of God.
3. The Everlasting Word of God.
4. The Ever-present Word of God.

6: 6–7
1. A Glorious Presence.
2. A Glorious Promise.
3. A Glorious Privilege.
4. A Glorious Possession.

6: 9–13
1. Disappointment.
2. Dismay.
3. Distress.
4. Determination.

7: 3, 6–13
1. Frustration to Faith.
2. Partnership in Purpose.
3. Encouragement in Enterprise.

7: 14, 17; 8: 1
1. When God permits.
2. What God promises.
3. When God perseveres.

8: 1, 5, 15
1. The Training continues.
2. The Terror continues.
3. The Test continues.

8: 19
1. Lord of all His creation.
2. Lord of all His creatures.
3. Lord of all His children.

8: 22, 27, 30
1. Come ye apart.
2. Be ye separate.
3. Turn ye unto Me.

9: 35–10: 3
1. Unappreciative of Opportunity.
2. Unwearying in Obedience.
3. Unafraid of Opposition.

10: 7, 9, 11
1. Discussion.
2. Decision.
3. Dedication.

10: 19–23
1. Forgiven but not Forgiving.
2. Frustrated but still Fighting.
3. Fogbound but Faithful.

10: 25–29
1. His Resolve.
2. The Lord's Requirements.
3. His Readiness.
4. His Rebuke.

11: 6–8
1. Panic among unbelievers.
2. Preservation of believers.
3. Proclamation to all.

12: 1, 2, 12, 17

1. A New Beginning with God.
2. A New Bondage with God.
3. A New Blessing from God.

12: 21–28

1. The Sacrifice.
2. The Safeguards.
3. The Service.
4. The Salvation.

12: 30–32

1. The Beaten Monarch.
2. The Beckoning Monarch.
3. The Blessing sought.

12: 40–42

1. The Detention.
2. The Deliverance.
3. The Duty.

13: 17–18

1. Unfettered at last.
2. Unlettered in war.
3. Undertaking before them.
4. Undergirding they would know.

13: 17–18

1. Departure at last.
2. Discipline to continue.
3. Direction will be given them.

13: 21–22

1. The Guidance they needed.
2. The Guidance they received.
3. The Guidance that remained.

14: 10–14

1. The Meeting.
2. The Murmuring.
3. The Miracle.

14: 13

1. Belief.
2. Behaviour.
3. Beholding.

14: 15

1. The Temptation to look back.
2. The Time to look up.
3. The Task—to look forward.

14: 23, 27, 31

1. The Interruption.
2. The Intervention.
3. The Intention.

15: 9–12

1. A Great Boast.
2. A Gentle Breath.
3. A Glorious Beginning.

15: 16–17

1. Brought out from Bondage.
2. Bought with a Price.
3. Brought in to Blessing.

15: 22–26

1. Deliverance.
2. Discipline.
3. Disappointment.
4. Discovery.
5. Dedication.

15: 27

1. Rejoicing or Shade.
2. Refreshment or Satisfaction.
3. Riches or Security.

16: 2–7

1. They begin to Grumble.
2. They are promised Grace.
3. They will behold the Glory.

16: 3–8

1. The Murmurings of the Multitude.
2. The Modesty of Leadership (Moses).
3. The Miracle of God's Provision.

16: 18

1. The Standard.
2. The Satisfaction.
3. The Sanity.

16: 25–27

1. Dedication.
2. Disobedience.
3. Disappointment.

16: 31

1. Sweet.
2. Strengthening.
3. Satisfying.

16: 32–3
1. The Record.
2. The Remembrance.
3. The Redemption.

17: 1–7
1. They ask for Essentials.
2. They are not yet Established.
3. They are set an Example.
4. They share an Experience.

17: 8–13
1. The Prayer.
2. The Partnership in Prayer.
3. The Prevailing Prayer.

18: 17–26
1. A Wholesome Intervention.
2. A happy Inspiration.
3. A Holy Institution.

19: 3–4
1. Symbol of Salvation.
2. Symbol of Support.
3. Symbol of Shelter.

19: 5–6
1. The Call.
2. The Conditions.
3. The Consequence.
4. The Consecration.

19: 7–9
1. The Message of God.
2. The Miracle.
3. The Majesty of God.

19: 10–17
1. A Waiting Community.
2. A Watchful Community.
3. A Witnessing Community.

19: 21–24
1. The Multitude.
2. The Ministry.
3. The Mystics.

20: 1–2
1. The Introduction.
2. The Inspiration.
3. The Intervention.

20: 3
1. Must man worship at all?
2. Must man worship one God?
3. Must man worship one God only?

20: 4–5
1. Reality is Spiritual.
2. Real Religion is Spiritual.
3. Real Reverence is Spiritual.

20: 7
1. Profanity not to be encouraged.
2. Promises not to be broken.
3. Perjury not to be encouraged.
4. Pardon not to be assumed.

20: 8–11
1. An honoured Custom.
2. A helpful Custom.
3. A harmless Custom.

20: 12
1. Family life demands it.
2. National life depends upon it.
3. Future life will justify it.

20: 13, 14, 16
1. Destruction of human life condemned.
2. Destruction of home life condemned.
3. Destruction of an honest name condemned.

20: 15
1. Dishonesty in speech condemned.
2. Dishonesty of Spirit condemned.
3. Dishonesty in Service condemned.

20: 17
1. Covetousness is undesirable.
2. Covetousness is unworthy.
3. Covetousness is unsocial.

20: 18–20
1. The Revelation evokes Reverence.
2. The Revelation evokes Repentance.
3. The Revelation evokes Righteousness.

B

20: 21
1. Fear of God shown by Multitudes.
2. Faith in God shown by Moses.
3. Fact of God shrouded in Mystery.

20: 22–26
1. His Word is made known.
2. His Will is made known.
3. His Worship is made plain.

23: 1–3
1. Be sure of your Facts.
2. Be sure you keep Faith.
3. Be sure whom you Follow.
4. Be sure your judgement is Fearless.

23: 9
1. An Example we can all set.
2. An Experience we all know.
3. An Experiment we can all make.

23: 20
1. The Promise of Guidance.
2. The Promise of Protection.
3. The Promise of Performance.

23: 30
1. Life's little disciplines.
2. Life's little disappointments.
3. Life's little delays.
4. Life's large dividends.

23: 31–33
1. The future is His.
2. The Faith is in Him.
3. The Fight is on.

24: 1, 6, 8
1. A Partnership begun.
2. A Promise made.
3. A Partnership confirmed.
   or
1. The Call.
2. The Covenant.
3. The Confirmation.

24: 9–11
1. The Obedience they rendered.
2. The Ordeal they shared.
3. The Occasion they celebrated.

24: 12
The Moral Law:
1. Not of man but of God.
2. Not a discovery but a disclosure.
3. Not only true but to be taught.

25: 1–9
1. The Revelation.
2. The Response.
3. The Requirement.

25: 10–11
1. The Symbol of the Majesty of God.
2. The Symbol of the Moral Law of God.
3. The Symbol of the Most man has to offer.

25: 16
1. Revealed Guidance of God.
2. Received Guidance of God.
3. Recorded Guidance of God.

25: 17, 20, 22
1. The Majesty of God.
2. The Mystery of God.
3. The Mercy of God.

25: 10, 30, 31; 26: 1
1. The Ark—The Presence.
2. The Table—The Praise.
3. The Candlestick—The Prayers.
4. The Curtains—The Partition, *or* The Purpose.

28: 36–38
1. A Royal Claim.
2. A Responsible Charge.
3. A Reasonable Concern.

29: 14
1. A Prophecy of the Passion of our Lord.
2. A Prophecy of the People for whom He died.
3. A Prophecy of the Pattern of our Salvation.

29: 46
1. The sober Certainty.
2. The safe Conduct.
3. The sure Covenant.

30: 10
1. Then, once a year.
2. Then, once every year.
3. Now, once for all, for ever.

31: 3
1. All knowledge is from God.
2. All knowledge is of God.
3. All knowledge is for God.

31: 16–17
1. Divine Command.
2. Divine Covenant.
3. Divine Counsel.

32: 1–5, 11–14
1. An Ancient Failure.
2. A Modern Folly.
3. A Great Fear.
4. A Wonderful Faith.

32: 26
1. The Challenge to think.
2. The Choice they must make.
3. The Call to be separate.

32: 27–29
1. SIN disrupts.
2. SIN destroys.
3. SIN demands Decision.

32: 30–32
1. The Accusation.
2. The Atonement.
3. The Advocacy.

32: 33–35
1. Rebellion.
2. Reconciliation.
3. Retribution.

33: 1–6
1. Programme to be continued.
2. Promise to be kept.
3. Pride to be acknowledged.

33: 7–11
1. The Place of Meeting.
2. The Preparation for the Meeting.
3. The Personal nature of the Meeting.

33: 12b–13
1. Divinely chosen.
2. Divinely cherished.
3. Divinely charged.

33: 14–16
1. Guidance will be given.
2. Goal will be realised.
3. Glory that will be known.

33: 18–23
1. The Request.
2. The Response.
3. The Restraint.
4. The Result.

34: 1, 2, 10
1. The Second Chance.
2. The Second Challenge.
3. The Second Covenant.

34: 5–7
1. The Majesty.
2. The Meeting.
3. The Meaning.
4. The Mercy.

34: 10–11
1. The Initiative is of God.
2. The Inspiration is of God.
3. The Instruction is of God.

34: 29–31
1. The Glory he had known.
2. The Glow he did not know.
3. The Grace he shared.

40: 25
1. The Lamp of Truth.
2. The Lamp of Testimony.
3. The Lamp of Tribute.

40: 34–38
1. There is a Limit to our Knowledge.
2. There is a Limit to our Experience.
3. There is a Light that is sometimes withheld.
4. There is a Love that is Freely Given.

Leviticus

1: 1–17
1. Do we worship because we are free?
2. Do we worship in faith?
3. Do we worship for the sake of the fellowship?
4. Do we worship with the finest gifts we have to offer?

2: 1–16
1. Does our worship involve preparation?
2. Does our worship cost us anything?
3. Does our worship mean anything to us?

3: 1–17
1. The value of our communion with God.
2. The vow to commune with God.
3. The vision that comes from communion with God.

4: 1–35
1. Do we acknowledge a Moral Law?
2. Do we acknowledge a Moral Law-Giver?
3. Do we acknowledge our moral responsibility towards others?

5: 1–13
1. Silent when we ought to have spoken.
2. Corrupt when we ought to have been clean.
3. Thoughtless when we ought to have been thorough.
4. Repentance, the road to reconciliation.

5: 14–19
1. The fact of forgiveness.
2. The fear of forgiveness.
3. The faith of forgiveness.

6: 1–7
1. Do we offend God when we offend a neighbour?
2. Do we offend the fellowship when we offend a neighbour?
3. Do we restore fellowship when we make restitution?

6: 8–13
1. Is the flame of reverence still burning?
2. Is the fire of devotion still ablaze?
3. Is the faith of loyalty still strong?

6: 14–18
1. Have we lost our sense of the holiness of God?
2. Have we lost our sense of the high claims of God?
3. Have we lost our sense of the wholesomeness of life?

6: 19–23
1. Are we fully committed to the Lord?
2. Are we fully convinced of the Lord?
3. Are we fully convicted by the Lord?

6: 24–30*
1. Foreshadowing of the Lord's sacrifice for sin.
2. Foreshadowing of the Lord's cleansing from sin.
3. Foreshadowing of the Lord's completed work.

7: 1–10

1. The place of forgiveness.
2. The price of forgiveness.
3. The partnership in forgiveness.

7: 11–21

1. The acknowledgement of God's grace.
2. The anticipation of God's grace.
3. The appropriation of God's grace.

7: 22–27

1. Discipline in the interests of faith.
2. Discipline in the interests of fellowship.
3. Discipline in the interests of the full life.

7: 28–34

1. Are we making personal contribution towards the work of the Church?
2. Are we making personal contribution towards the worship of the Church?
3. Are we making personal contribution towards the warfare of the Church?

7: 35–38

1. Is our service imaginative?
2. Is our service instructed?
3. Is our service individual?

8: 1–36

1. They were called out, are we?
2. They were cleansed, are we?
3. They were consecrated, are we?
4. They were committed, are we?

9: 1–24

1. The preparation they made.
2. The promise they were given.
3. The presence that was revealed.

10: 1–3

1. They misunderstood their privileges.
2. They misused their powers
3. They miscalculated the penalty.

10: 4–20

1. The solidarity of sin.
2. The certainty of salvation.
3. The sincerity of a soul.

11: 1–47

1. The holiness of God—are we forgetting it?
2. The sacredness of life—are we forgetting that?
3. The sacrifice of love—are we forgetting that, too?

12: 1–8

1. Discipline for the sake of the servant.
2. Discipline for the sake of society.
3. Discipline for the sake of the sanctuary.

13: 1–59

1. Religion and health.
2. Ritual and holiness.
3. Holiness and healing.

14: 1–57

1. Religion and the common life.
2. Religion and the purity of the common life.
3. Reconciliation to God and to the common life.

15: 1–33

1. Personal hygiene and personal holiness.
2. Personal holiness and community health.
3. Community health and divine holiness.

16: 1–34

1. Sacrifice reveals the soul of religion.
2. Service reveals the sincerity of religion.
3. Simplicity reveals the saving power of religion.

17: 1–16

1. Is worship the holiest moment of life?
2. Is sacrifice the highest moment of life?
3. Is salvation the most humbling moment of life?

18: 1–5

1. Are we different because we are Christian?
2. Are we dedicated because we are Christian?
3. Are we dead to self because we are Christian?

18: 6–30

1. Does our religion keep us clean?
2. Does our religion keep God clear?
3. Does our religion keep the needs of the community clear?

19: 1–37

1. What is our attitude to the Lord God?
2. What is our attitude towards those at home?
3. What is our attitude towards our fellow-men?
4. What is our attitude towards the world's prizes?

20: 1–5

1. Do we stand by when evil is done?
2. Do we stand idle when God is blasphemed?
3. Do we stay indifferent when the Church of God is defamed?

21: 1–24

1. He was to be different—how different is our Great High Priest?
2. He was to be devoted—how devoted is our Great High Priest?
3. He was to be undefiled—how undefiled is our Great High Priest?

22: 1–33

1. Their offering was to be perfect.
2. Their obedience was to be perfect.
3. Their objective was purity of religion.

23: 1–44

1. God is acknowledged as the Author of life.
2. God is acknowledged as the Architect of their welfare.
3. God is acknowledged as the Object of their love.

24: 1–23

1. Holy Lamp—symbol of the Presence of God.
2. Holy Table—symbol of the Providence of God.
3. Holy Name—symbol of the Personality of God.
4. Holy Law—symbol of the Purpose of God.

25: 1–55

1. They safeguarded the health of the soil.
2. They safeguarded the moral health of the community.
3. They safeguarded the honour of the Lord.

25: 55

1. The Lord God thinks of us.
2. The Lord God thinks of us as persons.
3. The Lord God thinks of us as His possession.

26: 1–2

1. The sin that so easily besets us.
2. The secular life that so easily absorbs us.
3. The secret Love that saves us.

26: 3-13

1. Are the God-fearing more prosperous than others?
2. Are the God-fearing more powerful than others?
3. Are the God-fearing more practical than others?

26: 14-39

1. Disobedience still needs discipline.
2. Irreligion still breeds irreverence.
3. A bad conscience still breeds cowardice.

26: 40-46

1. Repentance unto life.
2. Restoration into living fellowship.
3. Reconciliation is the last word.

27: 1-34

1. Are we paying our way in life?
2. Are we praying our way through life?
3. Are we preparing for Life?

Numbers

1: 1–46
1. God's interest in us is personal.
2. God's interest in us is permanent.
3. God's interest in us is for a purpose.

1: 47–54
1. They were privileged but for a purpose.
2. They were men of the world but called to an unworldly mission.
3. They were servants but in the best service.

2: 1–34
1. Local responsibility.
2. Central responsibility.
3. Equal responsibility.

3: 1–39
1. Removed from the people.
2. Representative of the people.
3. Responsible to the Lord.

3: 40–51
1. The consideration.
2. The cost.
3. The consequence.

4: 1–20
1. For every man his duty.
2. For every man his discipline.
3. For every man his deliverance.

4: 21–28
1. A common cause.
2. A common contribution.
3. A common conscience.

4: 29–49
1. The privilege to which they were appointed.
2. The purpose to which they were contributing.
3. The patience in which they were sharing.

5: 1–4
1. Has the Church room for the unwanted?
2. Is the Church ready for the unwanted?
3. Does the Church rejoice in the unwanted?

5: 5–10
1. Repentance for wrong done.
2. Restitution for wrong done.
3. Restoration of wrong relationship.

5: 11–31
1. Do we bring our doubts to God?
2. Do we believe our doubts cans be resolved?
3. Do we believe our doubts honour God?

6: 1–21
1. Were they extremists or enthusiasts?
2. Were they pious only or practical also?
3. Were they contentious or constructive?

6: 22–27
1. The blessing of Providence.
2. The blessing of Pardon.
3. The blessing of Peace.
4. The blessing of Personal Knowledge.

7: 1–89

1. They were pioneers for God—Purpose.
2. They were pioneers with God—Partnership.
3. They were pioneers proving God—Promises.

8: 1–4

1. Does the ministry of the Word enlighten the mystery of God?
2. Does the ministry of the Word enlighten the mystery of Sin?
3. Does the ministry of the Word enlighten the meaning of life?

8: 5–26

1. Chosen to render service.
2. Chosen to represent the people.
3. Chosen to renounce the world.

9: 6–12

1. The confession made.
2. The conference sought.
3. The conclusion reached.

9: 9–14

1. We cannot run away from God.
2. We cannot excuse ourselves before God.
3. We cannot neglect God without cost.

9: 15–23

1. The guidance of God was disclosed to them.
2. The guidance of God was continuous.
3. The guidance of God was obeyed by them.

10: 1–10

1. Has the Church lost her authority?
2. Does the Church need an awakening?
3. Is the Church advancing?

10: 11–28

1. Have we a standard of faith?
2. Have we a standard of fellowship?
3. Have we a standard of following?

10: 29–36

1. God seeks human co-operation.
2. God finds human co-operation.
3. God depends upon human co-operation.

11: 1–9

1. Do we murmur at the ways of God?
2. Do we ever doubt the wisdom of God?
3. Do we ever invite the wrath of God?

11: 9

1. The Silence.
2. The Secrecy.
3. The Sustenance.

11: 10–15

1. The compassion he felt.
2. The complaint he made.
3. The courage he showed.

11: 16–7, 24–5

1. Are we carrying too heavy a burden?
2. Are we caring too much?
3. Are we confiding as we ought?

11: 18–23

1. We can hinder God's purpose but cannot halt it.
2. We can doubt God's purpose but cannot destroy it.
3. We can challenge God's power but cannot change it.

11: 26–30

1. God is no respecter of persons.
2. God is no respecter of places.
3. God is no respecter of prejudice.

11: 31–35

1. God is working His purpose out.
2. God is making provision to that end.
3. God imposes penalty on unfaithfulness.

12: 1–16

1. God calls whom he chooses.
2. God equips whom He chooses.
3. God convinces those whom He chooses.

13: 1–20
1. Were they counting the cost?
2. Were they lacking in courage?
3. Were they losing confidence?

13: 21–33
1. The venture, then the vision.
2. The facts, then the fear.
3. The prophecy, then the protest.

14: 1–10
1. The consequences of falsehood.
2. The conspiracy of fear.
3. The conviction of faith.
4. The comfort of Divine Fellowship.

14: 11–12
1. We can obstruct the purpose of God.
2. We must believe that purpose is good.
3. We must believe that power is with God.

14: 13–19
1. Are we concerned about the honour of the Lord?
2. Are we convinced of the hospitality of the Lord?
3. Are we convinced of the hand of God upon us?

14: 20–25
1. Pardon—an act of the free grace of God.
2. Purpose—a continuing act of God.
3. Person—a contributor to the purpose of God.
4. Practical measures—also contributing to the purpose of God.

14: 26–39
1. Is our attitude towards God a responsible one?
2. Is our attitude towards the future a responsible one?
3. Is our attitude towards the past a repentant one?

14: 40–45
1. Life without God—does it work?
2. Life without God—does it pay?
3. Life without God—does it last?

15: 1–40
1. Let not our worship be thoughtless.
2. Let not our forgiveness be taken for granted.
3. Let not our freedom be taken for granted.
4. Let not the facts of faith be forgotten.

16: 1–11
1. Authority is challenged.
2. Authority is chastened.
3. Authority is confident.

16: 12–35
1. Do we see the hand of God in disappointment?
2. Do we see the hand of God in discipline?
3. Do we see the hand of God in destiny?

16: 36–50
1. Is any service for the Lord ever wasted?
2. Is any service for the Lord ever wicked?
3. Is any supplication to the Lord ever wasted?
4. Is there any salvation without a Saviour?

17: 1–13
1. The unworthy doubt of God's leadership.
2. The unexpected decision to prove God's leadership.
3. The unexpected disclosure of God's leadership.

18: 1–20
1. What is our reaction to the majesty of God?
2. What is our reaction to the Mercy of God?
3. What is our reaction to the miracle of God's provision?

18: 21-32
1. The justice of regular giving.
2. The joy of regular giving.
3. The jewel of regular giving.

19: 1-22
1. Does forgiveness bring new life?
2. Does faith maintain life?
3. Does fear serve life?

20: 1-13
1. Can we keep going without murmuring?
2. Can we keep faith without wavering?
3. Can we trust, and OBEY?

20: 14-29
1. Discouragement—the test of faith.
2. Death—the challenge to faith.
3. Discovery—the encouragement to faith.

21: 4-9
1. The wisdom of the long way round.
2. The weariness of the long way round.
3. The warfare on the long way round.
4. The wonder on the long way round

21: 10-30
1. Hopefulness—they march on.
2. Hostility—they make contact.
3. Help—they find refreshment.
4. Hand of God—they almost arrive.

21: 31; 22: 1
1. We are never safe.
2. We are never forsaken.
3. We must fight on.

22: 2-41
1. Human and divine encounter.
2. Human and divine enterprise.
3. Human and divine exchanges.
4. Human and divine enlightenment.

23: 1-12
1. Reverence does not fail him.
2. Response does not fail him.
3. Resolution does not fail him.

23: 13-30
1. God's purpose will be fulfilled.
2. God's power will not fail.
3. God's patience will not fail.

24: 1-9
1. The confirmation of God's word to him.
2. The constraint of God's word upon him.
3. The confidence in God's will for him.

24: 10-25
1. God chooses whom He will to serve Him.
2. God challenges those who will not serve Him.
3. God cheers those who do serve Him.

25: 1-5
1. New surroundings—new temptations facing them.
2. New surroundings—new triumph expected of them.
3. New surroundings—new trust demanded of them.

25: 6-9
1. Irreverence is not new.
2. Idolatry is not new.
3. Irresponsibility is hot new.

25: 10-18
1. The message God would convey.
2. The mediator God would honour.
3. The ministry God would give.

26: 1-62
1. Persons—important in the sight of God.
2. Portions—indicated by God.
3. Privilege—inheritance is in God.

26: 63-65
1. New generation but the same Person leading.
2. New generation but the same Purpose.
3. New generation but still on pilgrimage.

27: 1–11
1. They believed the Promise was for them.
2. They fought for a principle.
3. They became pioneers for others.

27: 12–17
1. His call.
2. His courage.
3. His concern.

27: 18–23
1. The divine call to leadership.
2. The divine equipment for leadership.
3. The divine challenge to lead.

28: 1–29: 40
1. Sacred obligations were renewed —how easily forgotten.
2. Sacred obligations ready for new generation—how early they forget.
3. Sacred obligations were to bring rejoicing—how easily that is forgotten.

30: 1–16
1. Are we people of our word?
2. Are we people of the Word?
3. Have we principles for the world?

31: 1–54
1. A common enemy.
2. A common effort.
3. A common encouragement.

32: 1–42
1. Conflict—art of war against arts of peace.
2. Conquest—art of war and the arts of peace
3. Consummation—art of war into arts of peace.

33: 1–56
1. From wonderland to wilderness.
2. From wilderness to warfare.
3. From warfare to another wonderland.

34: 1–29
1. Kingdoms of men have frontiers.
2. Kingdom of God has no frontiers.
3. Kingdoms of men are an inheritance from the past.
4. Kingdom of God is a present inheritance pointing to the future.

35: 1–34
1. Religion would be domesticated.
2. Law would be declared.
3. Grace would be demonstrated.

35: 22–28
1. He would be free when the high priest died.
2. We are free because our Great High Priest did die.
3. We are free because we are forgiven.

36: 1–13
1. No joy without justice.
2. No order without obedience.
3. No happiness without honour.

Deuteronomy

1: 6–8
1. Their Training is over.
2. Their Task awaits them.
3. Great Treasure awaits them, also.

1: 9–16
1. He knew his limitations.
2. He gave them leaders.
3. He gave them law.

1: 17–18
1. Law must show no Favouritism.
2. Law must show no Fear of Man.
3. Law must show forth the Fear of God.

1: 19–25
1. They struggled all the way.
2. The Lord was Steadfast all the way.
3. The Lord gave Strength all the way.

1: 22–25
1. Foretaste (*v. 22*).
2. Taste (*v. 24b*).
3. Testimony (*v. 25*).

1: 26–33
1. They change their minds.
2. They charge the Lord.
3. They judge by what they see, only.
4. They are judged by what they see.

1: 34–39
1. The Kingdom of Promise.
2. The Qualification of the Pioneers.
3. The Completeness of the Preparations.

1: 39
1. The Inheritance of the Kingdom.
2. The Inheritors of the Kingdom.
3. The Innocency in the Kingdom.

1: 41–46
1. They were undisciplined.
2. They were unprepared.
3. They were unblessed.
4. They were unheard.

2: 4–7
1. The Lord keeps His Word.
2. The Lord keeps company with His Warriors.
3. The Lord cares for His Warriors.

2: 25
1. A Revelation will be made.
2. A Reputation will be known.
3. A Revolution will begin.

2: 26–33
1. Destination is published.
2. Diligence is promised.
3. Difficulty presents itself.
4. Deliverance is proclaimed.

3: 18–22
1. The Promise given them.
2. The Preparation demanded of them.
3. The Plan explained to them.
4. The Providence in their midst.

3: 23–29
1. The Prayer that was made.
2. The Prayer that was refused.
3. The Punishment endured.
4. The Purpose made clear.

4: 1–5

1. The Revealed Law for Life.
2. The Complete Law for Life.
3. The Continuous Law for Life.

4: 9–10

1. The Special Task.
2. The Spiritual Task.
3. The Saving Task.

4: 12

1. Through the Fire of Affirmation.
2. Through the Fire of Affliction.
3. Through the Fire of Affection.

4: 15–20

1. The Temptation.
2. The Tribute.
3. The Trust.

4: 21–23

1. He was a Prophet of the Promise but not a Pioneer.
2. He had been chosen and yet was chastised.
3. He was utterly Dedicated but destined to be Disappointed.

4: 24

1. Deserving of Respect.
2. Destroying Evil.
3. Dedicated to the Fulfilment of His Purpose.

4: 25–27

1. The Prophet's Warning.
2. The Prophecy made.
3. The Prophecy fulfilled.

4: 28–31

1. The Evil besetting them.
2. The Evangel awaiting them.
3. The Everlasting Mercy.

4: 32–35

1. Beyond Comparison.
2. Beyond Contradiction.
3. Beyond Controversy.

4: 39–40

1. The Lord God is One and Alone.
2. The Lord God is Working.
3. The Lord God is Worthy.

4: 41–43

1. A Place of Refuge.
2. A Place for Repentance
3. A Place for Reconciliation.

5: 6–21
(See EXODUS 20: 1–10)

5: 24–27

1. The Authority they recognised.
2. The Access they found.
3. The Alarm they experienced.
4. The Advocate they sought.

5: 28–29

1. The Word of their prayers was heard.
2. The Will of the people was essential.
3. The Welfare of the people was at stake.

6: 4–7

1. The Unity of God Most High.
2. The Uniqueness of God Most High.
3. The Unchanging nature of God Most High.

6: 8–9

1 Religion and Work.
2. Religion and the World.
3. Religion and the Home.
4. Religion and daily Conduct.

6: 10–12

1. The unmerited Grace of God.
2. The unremembered Grace of God.
3. The unremembered Guidance of God.

6: 20–23

1. The Enquiry.
2. The Explanation.
3. The Exodus.
4. The Entrance.

6: 24–5
1. Reverence for God.
2. Righteousness is of God.
3. Remembrance of God.

7: 1–9
1. The God of the Impossible.
2. The God of the Incredible.
3. The God of the Inheritance.

7: 9–11
1. God is Faithful to those who trust Him.
2. God is Fearful to those who despise Him.
3. God is Faithful to Himself.

7: 14–16
1. The Faithful will suffer no Reproach.
2. The Faithful will abide in Strength.
3. The Faithful will fulfil the Purpose of God.

7: 17–24
1. The Inspiration of the Past.
2. The Inspiration in the Present.
3. The Inspiration for the Future.

8: 1–2
1. Power comes through Obedience.
2. Promise is to the Obedient.
3. Providence through Obstacles.

8: 3
1. We live by what we see.
2. We live by what we do not see.
3. We live by what we can not see.

8: 4–10
1. Love's Diligence.
2. Love's Discipline.
3. Love's Duty.

8: 11–18
1. The Perils of Prosperity.
2. The Privilege of Prosperity.
3. The Purpose of Prosperity.

9: 1–3
1. The Task to be undertaken.
2. The Trembling they feel.
3. The Triumph is not theirs.

9: 4–5
1. Not by our Goodness but His.
2. Not by our Achievement but His.
3. Not by our Faithfulness but His.

9: 9–29
1. The Man of Patience.
2. The Mediator of Pardon.
3. The Master of His People.

10: 1–5
1. The Second Chance.
2. The Sacred Covenant.
3. The Solemn Charge.
4. The Signature of Charity.

10: 8
1. Separated to show Him forth to men.
2. Separated to serve Him faithfully.
3. Separated to save in His Name.

10 :9
1. Not land but Love.
2. Not goods but Grace.
3. Not glitter but Glory.

10: 10–11
1. The Enjoyment of Fellowship with God.
2. The Encouragement to Faith.
3. The Enterprise of Faith.

10: 12–13
1. True Religion—Reverence for God.
2. True Religion—Righteousness of Life.
3. True Religion—Rejoicing in Him.

10: 14–15
1. The Perfection of God the Creator.
2. The Preference of God the Father.
3. The Pre-eminence amongst His Creatures.

10: 17–18
1. The Lord God is impartial.
2. The Lord God is incorruptible.
3. The Lord God intercedes for the lonely.
4. The Lord God is interested in the outcaste.

10: 22
1. The Goodness of the Lord is beyond Calculation.
2. The Goodness of the Lord is beyond Change.
3. The Goodness of the Lord is beyond Challenge.

11: 1–9
1. The Requirements of Pioneers.
2. The Responsibility of Parents.
3. The Remembrance of Posterity.

11: 10–12
1. The Country of Reward.
2. The Country of Refreshment.
3. The Country of Renewal.

11: 13–17
1. The Harvest that is sure.
2. The Heart must be right.
3. The Happiness that is threatened.

11: 26–28
1. The Challenge presented.
2. The Choice we must make.
3. The Chastening we may expect.

12: 2–12
1. Where God is, there His Church is.
2. Where God is, there His Challenge is.
3. Where God is, there His Comfort is.
4. Where God is, there His Charity is.

12: 29–32
1. The Danger of Success.
2. The Duty of Sincerity.
3. The Dignity of Simplicity.

13: 1–15
1. Beware of the Irreligion of False Prophets.
2. Beware of the Irreligion of False Friends.
3. Beware of the Irreligion of False Community Life.

13: 16–18
1. The Offering must be complete.
2. The Obedience must be complete.
3. The Overflow will be complete.

14: 1–2
1. The Lord claims us.
2. The Lord wants us as we are.
3. The Lord needs us.

14: 3–29
1. Divine Provision.
2. Divine Prohibition.
3. Divine Priority.

15: 1–23
1. They are to cancel all Debts.
2. They are to be compassionate towards the Down and Out.
3. They are to be conscientious towards servants.
4. They are to be completely committed to God.

16: 1–8
1. Remembrance is enjoined.
2. Realisation is to be experienced.
3. Reconciliation is to be known.

16: 9–17
1. Thanksgiving is encouraged.
2. Thoughtfulness is encouraged.
3. Thoughtful giving is encouraged.

16: 18–20
1. Justice must be impersonal.
2. Justice must be impartial.
3. Justice must be incorruptible.

16: 21–22
1. No Competitor to be set up.
2. No Comparisons to be made.
3. No Condemnation to be feared.

17: 13

1. Hearing the Word of the Lord.
2. Fearing the Word of the Lord.
3. Following the Word of the Lord.

17: 14–20

1. The Desire for a King.
2. The Divine choice of a King.
3. The Discipline of the King.
4. The Dedication of the King.
5. The Devotion of the King.

18: 9–14

1. The Demand.
2. The Danger.
3. The Dedication.

18: 15–22

1. The Promise made.
2. The Person described.
3. The Pattern drawn.

19: 1–10

1. The Charitable Provision—Refuge.
2. The Challenging Proclamation—Righteousness.
3. The Cherished Purpose—Reconciliation.

19: 14

1. A Symbol of Agreement.
2. A Symbol of Access.
3. A Symbol of Adoption.

19: 16–21

1. The Perjury committed.
2. The Penalty laid down.
3. The Purpose proclaimed.

20: 1–8

1. Life's constant Struggle.
2. Life's comforting Strength.
3. Life's constant Stimulation.

20: 19–20

1. The Warfare in which we are engaged.
2. The Wisdom of our Enterprise.
3. The Work we have to do.

22: 10

1. Each one a Task that is different.
2. Each one a Temperament that is different.
3. Each one a Training that is different.

26: 1–11

1. The Best alone for God.
2. The Blessing of God acknowledged.
3. The Bounty of God Accepted.

27: 1–8

1. The Law of the Lord—Sacred.
2. The Law of the Lord—Central
3. The Law of the Lord—Satisfying.

27: 9–10

1. The Privilege bestowed upon them.
2. The Possession they must acknowledge.
3. The Purpose they must fulfil.

27: 14–26

1. Safeguarding of Purity of Worship.
2. Safeguarding of the Honour of Family Life.
3. Safeguarding Social Obligations.
4. Safeguarding Personal Purity.
5. Safeguarding Social Conscience.

28: 1–9

1. Obedience to the Lord issues in Moral Pre-eminence amongst the Nations.
2. Obedience to the Lord issues in Spiritual Prosperity within the Nation.
3. Obedience to the Lord issues in realisation of Eternal Promises.

28: 15–24

1. Conscious Disobedience issues in Dismay.
2. Conscious Disobedience issues in Discouragement.
3. Conscious Disobedience issues in Despair.
4. Conscious Disobedience issues in Disaster.

28: 36–37

1. The Condemnation if they are disobedient.
2. The Chastisement if they are disobedient.
3. The Consequences if they are disobedient.

28: 67

1. When the day is too long—Weariness.
2. When the night is too long—Worry.
3. When the heart is all wrong—Wickedness.

28: 68

1. The unexpected Changes of Life.
2. The Unexpected Chastenings of Life.
3. The Unwanted Children of Life.

29: 2–18

1. He raises the Banner again.
2. He rebukes their Blindness again.
3. He rouses their Belief again.

29: 29

1. The Future is with God.
2. There are Facts we already know.
3. Let our Faith be based upon those known Facts.

30: 1–3

1. The Privilege of Repentance.
2. The Pain of Rejection.
3. The Promise of Restoration.

30: 11–14

1. We are not asked to do the Impossible.
2. We are not asked to believe the Incredible.
3. We are not Ignorant of God's Will.

30: 15–20

1. The Announcement.
2. The Alternative.
3. The Answer.

30: 19–20

1. The Legacy he leaves them.
2. The Life he offers them.
3. The Liberty he bestows upon them.

31: 1–3

1. The Disappointment.
2. The Dividing Line.
3. The Distinction.

31: 6

1. These are Campaign Orders.
2. There is Holy Companionship always.
3. He is Constant always.

31: 7–8

1. The Source of Encouragement.
2. The Source of the Enterprise.
3. The Source of Endurance.

31: 10–13

1. The Instruction.
2. The Inspiration.
3. The Initiation.

31: 14–19

1. The Promised Revelation.
2. The Proper Reverence.
3. The Prophetic Rebuke.
4. The Proposed Repentance.

31: 26–30

1. The Insurance.
2. The Insight.
3. The Instruction.
4. The Iniquity.

32: 1–3

1. The Truth of God is necessary.
2. The Truth of God is precious.
3. The Truth of God is made known.
4. The Truth of God is big enough for life.

32: 4

1. Steadfast in midst of Change.
2. Sure in midst of Uncertainty.
3. Sincere in midst of evil.

32: 5
1. They have been unworthy.
2. They are now unrecognisable.
3. They have been unruly.

32: 6–9
1. He appeals to history.
2. He appeals to their hearts.
3. He appeals to their heritage.

32: 10–12
1. Found of God.
2. Favoured of God.
3. Forgiven of God.

32: 13–20
1. They flourished but forgot the Lord.
2. They flourished and sought other Gods.
3. They flourished and were faithless.

32: 21–25
1. No escape from the Wrath of God.
2. No escape from Strife around us.
3. No escape from Struggle within us.

32: 26–34
1. The Lord's Consideration for a People at Fault.
2. The Lord's Concern for a People without Faith.
3. The Lord's Compassion for a People fighting still.

32: 35–43
1. The Will of God cannot be broken.
2. The Work of God concerns those who are broken.
3. The Wisdom of God controls our beginning and our end.

32: 48–50
1. The Glimpse but not the Glory.
2. The Climb but not the Conquest.
3. The Hour and the Honour.

33: 1
1. The Mediator between God and Man.
2. The Mediator between Man and Man.
3. The Mediator between Today and Tomorrow.

33: 2–3
1. The Revelation given.
2. The Radiance therein.
3. The Revolution resulting therefrom.

33: 6–24
1. Differing in Character—differing in Conduct.
2. Differing in Talent—different Tasks.
3. Differing Burdens—different Blessing.

33: 25b–26
1. A Fear acknowledged.
2. A Fear banished.
3. A Faith born.

33: 27
1. Man's real Home.
2. Man's abiding Home.
3. Man's abiding Help.

33: 29
1. They know the Blessing.
2. They alone know the Blessing.
3. They will never be without the Blessing.

34: 1–5
1. The Call upwards.
2. The Kingdom unveiled.
3. The Call homewards.
4. The Character revealed.

34: 10–12
1. A Prince among the Prophets.
2. A Power among the People.
3. A Person with a Pilgrimage.

Joshua

1: 1–5
1. The Divine Revelation continues.
2. The Divine Revolution continues.
3. The Divine Resources continue.

1: 6–7
1. The Encouragement.
2. The Enterprise.
3. The Entreaty.

1: 8–9
1. His Final Authority.
2. His First Admonition.
3. His Future Advance.

1: 12–16
1. A Partnership that was cultivated.
2. A Partition that was agreed to.
3. A Promise that was kept.

1: 17–18
1. The Full Obedience they gave.
2. The Full Obedience they promise.
3. The Oversight they prayed for.
4. The Obedience unto life.

2: 1–7
1. Planning in advance (*v. 1a*).
2. Planned in advance. (*v. 1b*).
3. Precaution observed (*v. 4*).
4. Providence is served (*v. 7*).

2: 9–11
1. The Lord's Works are known.
2. The Lord's Witness is known.
3. The Lord's Wonders are known.
4. The Lord's Wisdom is known.

2: 12–16
1. The Sign of Grace.
2. The Symbol of Grace.
3. The Simplicity of Grace.
4. The Strategy of Grace.

2: 18–24
1. The Command that was issued.
2. The Company that was chosen.
3. The Consequences made clear.
4. The Command carried out.
5. The Conviction of Divine action.

3: 3
1. The Symbol of Divine Law.
2. The Symbol of Divine Leadership.
3. The Symbol of Divine Light.

3: 4
1. A New Beginning with God.
2. New Behaviour towards God.
3. New Blessing from God.

3: 5
1. Not our Possessions but Ourselves.
2. Not our Prayers but Ourselves.
3. Not Parts of us but Ourselves.
4. Not Promise but Performance.

3: 7
1. The Divine Enlightenment.
2. The Divine Equipment.
3. The Divine Encouragement.

3: 9–11
1. Not my Words but His.
2. Not my Wisdom but His.
3. Not my Power but His.
4. Not my Presence but His.

3: 12–17
1. Divine Precedent.
2. Divine Prerogative.
3. Divine Purpose.

4: 6–7, 14
1. The Memorial of a Miracle.
2. The Meaning of the Miracle.
3. The Message of the Miracle.

4: 22–24
1. Divine Deliverance.
2. Divine Destiny.
3. Divine Dominion.
4. Divine Doctrine.

4: 23–24
1. God's Power has been revealed.
2. God's Power has been recorded.
3. God's Power is waiting to be realised.
4. God's Power is our redemption.

5: 1
1. Working His purpose out.
2. Working His way in.
3. Working His way through.

5: 2–9
1. Discipline for God's Work.
2. Dedication for God's Glory.
3. Disobedience to God's Will.
4. Declaration of God's Mercy.

5: 12
1. Special Providence now at an end.
2. Special Purpose now to begin.
3. Special Provision will be made.

5: 13–15
1. A Vision of Divine Authority.
2. A Vesture of Divine Action.
3. A Voice of Divine Appointment.

6: 1
1. The City had lost Heart.
2. The City had lost Hope.
3. The City had lost touch with Help.

6: 2–21
1. The Calm Word to Joshua.
2. The Cold War of Jericho.
3. The Collapsed Walls of Jericho.

6: 2–10
1. Deliverance is announced.
2. Direction is given.
3. Deviation is forbidden.
4. Demand is made.

6: 22–25
1. The Promise of God to those who trust Him.
2. The Purpose of God through those who trust Him.
3. The Praise of God through those who trust Him.

7: 1
1. Rebellion.
2. Reproach.
3. Retribution.

7: 7–9
1. The Question.
2. The Querulousness.
3. The Quandary.
4. The Quest.

7: 11–21
1. The Exposure.
2. The Explanation.
3. The Exhortation.
4. The Examination.
5. The Evangelism.

7: 19–26
1. The Appeal of Joshua.
2. The Acknowledgement of Achan.
3. The Affliction of Israel.
4. The Atonement made.

8: 1
1. The Constraint.
2. The Counsel.
3. The Confidence.

8: 3-9
1. The Warfare continues.
2. The Warrior takes command.
3. The Warrior cares.

8: 17, 18, 21
1. A People over-eager.
2. A People overwhelmed.
3. A Pioneer Overshadowed.

8: 18, 26, 30
1. An Instruction received.
2. An Inspiration known.
3. An Inheritance assured.

9: 1-2, 3, 4,
1. The Enemies of God are uneasy.
2. The Enemies of God are united.
3. The Enemies of God are unprepared for treachery.

9: 4-5, 6, 12, 21
1. The Deceit of Sin.
2. The Diligence of Sin.
3. The Dishonesty of Sin.
4. The Disgrace of Sin.

9: 21-27
1. The Condemnation.
2. The Confirmation.
3. The Consideration.

10: 3-11
1. The Enemies of Israel are alarmed.
2. The Enemies of Israel are aggressive.
3. The Enterprise of Israel is approved.
4. The Elements in Israel are active.

10: 25
1. A Word of Encouragement to Faith.
2. A Word of Encouragement to Fortitude.
3. A Word of Encouragement to Fearlessness.

10: 28-43
1. The Campaign proceeds.
2. The Campaign prospers.
3. The Campaign's Partnership.

11: 6
1. Divine Encouragement.
2. Divine Enterprise.
3. Divine Expectation.

11: 23
1. The Venture of God into Palestine.
2. The Vigilance of Joshua in Palestine.
3. The Victory over Palestine.

14: 6-12
1. Claims the Lord has kept him faithful.
2. Claims the Lord has kept him fit.
3. Claims the Lord's Inheritance.

15: 18-19
1. An Appeal is made.
2. An Answer is given.
3. Abundance is provided.

15: 63
1. The Pocket of Resistance.
2. The Price of Compromise.
3. The Purpose of Defeat.

17: 3-4
1. They command the hearing of Joshua.
2. They claim the Promise.
3. They are convinced Pioneers.

17: 17-18
1. A Reputation to maintain.
2. Resources to count upon.
3. Results to be convinced of.

18: 8-10
1. The Orders.
2. The Obedience.
3. The Outcome.

19 : 49-50
1. The Inheritance.
2. The Inspiration.
3. The Instruction.
4. The Initiative.

20: 1–3
1. Proclamation is made.
2. Provision is arranged.
3. Promises are kept.
4. Providence is served.

21: 1–3
1. Religion stakes its claim.
2. Revelation confirms the claim.
3. Resolution grants the claim.

21: 43–45
1. Divine Promises are fulfilled.
2. Divine Peace is realised.
3. Divine Plan is completed.

22: 2–4
1. They have been Diligent in remembrance of Divine Orders.
2. They have been Dutiful towards Joshua.
3. They are now Discharged for further duty at home.

22: 5–6
1. A call to Discipline.
2. A challenge to Discipleship.
3. A clear Duty.
4. An encouraging Dismissal.

22: 7b–8
1. The Will of the King.
2. The Wealth of the Kingdom.
3. The Wisdom of the King.

22: 10, 13, 16, 29, 31, 33
1. An acknowledgement of God's Goodness and Mercy.
2. An act of Godly Jealousy and Suspicion.
3. An Affirmation of Godly Fear and Trust.
4. An achievement of Good Sense.
5. An acceptance of Goodly Fellowship.

23: 3–8
1. The Undertaking is of God.
2. The Upholding is of God.
3. The Overtaking is of God.
4. The Utmost for God.

23: 10
1. Power unlimited.
2. Providence unrecognised.
3. Prophecy (Promise) unaltered.

23: 10
1. An Affirmation of Faith.
2. An Admission of Faith.
3. An Acceptance in Faith.

23: 11–13
1. The Demands of the Kingdom.
2. The Danger of Rebellion.
3. The Duty of Remembrance.

23: 14–16
1. Behold the Sojourner before God!
2. Behold the Salvation of God!
3. Behold the Severity of God!

24: 1–13
1. They bow before the Authority of God.
2. They bring to remembrance the Leadership of God.
3. They rejoice in free gift of the Salvation of God.

24: 14–18
1. The Call to Loyalty.
2. The Challenge to Decision.
3. The Choice set before them.
4. The Confession they made.

24: 19–22
1. They must consider the character of God.
2. They must count the cost of their loyalty.
3. They must have the Courage of their convictions.

24: 23–25
1. A new Command.
2. A new Confession.
3. A new Covenant.

24: 29, 31
1. His Warfare is over.
2. His Work continues.
3. His Witness remains.

Judges

1: 1–2
1. The Objective.
2. The Obedience.
3. The Overcoming.

1: 3–4
1. The Brothers.
2. The Bargain.
3. The Benefit.

1: 12–15
1. The Reward.
2. The Request.
3. The Response.

1: 22–26
1. A Partnership acknowledged.
2. A Promise made.
3. A Promise kept.
4. A Purpose is served.

2: 1–5
1. The Reminder.
2. Their Refreshment.
3. Their Rebellion.
4. Retribution.

2: 6–10
1. Time for Leadership to be withdrawn.
2. Time for everyone to find his corner in life.
3. Time for Loyalty is always with us.

2: 11–15
1. No Leader—No Loyalty.
2. No Love—No Life.
3. No Obedience—No Overcoming.

2: 16–23
1. The Covenant of Love is renewed.
2. The Cost of Loyalty is resented.
3. The Character of Loving-kindness is redemptive.

3: 1–6
1. The Nation's Experiences in the Past.
2. The Nation's Enticements in the Present.
3. The Need for Encounter today.

3: 7–11
1. The Popularity of Idolatry.
2. The Power of Idolatry.
3. The Purpose of Idolatry.
4. The Poverty of Idolatry.
5. The Power that redeemed Idolatry.

3: 12–30
1. The Enchantment of Evil.
2. The Enslavement of Evil.
3. The Escape from Evil.

4: 4–10
1. The Excellence of Deborah.
2. The Enterprise of Deborah.
3. The Encouragement of Deborah.

4: 14
1. Her Challenge.
2. Her Conviction.
3. Her Confession.

5: 7c
1. She was experienced in the ways of God.
2. She was an example to the people of God.
3. She was an enrichment to the people of God.

5: 20

1. Nature seeks man's Good.
2. Nature serves man's Good.
3. Nature safeguards man's Good.

5: 28

1. The Cry of Everyman.
2. The Call to Everyman.
3. The Coming to Everyman.

5: 31

1. They obtained Rest from Unrest.
2. They obtained Rest from Unbelief.
3. They obtained Rest from Unrighteousness.

6: 1–10

1. Their Circumstances.
2. Their Cry.
3. Their Consolation.
4. Their Condemnation.

6: 11–24

1. Called whilst working.
2. Competent but not willing.
3. Convinced but still wondering.

6: 14, 21–24

1. The Commission.
2. The Confirmation.
3. The Comfort.
4. The Confession.

6: 25–32

1. The Obstacle to real Faith.
2. The Obedience of real Faith.
3. The Opportunity of real Faith.

6: 36–40

1. The Search for Certainty.
2. The Signs of Certainty.
3. The Signature of Certainty.

7: 1–4

1. A Word concerning Pride.
2. A Word concerning Power.
3. A Word concerning Privilege.

7: 9–15

1. The Command.
2. The Confusion.
3. The Comfort.
4. The Confirmation.

7: 19–25

1. The Battle in Faith.
2. The Battle-cry of Faith.
3. The Battle won for Faith.

8: 1–3

1. Pride is hurt.
2. Patience is shown.
3. Peace is restored.

8: 4

1. The Resolution implied.
2. The Fellowship implied.
3. The Leadership implied.

8: 22–23

1. The Request they make.
2. The Reason they offer.
3. The Refusal he gives.
4. The Reign that matters.

8: 23–27

1. He was big enough to say No.
2. He was big enough to ask a Favour.
3. He was big enough to make a mistake.

8: 33–35

1. They remembered not their Leader.
2. They honoured not their Lord.
3. They valued not their Legacy.

9: 1–6

1. His Motive was commendable.
2. His Method was clumsy.
3. His Malice was contemptible.

9: 7–20

1. The Presumption.
2. The Parable.
3. The Prayer.

9: 22–31
1. Friendship is broken.
2. Fears are betrayed.
3. Friend is bold.

9: 36–40
1. His Vision is distorted.
2. His Vanity is challenged.
3. His Valour is challenged.

9: 45
1. He fought.
2. He fought with fervour.
3. He fought to a finish.

9: 48–49
1. The Fire of Enthusiasm.
2. The Force of Example.
3. The Finality of the Effort.

9: 50–57
1. Unexpected Defence.
2. Unexpected Disaster.
3. Unexpected Destiny.

10: 1–2
1. He was unknown but not un-important.
2. He was unsung but not unworthy.
3. He was undistinguished but not unloved.

10: 14–16
1. The Message to the People.
2. The Misery of the People.
3. The Mercy of their Lord.

10: 17–11: 1
1. The Dispute.
2. The Distress.
3. The Distinction.

11: 1–35
1. Dishonoured because of his origins.
2. Honoured because of his courage.
3. Honourable in his promises.

11: 29–35
1. The Vow he made.
2. The Victory he was given.
3. The Valour he showed.

11: 34–40
1. Anonymous but anointed.
2. Appointed to die but assenting in faith.
3. Afflicted but what an advertisement of faith!

12: 6
1. The Simplicity of the Test.
2. The Certainty of the Test.
3. The Self-Revelation of the Test.

13: 1–5
1. The Disclosure.
2. The Discipline.
3. The Distinction.

13: 12
1. Their Concern.
2. His Career.
3. His Character.

13: 21–25
1. The Common Idea.
2. The Common Sense.
3. The Communication..

14: 1
1. Samson begins with Promise.
2. Samson blinded by Passion.
3. Samson betrayed by Pride.
4. Samson broken by Punishment.

14: 1, 4–6; 16: 3, 8, 30
1. A Man with a Mission.
2. A Man of Moods.
3. A Man of Miracle.
4. A Man with a Message.

15: 11–15
1. His strong sense of Purpose.
2. No suggestion of self-pity.
3. His strong sense of Power.

15: 18–19
1. The Cry of a Warrior.
2. The Contrast in Experience.
3. The Consequence.

16: 1–6, 20
1. The Enlightenment they sought.
2. The Enticement they encouraged.
3. The Evidence they found.

16: 28–31
1. Hatred consumed him but no honour was won.
2. Vengeance he sought, but no Victory was won.
3. Sacrifice was made but no Salvation was won.

17: 1–3
1. A guilty conscience.
2. A godly conscience.
3. A good cause.

18: 1–7
1. Without religion—without restraint.
2. Without leadership—without common loyalty.
3. Without Community life—without public conscience.

18: 7
1. They were unsuspecting.
2. They were undisturbed.
3. They were unfriendly.

18: 9–10
1. The Enterprise commended to them.
2. The Enthusiasm required of them.
3. The End before them.

20: 8–28
1. The Concerted Plan of Campaign.
2. The Courageous Persistence.
3. The Encouraging Promise.

21: 1–25
1. Their Vengeance—to preserve racial Purity.
2. Their Vows—to preserve religious Unity.
3. Their Venture—to preserve their sense of Duty.

Ruth

1: 1–4
1. The Courage that was shown.
2. The Convention that was ignored.
3. The Contentment that was known

1: 6–14
1. The Resolution that was made.
2. The Reward they deserved.
3. The Response shown.

1: 16–18
1. The Devotion shown.
2. The Dedication promised.
3. The Destiny accepted.
4. The Decision made.

1: 19–22
1. Their arrival in Bethlehem.
2. The Affection shown.
3. The acceptance of her lot.

2: 2–13
1. She seeks Work for her hands.
2. She finds Work for her heart.
3. She experiences Wonder in her heart.
4. She offers Worship in her heart.

2: 14
1. The Feast to which she was invited.
2. The Fellowship in which she shared.
3. The Fullness she knew.

2: 15, 16
1. The Command that was obeyed.
2. The kindness that overflowed.
3. The Concern that overshadowed.

2: 17–23
1. Thoughtfulness asserts itself.
2. Thankfulness returns.
3. Thorough-going advice is given.

3: 1–12
1. A Home of her own.
2. An Honour awaiting her.
3. Her Humility commends her.
4. His Honesty commends him.

3: 14–4: 9
1. His regard for her Honour.
2. His regard for her Mother-in-law.
3. His regard for her Heritage.

4: 9–12
1. He redeemed them from Poverty.
2. He redeemed them to Protect them.
3. He redeemed them to Preserve the Inheritance.

4: 13–17
1. An acknowledgement of the Providence of God.
2. An acknowledgement of the Power of God.
3. An acknowledgement of the Privilege from God.
4. An acknowledgement of the Prophetic Succession.

I Samuel

1: 1–8
1. A man with a sense of shame.
2. A man with a sense of loyalty.
3. A man with a sense of responsibility.
4. A man with a sense of pride.

1: 9–18
1. A Woman's Prayer for Mercy.
2. A Woman's Prayer with a Mission.
3. A Woman's Prayer misunderstood.
4. A Woman's Prayer that worked a miracle.

1: 19–28; 2: 11
1. Her prayer is answered.
2. Her promise is kept.
3. Her piety is rewarded.

2: 12–17, 22–25
1. They were unworthy before the Lord.
2. They were unscrupulous towards their fellows.
3. They were unashamed before their father.

2: 18–21, 26
1. His discipleship began at the right time.
2. His discipleship began at the right place.
3. His discipleship began with the right people.

2: 27–34
1. The man who forgot his duty.
2. The man who forfeited his privileges.
3. The man who failed in authority.

2: 35–36
1. The continuation of the ministry.
2. The character of the ministry.
3. The conditions of the ministry.
4. The consequences to the ministry.

3: 1–9
1. He serves his probation.
2. He enters upon personal experience.
3. He enters into privilege.

3: 1–9
1. A time for discipline.
2. A time for discovery.
3. A time for duty.

3: 10
1. First the Voice.
2. Then the Vision.
3. Then the Volunteer.

3: 10–15
1. He listened.
2. He learnt.
3. He lingered.

3: 16–18
1. The Obedience he gave.
2. The Opportunity he accepted.
3. The Outcome.

3: 19–4: 1a
1. His growth in experience.
2. His growth in authority.
3. His growth in service.

4: 1–11
1. Do we live as unto God?
2. Do we localize God?
3. Do we love God for Himself?

4: 12–18

1. A man who cared.
2. A man who collapsed.
3. A man who confessed.

4: 19–22

1. An example of faith shaken.
2. An example of faith's sacrifice.
3. An example of faith's certainty.

5: 1–12

1. The humiliation they imposed.
2. The honour they refused.
3. The hostage they despised.

6: 1–13

1. Respect.
2. Response.
3. Rejoicing.

6: 14–18

1. Emotions find expression in—
   (a) Work.
   (b) Worship.
   (c) Witness.

6: 19–7: 1

1. There are things we should not see
   —Irreverence.
2. There are things we should not
   know—Ignorance.
3. There are things we should not do
   —Irresponsibility.

7: 2–4

1. Divine relationship is remembered.
2. Divine requirements are respected.
3. Divine Right is recognised.

7: 5–12

1. They repent of their Idolatry.
2. They realise their Impotence.
3. They recognise they are not independent.
4. They rejoice in their Inspiration.

7: 12

1. An acknowledgement of God.
2. An acknowledgement of God's
   Goodness.
3. An acknowledgement of God's
   Grace.

7: 13–14

1. Rest He gave them.
2. Restoration He granted them.
3. Reconciliation He made possible.

7: 15–17

1. Where the world saw him.
2. Where his relatives saw him.
3. Where God saw him.

8: 1–9

1. The renegade sons.
2. The rebellious people.
3. The rejected Lord.
4. The royal Word.

8: 10–22

1. The King they wanted—do we
   know what is good for us?
2. The King they despised—do we
   resent advice?
3. The King they were given—do we
   get what we deserve?

9: 1–27

1. He sought Guidance and found a
   Guide.
2. He sought something lost and
   himself was found.
3. He sought his way back and found
   his way forward.

9: 21

1. No ancestry of which to boast.
2. No family of which to boast.
3. No claim at all of which to boast.

9: 18

1. What are we looking for in life?
2. Why are we looking for it?
3. Where are we looking for it?

10: 1–9a
1. The Consecration.
2. The Confirmation.
3. The Conviction.

10: 9–13
1. Does the fact of conversion surprise us?
2. Does the fact of conversion convince us?
3. Does the fact of conversion concern us?

10: 24–27
1. His Call.
2. His Companions.
3. His Critics.
4. His Comprehension.

11: 1–15
1. A chosen warrior and yet a worker.
2. A man of greatness and yet of goodwill.
3. A man of privilege and yet one of the people.

12: 1–25
1. His unchallenged Integrity is declared.
2. His undying interest in their destiny.
3. His unwavering indictment of their disobedience.
4. His untiring Inspiration of their duty.

13: 1–15
1. Dishonesty—takes to himself praise due to another.
2. Disobedience—takes upon himself a privilege not his.
3. Disgrace—takes second place in affections of his people.

14: 1–16
1. Enterprise in the service of the King.
2. Enthusiasm in the service of the King.
3. Expectation in the service of the King.

14: 17–23
1. A common foe calls for a common faith.
2. Enthusiasm creates enthusiasm.
3. Defeat is turned into Deliverance.

14: 24–35
1. Denial in the interest of Discipline.
2. Patriotism greater than personal relationship.
3. Rebellion and Repentance.

14: 36–46
1. There was diligence to know God's Will.
2. There was delay in knowing God's Will.
3. There was decision on knowing God's Will.
4. There was Deliverance in God's Will.

15: 1–21
1. The arm of the Lord is not shortened.
2. The Word of the Lord is not silent.
3. The Will of the Lord is not swept away.

15: 22–23
1. The Condemnation.
2. The Cause.
3. The Consequence.

15: 24–31
1. He was afraid to be unpopular.
2. He was afraid to be unforgiven.
3. He was afraid.

16: 1–13
1. The Lord's Provision for the maintenance of His Work.
2. The Lord's Preference in the choice of His Witness.
3. The Lord's Power is given His Warrior.

16: 14–23
1. The Costliness of Disobedience.
2. The Cure was not in himself.
3. The Cure was available.

17: 1–3
1. The Mountain of Pride—the Valley of Humiliation.
2. The Mountain of Success—the Valley of Failure.
3. The Mountain of Honour—the Valley of Shame.

17: 4–49
1. Organization complete—warrior a failure.
2. Organization absent—warrior a success.
3. Object is his victim—objective is Victory.

17: 45–47
1. The Challenge accepted.
2. The Confidence expressed.
3. The Conviction shared.
4. The Confession made.

17: 50–58
1. The Honour he restored.
2. The Honour he received.
3. The Honour he resigned.

18: 1–5a
1. Love expressed.
2. Love demonstrated.
3. Love obedient.

18: 5b
1. Authority is given him.
2. Authority is recognised.
3. Authority is confirmed.

18: 6–14
1. The Joy of their welcome.
2. The jealousy of their warrior.
3. The injustice of their warrior.

18: 14–16
1. The Patience shown.
2. The Prejudice revealed.
3. The Pride expressed.

18: 17–30
1. The humility of the one.
2. The hypocrisy of the other.
3. The honour of the one.
4. The hatred of the other.

19: 1–7
1. A plot is announced.
2. A plan is arranged.
3. A protest is made.
4. A pledge is given.

19: 8–17
1. The Wisdom of Love.
2. The Way of Love.
3. The Warfare of Love.

19: 18–24
1. The Wisdom from above is Peaceable
2. The Wisdom from above is Pure.
3. The Wisdom from above is Practical.

20: 1–2
1. The Perplexity of man.
2. The Promise of mercy.
3. The Priesthood of mercy.

20: 3–4
1. The Doubt that troubled him.
2. The Danger that threatened him.
3. The Devotion that strengthened him.

20: 5–17
1. The Friendship that trusts.
2. The Friendship that stands by.
3. The Friendship that stands unshaken.

20: 18–42
1. Friendship put to the test.
2. Friendship is put to shame.
3. Friendship is found to endure.

21: 1–6
1. Need to be met.
2. Nourishment is available.
3. Necessity is laid upon us.

21: 7-9

1. No time to lose.
2. No trouble too great.
3. No talent to be withheld.
4. No testimony to be refused.

21: 10; 22: 2

1. The Wisdom of Flight.
2. The Wisdom of Fear.
3. The Wisdom of Friends.

22: 3-19

1. His concern for his parents.
2. His concern for his purpose.
3. His character is defended.
4. His cause is upheld.

22: 20-23

1. He was saved to serve.
2. They were sacrificed in service.
3. He was steadfast in strife.

23: 1-5

1. He seeks guidance of the Lord.
2. He checks his guidance because of his men.
3. He justifies his guidance before his men.

23: 6-14

1. Pursuit is planned.
2. Prayer is offered.
3. Purpose is made clear.
4. Providence is kind.

23: 15-18

1. Caught in the Wilderness.
2. Comfort in the Wilderness.
3. Covenant in the Wilderness.

23: 19-29

1. Betrayal.
2. Boldness.
3. Blessing.

C

24: 1-15

1. A man who was hunted.
2. A man who would heal.
3. A man who was big-hearted.
4. A man who was humble.

24: 16-22

1. Loyalty finds a response.
2. Loyalty prepares for Reconciliation.
2. Loyalty finds its reward.

25: 1-35

1. One rich in possessions—the other in personality.
2. One was courteous—the other was callous.
3. One sought revenge—the other urged restraint.
4. One was humble—the other was made happy.

25: 36-44

1. The Price paid.
2. The prayer offered.
3. The partnership that emerged.

26: 1-20

1. An attitude towards personal leadership.
2. An attitude towards personal loyalty.
3. An attitude towards personal liberty.
4. An attitude towards personal life.

26: 21-25

1. An acknowledgement of Folly.
2. An appeal of faith.
3. An appeal for favour.
4. An acknowledgement of fact.

27: 1-28: 2

1. He falls back on old friends.
2. He fights for his homeland when in exile.
3. He fights for his own good name.

29: 1-11

1. A false accusation.
2. A full approval.
3. A fighting appeal.
4. A final argument.

30: 1–20
1. He returns and finds Devastation.
2. He meets Distress.
3. He exercises Discipline.
4. He brings Deliverance.

30: 21–25
1. They had a common objective.
2. They shared a common obedience.
3. They shared a common ordinance.

30: 26–31
1. His remembrance.
2. His resources.
3. His reverence.

28: 3–19
1. The Panic of a King (without God).
2. The Pride of a King (how thou art fallen)
3. The Premonition of a King (the end).

28: 20–25
1. The Memory haunts him.
2. The Message horrifies him.
3. The Moment humiliates him.

31: 11–13
1. A Gleam of light on a dark day.
2. A Gallantry on a dark night.
3. A Golden deed in a dark hour.

II Samuel

1: 1–16
1. He was jealous for God.
2. He was jealous for God's Servant.
3. He was jealous for God's Purpose.

1: 17–27
1. The tragedy.
2. The tribute.
3. The tenderness.

2: 1–7
1. His response is immediate.
2. His responsibility increases.
3. His remembrance is inspiring.

2: 8–17
1. Safe when separated.
2. Strong when separated.
3. Strife when not separated.

2: 18–23
1. The Pursuit of evil.
2. The Subtlety of evil.
3. The cruélty of evil.
4. The cowardice of evil.

3: 1–21
1. Does the wrath of man serve the Purpose of God?
2. Does the weakness of man reveal the Power of God?
3. Does the work of man disclose the Plan of God?

3: 22–30
1. His loyalty was on fire.
2. His loyalty was not without fear.
3. His loyalty never failed.

3: 31–39
1. He did not underestimate his opponent.
2. He did not understand his own officers.
3. He did not underrate the offence.

4: 1–12
1. Their enthusiasm was misguided.
2. Their enterprise was mistaken.
3. Their end was misery.

5: 1–3
1. The appeal to his humanity.
2. The acknowledgement of his greatness.
3. The acceptance of his kingship.
4. His acceptance of the kingdom.

5: 6–12
1. Men still belittle the kingdom.
2. Men still bow before the King.
3. Men still are brought into the Kingdom.

5: 17–25
1. A man with a Master.
2. A man with a Mission.
3. A man with a Method.

5: 24
1. Are we waiting on the Lord?
2. Are we witnesses to the Lord?
3. Are we warriors of the Lord?

6: 1–15
1. No power without the Presence of God.
2. No religion without Reverence for God.
3. No conviction without Confidence in God.

6: 16–23
1. Was his rejoicing overdone?
2. Was his religion outward or inward?
3. Was her rebuke deserved?

7: 1–17
1. A growing sense of the Majesty of God.
2. A growing sense of the Providence of God.
3. A growing sense of the Purpose of God.
4. A growing sense of the Patience of God.

7: 18–24
1. He is conscious of a great honour.
2. He is conscious of a great hour.
3. He is conscious of a great revelation.
4. He is conscious of a great redemption.

7: 25–29
1. He is great but not self sufficient.
2. He is great but not self satisfied.
3. He is great but not self-centred.

8: 1–18
1. The Conquest continues.
2. The Kingdom is extended.
3. The King is extolled.
4. The Community is organized.

9: 1–13
1. An act of remembrance.
2. An act of repentance.
3. An act of restitution.
4. An act of restoration.

10: 1–5
1. They were received with suspicion.
2. They returned with shame.
3. They were banished from society.

10: 6–14
1. Brotherly agreement in battle.
2. Manly acceptance of their duty.
3. Divine purpose will overrule.

10: 15–19
1. The Opposition reorganizes.
2. The Opposition is overcome.
3. The Opposition is won over.

11: 1–5
1. He was relaxed but not on guard.
2. He was religious but not a god.
3. He conquered others but not himself.

11: 6–27
1. How are the mighty fallen in dignity!
2. How are the mighty fallen in duty!
3. How are the mighty fallen into disgrace!
4. How are the mighty fallen into deceit!

12: 1–23
1. The Sin of wanting too much.
2. The sorrow from wanting too much.
3. The suffering inflicted by wanting too much.

12: 26–31
1. Another venture.
2. Another victory.
3. Another victim.

13: 1–22
1. The poison of sinful behaviour.
2. The pride of sinful behaviour.
3. The punishment of sinful behaviour.

13: 23–39
Some effects of sin:—
1. Craftiness.
2. Cruelty.
3. Cowardice.

14: 12–17
1. She pleads for reconciliation.
2. She pleads for restoration.
3. She pleads for return.

14: 24b–28
1. Was it because of injured pride?
2. Was it because of jealousy?
3. Was it because of fear?

14: 28-33
1. Endurance was at breaking point.
2. Enlightenment must be forthcoming.
3. Encounter must be made.

15: 1-12
1. He sought popularity by false pretences.
2. He sought power by false pretences.
3. He sought to fulfil his purpose by false pretences.

15: 13-23
1. He provided for continuation of the royal house.
2. He provided for continuation of the royal city.
3. He provided for continuation of royal hospitality.

15: 24-29
1. His sense of reverence does not depart from him.
2. His sense of resignation does not discourage him.
3. His sense of responsibility does not desert him.

15: 30-37
1. In prosperity he was surrounded by friends.
2. In adversity he discovered his friends.
3. In adversity and in prosperity he was faithful to his friends.

16: 1-14
1. Remembrance is abused.
2. Rebuke is accepted.
3. Redemption is anticipated.

16: 15-23
1. The working out of his purpose.
2. The wanting his purpose made known.
3. The warrant for his purpose.

17: 1-22
1. When friends lead us astray.
2. When faith has to fight its own battles.
3. When faithfulness is put to the test.

17: 26-29
1. The hostilities of life.
2. The hospitalities of life.
3. The hunger of life.

18: 1-8
1. His comfort.
2. His Compassion.
3. His Conquest.

18: 9-18
1. Lawlessness has to be paid for.
2. Law must be respected.
3. Life is sacrificial.

18: 19-33
1. The warrior who was broken.
2. The warfare that was over.
3. The warrior who was heart-broken.

19: 1-15
1. They acknowledge their need of a Leader.
2. They acknowledge they have no Leader amongst them.
3. They accept the offer of a Leader.

19: 16-30
1. He who cursed lived to bless.
2. He who conquered lived to forgive.
3. He who was lame lived to love.

19: 31-39
1. A kindness remembered.
2. A courtesy returned.
3. A kindness refused.
4. A compromise recorded.

19: 40-20: 26
1. After the High moment, the Low moment.
2. After the Conquest, the Quarrel.
3. After the Triumph, the Treachery.

21: 1–14

1. The Entail of Sin.
2. The End of Sacrifice.
3. The Enduring Sacrifice.

23: 3–4

1. He must be good living.
2. He must be God-fearing.
3. He must be generous in heart.
4. He will gladden the hearts of others.

23: 5

1. The Believer's Hope.
2. The Believer's Help.
3. The Believer's Happiness.

23: 13–17

1. Life is promised us.
2. Life is precious to us.
3. Life is purchased for us.

24: 10–17

1. He fought a good fight.
2. He fought for his people.
3. He founded a dynasty.
4. He fulfilled his destiny.

24: 18–25

1. The Offence of a warrior.
2. The Obedience of a warrior.
3. The Offering of a warrior.

I Kings

1: 1–40
1. The Purpose of God is threatened.
2. The Promise of God is remembered.
3. The Praise of God is restored.

1: 41–53
1. The Noises that were heard.
2. The News that was not expected.
3. The News that encouraged.

2: 1–9
1. He is being called home.
2. He consolidates his heritage.
3. He counsels wisely.

2: 10
1. He was great but not without sin.
2. He was great enough to repent.
3. He was great but believed in a greater mercy.

2: 13–25
1. Enemies of the Kingdom are:
   (1) Cowardly.
   (2) Crafty.
   (3) Conscienceless and
   (4) Called to account.

2: 26–27
1. How keen is our sense of loyalty?
2. How considerate are we towards others?
3. How concerned are we to do what is right?

2: 28–35
1. What many do in an emergency: run to religion.
2. What many forget: retribution.
3. What many have found: rest.

2: 36–46
1. The Promise made.
2. The Promise broken.
3. The Penalty imposed.

3: 1–4
1. Tribute but no Temple.
2. Response but no less remembrance.
3. Kingly and yet a commoner.

3: 5–12
1. The Understanding he already has.
2. The Understanding he would be given.
3. The Understanding he received.

3: 13–15
1. His Mercies are beyond our asking.
2. His Mercies are beyond our deserving.
3. His Mercies are beyond our realization.

3: 16–28
1. The appeal that protested too much.
2. The answer that was unexpected.
3. The affection that prevailed.

4: 1–19
1. He knew his limitations.
2. He knew life demanded law.
3. He knew leadership was essential.

4: 20–31
1. The Kingdom was prosperous.
2. The Kingdom was powerful.
3. The Kingdom had a personality.

4: 30–34

1. The man God chose.
2. The man God challenged.
3. The man God equipped.

5: 1–18

1. Given the Task, the servants are ready.
2. Given the Task, the supplies are available.
3. Given the Task, the strength is given.

6: 1

1. Faith had survived the centuries.
2. Faith had grown stronger through the centuries.
3. Faith was now central in life.

6: 6b

1. Stone was prepared according to pattern.
2. Stone was ready for use.
3. Stone was useless without other stones.

6: 10

1. The Church still stands.
2. The Church still supports others.
3. The Church still shelters others.

6: 11–13

1. The Church—external sign of allegiance.
2. The Character—inner proof of allegiance.
3. The Contract—divine confirmation of our allegiance.

6: 20

1. Their offering was to the Highest they knew.
2. Their offering was of the best they possessed.
3. Their offering was by the most they could employ.

6: 27–28

1. Act of worship is to embrace the whole of life.
2. Act of worship is to enhance the whole of life.
3. Act of worship is to encourage the whole of life.

6: 37–38

1. Presence of God is now localized.
2. Worship of God is now centralized.
3. Power of God is now realized.

7: 22

1. It redeemed from harshness.
2. It redeemed from dullness.
3. It redeemed from strangeness.

7: 51

1. They would be reminded of God's Providence in the past.
2. They would be reminded of God's Promises in the present.
3. They would be reminded of God's Presence always.

8: 1–11

1. The Preparation for the Presence.
2. The Panoply of the Presence.
3. The Powerlessness before the Presence.

8: 12–13

1. Is our God approachable?
2. Is our God inaccessible?
3. Is our God beyond understanding?

8: 14–21

1. The Providence and the Promise.
2. The Purpose and the Person.
3. The Prayer and the Performance.

8: 22–26

1. He stands alone.
2. He serves those who trust Him.
3. He secures the future of the kingdom.

8: 27-30
1. Can the incredible come to pass?
2. Can the unworthy come with confidence?
3. Can the sinful count upon compassion?

8: 31-34
1. Is evil always punished?
2. Is innocence always rewarded?
3. Is prayer always answered?

8: 35-40
1. Has God favourites?
2. Does God forgive?
3. Can God control nature?
4. Does God know our hearts?
5. Does God expect our reverence?

8: 41-43
1. The God they would honour.
2. The greatness they would know.
3. The glory they would learn.

8: 44-53
1. When divinely sent, we are divinely served.
2. When the strain comes, the strength is given.
3. When the shame overwhelms, the salvation is near.

8: 54-61
1. The Faithfulness of God is acknowledged.
2. The Friendliness of God is acknowledged.
3. The Fear of God is advocated.
4. The Fact of God is proclaimed.

8: 62-66
1. Worship was an act of witness.
2. Sacrifices were symbolic of Salvation.
3. Religion was not without rejoicing.

9: 1-9
1. One task completed, another begins.
2. One promise kept, another is made.
3. One warning heeded, another has been issued.

9: 15-28
1. There is a place for the Outcast in the kingdom.
2. There is a place for the Obedient in the kingdom.
3. There is a place for the Outsider in the kingdom.

10: 1-10, 13
1. A Test from afar.
2. The Treasure from afar.
3. The Tribute from afar.

10: 21-22
1. Display was too prominent.
2. Double-mindedness was developing.
3. Decay was setting in.

10: 23; 11: 8
1. Great luxury surrounded him.
2. Great laxity characterised him.
3. Great loss overtook him.

11: 9-13
1. The Cost of Disobedience.
2. The Crisis of Division.
3. The Cause of David.

11: 14-22
1. He had been preserved.
2. He had prospered.
3. He was patriotic.

11: 26-39
1. A servant revolts—Plot.
2. A king is rejected—Punishment.
3. A city is reserved—Purpose.

12: 1-24
1. The Purpose of God will not be compromised.
2. The People of God must not compromise.
3. The Power of God must not be resisted.

12: 26–33

1. Do men worship false Gods today?
2. Do men have false values today?
3. Do men have false hopes today?

13: 1–32

1. The Protest of God through His servant.
2. The Power of God through His servant.
3. The Patience of God with His servant.
4. The Purpose of God for His servant.

13: 33–34

1. He knew no repentance.
2. He knew no reverence.
3. He knew no reward.

14: 1–20

1. The Mischief of Deceit.
2. The Miracle of Discovery.
3. The Mockery of Disobedience.
4. The Mercy of Death.

14: 21–31

1. He was handicapped at birth.
2. He was hasty in middle age.
3. He was humiliated when in power.

15: 1–8

1. He lived on the capital of the past.
2. He lived with no conscience about the past.
3. He died with no contribution to the past.

15: 9–24

1. He was faithful in an unfaithful world.
2. He was fearless in a challenging world.
3. He was frail but by no means feeble.

15: 25–26

1. He shunned the Law of the Lord.
2. He shared his father's faults.
3. He served his people badly.

15 : 27–34

1. When pure religion went out, pagan religion came in.
2. When pagan religion came in, morals went out.
3. When morals went out, vice came in.
4. When vice came in, virtue went out.

16: 1–20

1. Jealousy provokes division.
2. Weakness breeds disobedience.
3. Power promotes persecution.

16: 21–28

1. United loyalty was absent.
2. United leadership was absent.
3. Unbelief was everywhere.

16: 29–34

1. Idolatry was widespread.
2. Infidelity was general.
3. Integrity was disappearing.

17: 1–7

1. The prophet from nowhere.
2. The prophet without fear.
3. The prophet without favour.

17: 8–16

1. From the refreshment that failed to the refreshment that failed not.
2. From the halting place to the place of healing.
3. From a famine of friends to a family of friends.

17: 17–24

1. Sin and sickness.
2. Prayer and providence.
3. Persons and the purpose of God.

18: 1–15

1. A Witness in an unexpected place.
2. A Word from an unexpected person.
3. A Word with unexpected power.

18: 16–19
1. The Interview.
2. The Indictment.
3. The Instruction.

18: 20–24
1. The courage of a hunted man of God.
2. The challenge of a hunted man of God.
3. The conviction of a hunted man of God.

18: 25–40
1. Their gods were unreal: their prayers were unheard.
2. His God was real: his prayers brought response.
3. They were silent when challenged but sensible when convinced.

18: 41–46
1. Prayer consequent upon victory.
2. Promise confirming victory.
3. Power confirming victor.

19: 1–8
1. After the courage, the seeming cowardice.
2. After the mountain-top, the valley of shadow.
3. After the humiliation, the honour.

19: 9–18
1. Escaped from the world but not from God.
2. Escaped from the world but not from himself.
3. Escaped from the tumult but not from the Truth.
4. Escaped from despair and made a discovery.

19: 19–21
1. Called whilst working with his fellow men.
2. Called to witness to his fellow men.
3. Called to warfare for his fellow men.

20: 1–15
1. His readiness to part with some things.
2. His refusal to part with everything.
3. His reply.
4. His responsibility.

20: 16–21
1. Ill-prepared to meet opposition.
2. Irresponsible in his orders.
3. Invisible was his real opposition.

20: 22–30
1. In spiritual warfare, there is no relaxation.
2. In spiritual warfare, there can be no resignation.
3. In spiritual warfare, God reveals Himself.

20: 31–34
1. Broken but not beaten.
2. Humiliated but not without honour.
3. Captive but makes a covenant.

20: 35–43
1. The Purpose of the prophet.
2. The purpose of the acted parable.
3. The purpose of the punishment.

21: 1–16
1. The covetousness of a king.
2. The corruption of a queen.
3. The crime of a crowd.
4. The collapse of a creed.

21: 17–29
1. The Lust of Possession.
2. The Last Possession.
3. The Lost Possession.

22: 1–23
1. Cooperation is asked for.
2. Consent is given.
3. Confirmation is sought and given.
4. Conscience asserts itself.
5. Conviction speaks.

22: 24–28

1. The cost of loyalty to Truth.
2. The criterion of loyalty to Truth.
3. The cry of loyalty to Truth.

22: 29–36

1. Are we hiding from life?
2. Are we heeding the lessons of life?
3. Are we hopeful in life?
4. Are we heroic towards life?

22: 41–50

1. He feared the Lord.
2. He was faithful to his inheritance.
3. He fought with integrity.

22: 51–53

1. His heredity was against him.
2. His environment was against him.
3. His laziness was against him.

II Kings

1: 1–18
1. What makes us turn to God?
2. What kind of God do we turn to?
3. What response do we expect?

2: 1–8
1. The Ambassador about to leave.
2. The ambition about to be born.
3. The apprenticeship about to end.

2: 9–12a
1. The insight he sought.
2. The ignorance he confessed.
3. The inspiration he acknowledged.

2: 12b–14
1. The hour.
2. The humility.
3. The honour.
4. The hand of God.

2: 15–18
1. First, the vision.
2. Then the vocation.
3. Then the verification.

2: 19–22
1. They were poor in essentials.
2. They saw purification in symbol.
3. They were promised abundance.

2: 23–25
1. The jibe of irreverence.
2. The jealousy of irreverence.
3. The judgement upon irreverence.

3: 4–20
1. The concern.
2. The co-operation.
3. The consternation.
4. The consultation.
5. The consequences.

3: 21–27
1. They muster all available.
2. They misread the signs.
3. They misjudge the enemy.
4. The Miracle.

4: 1–7
1. Do we use the talents we have?
2. Do we exercise trust as we ought?
3. Do we expect treasure from stony ground?

4: 8–17
1. Hers was the gift of hospitality.
2. Hers was the grace of humility.
3. Hers was the gift of hope.

4: 18–37
1. Haste—she must do something.
2. Hopefulness—she must fall back on something.
3. Healing—she witnesses something new.
4. Happiness—she discovered something new.

4: 18–37
1. The reception he gave her.
2. The reason for her behaviour.
3. The restoration that failed.
4. The restoration that succeeded.
5. The reverence shown.

4: 38–44
1. Is the Church involved in human affairs?
2. Is the Church instructing human affairs?
3. Is the Church inspiring human affairs?

53

5: 2
1. She was a slave girl.
2. She was sympathetic.
3. She was serving the Lord.

5: 1–14
1. The misery of the man.
2. The misunderstanding of the man.
3. The meekness of the man.
4. The miracle of the new man.

5: 15–19
1. His Praise.
2. His Promise.
3. His Prayer.

5: 20–27
1. He was disloyal.
2. He was dishonest.
3. He was discomforted.
4. He was dispossessed.

6: 1–7
1. All our possessions are borrowed.
2. All our powers are borrowed.
3. All our privileges are borrowed.

6: 8–23
1. Resourcefulness in the service of God.
2. Resources for the service of God.
3. Reconciliation is the service of God.

6: 24–7: 2
1. Do we blame God for our troubles?
2. Do we expect God to intervene?
3. Do we doubt God's ability to control human affairs?

7: 3–10
1. Unwanted but unafraid.
2. Unwanted but not useless.
3. Unwanted but not unworthy.

7: 9
1. Their confession.
2. Their conviction.
3. Their conclusion.

7: 9
1. How often have we heard the Gospel?
2. Have we responded to the Gospel?
3. Have we shared the Gospel?

7: 11–20
1. Each one his duty in life.
2. Each one his decision about life.
3. Each one his destiny in life.

8: 1–6
1. Is kindness ever forgotten?
2. Is coincidence of God?
3. Is contentment of God?

8: 7–15
1. Religion comes to town.
2. Respect is shown.
3. Revelation is shared.
4. Realization is born.

8: 16–19
1. The Lord's Person is not honoured.
2. The Lord's Power is not recognized.
3. The Lord's Promise is honoured still.

8: 20–24
1. Are all our deeds recorded?
2. Are all our words remembered?
3. Are all our thoughts registered?

9: 1–10
1. Was religion interfering in politics?
2. Was religion attacking idolatry?
3. Was religion justifying the ways of God with men?

9: 11–13
1. The unknown who made an impression.
2. The unknown who conveyed his message.
3. The unknown who promoted a kingdom.

9: 14–26
1. He takes the initiative.
2. He tolerates iniquity no longer.
3. He claims the inheritance.
4. He justifies the cause of an innocent man.

9: 30–37
1. Rebellion lifts up its head.
2. Rejects offer their services.
3. Retribution claims its victim.
4. Remembrance is denied.

10: 1–11
1. Does the End justify the Means?
2. Does the enterprise justify the man?
3. Does the enthusiasm justify the mission?

10: 15–17
1. A Prince meets a Puritan.
2. A Pledge meets with a Promise.
3. A Prophecy meets with Performance.

10: 18–28
1. The claim in the name of religion.
2. The cunning for the sake of religion.
3. The collapse of a false religion.

10: 29–36
1. The Lord's servants are seldom perfect.
2. The Lord's service is always rewarding.
3. The Lord's service is never exhausted.

11: 1–16
1. Passion in high places.
2. Purpose in higher places.
3. Provision in higher places.
4. Pronouncement.

11: 17–21
1. The purpose of God is restored.
2. The promises of God are renewed.
3. The praise of God is re-established.

12: 1–16
1. Is our religion good enough?
2. Is our religion kept in good repair?
3. Is our religion glorifying God?

12: 17–21
1. Purpose of a prince.
2. Persons or possessions?
3. Price paid for power.

13: 1–9
1. Disobedience leads to distress.
2. Distress leads to discipline.
3. Discipline leads to discovery.

13: 14–20
1. He was well loved.
2. He was worth an army.
3. He was witnessing still.

13: 20–21
1. The past lives on in the present.
2. The past enlivens the present.
3. The past enlightens the present.

13: 22–25
1. Confirmation of the promises of old.
2. Confirmation of His Presence.
3. Confirmation of a prophecy.

14: 1–7
1. The value he placed on the past.
2. The vengeance he demanded.
3. The virtue he showed.
4. The victory he won.

14: 8–14
1. The pride that was reckless.
2. The pride that was rebuked.
3. The pride that repented not.

14: 17–22
1. The king who was humiliated.
2. The son who was crowned.
3. The kingdom which continued.

14: 23–29
1. He restored frontiers but not faith.
2. He re-established relationships but not religion.
3. He renewed prosperity but not its moral life.

15: 1–7
1. The trust he showed.
2. The tragedy of his life.
3. The tribute to his life.

15: 8–31
What destroys a nation?
1. Bad leadership—lack of character.
2. Broken loyalty—lack of continuity.
3. Blind living—lack of religion.

16: 1–18
1. He sacrificed principles.
2. He surrendered possessions.
3. He succumbed to pressure.

17: 1–6
1. The enterprise of evil.
2. The enchantment of evil.
3. The entanglement of evil.
4. The end of evil.

17: 7–18
1. Why do men forget the goodness of God?
2. Why do men ignore the guidance of God?
3. Why do men neglect the glory of God?

17: 19–23
1. A nation that dishonoured God.
2. A nation that distrusted God.
3. A nation that deserted God.
4. A nation that deserved God's displeasure.

17: 24–34
1. The restlessness that calls forth compassion.
2. The religion that called forth confusion.
3. The response that called forth condemnation.

17: 34–41
1. Men have many gods but there is only one Lord.
2. Men have many forms of worship but there is only one Lord.
3. Men have many loyalties but there is only one Lord!

18: 1–7
1. The pattern of his loyalty.
2. The practical nature of his loyalty.
3. The perseverance of his loyalty.
4. The personal inspiration of his loyalty.

18: 9–12
1. Does God work through unbelievers?
2. Does God punish the unfaithful?
3. Does God overrule unfaithfulness in His plan for us?

18: 13–18
1. The submission he made.
2. The sacrifice he offered.
3. The service he rendered.

18: 19–25
1. His confidence was exposed to ridicule.
2. His confidence was assumed to be wrong.
3. His confidence was rejected.

18: 26–37
1. Is the language of religion understood?
2. Is the leading of religion understood?
3. Is the loyalty of religion understood?

19: 1–4
1. The humiliation of a good man.
2. The honesty of a good man.
3. The hopefulness of a good man.

19: 5–14
1. The word of encouragement.
2. The way of the Eternal.
3. The wisdom of faith.

19: 15–19
1. He declares his faith in one living God.
2. He denounces the many false gods.
3. He would demonstrate the act of one God.

19: 20–28
1. The Lord who answers prayer.
2. The Lord's own who answer pride.
3. The Lord who uses opposition.

19: 29–34
1. The discipline of patience.
2. The duty of praise.
3. The deliverance promised.

19: 35–37
1. The visitation.
2. The vindication.
3. The victory.

20: 1–7
1. The prediction.
2. The protest.
3. The promise.

20: 8–11
1. The curiosity of the king.
2. The confidence of the prophet.
3. The confirmation of the promise.

20: 12–21
1. Are we proud of our inheritance?
2. Are we prepared to part with it?
3. Are we persuaded we must part with it?

21: 1–9
1. After reformation—reaction.
2. After industry—idleness and idolatry.
3. After illumination—ignorance.

21: 10–18
1. A man without a sense of shame.
2. A man without a sense of duty.
3. A man without a sense of destiny.

21: 19–26
1. The power of example.
2. The poverty of evil.
3. The patience of experience.

22: 1–2
1. He lived to some purpose.
2. He lived to please the Lord.
3. He lived according to plan.

22: 3–7
1. To God the glory.
2. To every man his due.
3. To the future a good example.

22: 8–20
1. The discovery made.
2. The decision registered.
3. The dismay experienced.
4. The diligence acknowledged.

22: 8–20
1. An exceptional book.
2. An exceptional woman.
3. An exception is made.

23: 1–4
1. The company called.
2. The contract agreed upon.
3. The consequences to all.

23: 4–20
1. Reformation began in the heart of one man.
2. Reformation was continued throughout the church.
3. Reformation challenged the whole nation.

23: 21–23
1. Celebration of God's Providence.
2. Celebration of God's continuing Providence.
3. Celebration of God's continuing patience.

23: 24–27

1. The environment was cleansed.
2. The enthusiasm was contagious.
3. The example was beyond comparison.

23: 28–30

1. He was courageous in life.
2. He was consecrated to the Lord.
3. He was courageous in death.

24: 1–7

1. God's ways are not as our ways.
2. God's thoughts are not as our thoughts.
3. God's wisdom is not as our wisdom.

24: 10–20

1. A nation disobedient.
2. A nation displaced.
3. A nation disgraced.

25: 1–12

1. The honour of the Lord.
2. The humiliation of the people.
3. The hope yet remaining.

25: 13–17

1. Raw material was beyond measurement.
2. Raw material of life is beyond measurement.
3. Raw material of Christianity is beyond measurement.

25: 18–21

1. The end of their uncertainty.
2. The end of their independence.
3. The end of their inheritance.

25: 22–30

1. The minority that fought.
2. The mission that fled.
3. The mercy that followed.

I Chronicles

1: 1–9; 44
1. The conception of faith.
2. The continuity of faith.
3. The conflicts of faith.
4. The care of faith.

10: 1–14
1. The resistance God encountered.
2. The risks God took.
3. The righteousness God would reveal.

11: 1–9
1. Coronation.
2. Conviction.
3. Challenge.
4. Confirmation.

11: 15–19
See 2nd Samuel 23: 13–17.

12: 1–40
1. They were a gathered community.
2. They were a grateful community.
3. They were a glad community.

13: 1–14
See 2nd Samuel 6: 1–11.

14: 1–17
See 2nd Samuel 5: 11–25.

15: 1–15
1. Worship is a universal fact.
2. Worship is an expression of faith.
3. Worship is expressed in many forms.

15: 16–28
1. To each, his part.
2. From each, his heart.
3. From all, co-operation.
4. By all, adoration.

15: 29–16: 3
See 2nd Samuel 6: 16–23.

16: 4–22
1. Why do we offer praise?
2. What have we to proclaim?
3. What prompts us to prayer?

16: 23–36
See Psalm 96.

16: 37–43
1. No sacrifice too great in the service of the Lord.
2. No task too small in the service of the Lord.
3. No praise too great in the service of the Lord.

17: 1–27
See 2nd Samuel 7: 1–29.

18: 1–17
See 2nd Samuel 8:1–18.

19: 1–19
See 2nd Samuel 10: 1–19.

20: 1
See 2nd Samuel 11: 1.

20: 2–3
See 2nd Samuel 12: 16–31.

20: 4–8
1. Can we deal with the unusual?
2. Can we deal with the unbelieving?
3. Can we deal with the unexpected.?

21: 1–7

1. Was it because of pride of position?
2. Was it because of pride of possessions?
3. Was it because of pride of person?

21: 8–17

See 2nd Samuel 24: 10–17.

21: 18–26

See 2nd Samuel 24: 18–25.

22: 1–11

1. Decision in life.
2. Diligence in life.
3. Disappointment in life.
4. Discipline in life.
5. Dedication in life.

22: 12–13

1. Without the blessing, no building.
2. Without obedience, no obtaining.
3. Without courage, no conquest.

22: 14–19

1. The building of the kingdom always needs money.
2. The building of the kingdom always needs materials.
3. The building of the kingdom always needs men and women.

23: 1–27: 34

1. There was a job for everyone.
2. There was justice for everyone.
3. There was joy for everyone.

28: 1–8

1. The intention was good.
2. The intervention was the Lord's.
3. The inheritance was Solomon's.
4. The intercession was for the people.

28: 9–10

1. The Prayer.
2. The psychology.
3. The partnership.

28: 11–21

1. Are we preparing for the future?
2. Are we passing on faith into the future?
3. Are we positive in our thoughts about the future?

29: 1–8

1. Let us ascribe greatness to God.
2. Let us acknowledge the goodness of God.
3. Let us acclaim the glory of God.

29: 9

1. They were happy because they were generous.
2. They were generous because their hearts were right.
3. Their hearts were right because the Lord was there.

29: 10–19

1. The utter majesty of God.
2. The undeserved magnanimity of God.
3. The unfailing mercy of God.
4. The unmerited meekness of God.

29: 20–30

1. Does worship gladden our hearts?
2. Does worship inspire our loyalty?
3. Does worship awaken our love?

II Chronicles

other than material in I Kings and II Kings

5: 11–14
1. The one purpose for which they met.
2. The one place where they met.
3. The one praise they offered.
4. The one Presence they experienced.

6: 40–42
See Psalm No. 132: 8–9.

11: 13–23
1. He respected the word of the Lord.
2. He restored confidence.
3. He restored central worship.
4. He restored community life.

13: 1–22
1. The purpose of God is frustrated.
2. The prayer of the faithful is offered.
3. The privilege of faith is claimed.
4. The power of God is known.

15: 1–7
1. Does God withdraw His Presence from man?
2. Does God withhold His Peace from man?
3. Does God withhold His Power from man?

15: 8–15
1. Faith in action.
2. Fellowship in worship.
3. Freedom in public life.

15: 16–19
1. He had no respect of persons.
2. He had no respect of position.
3. He had no respect of practices.

17: 1–9
1. He safeguarded his inheritance.
2. He set an example of faith.
3. He started an enterprise of faith.

19: 4–7
1. A royal witness to the people.
2. A loyal welcome from the people.
3. The real welfare of his people.

20: 1–13
1. Is prayer a form of cowardice?
2. Is prayer a confession of confidence?
3. Is prayer a claim upon God's care?

20: 14–19
1. God's purpose is His responsibility.
2. God's plan is our responsibility.
3. God's power is our redemption.

20: 20–30
1. Is our faith positive?
2. Is our faith informed?
3. Is our faith full of praise?

24: 15–22
1. Leadership departs.
2. Lawlessness enters.
3. Loyalty appeals.
4. Life is sacrificed.

25: 5–10; 13–16
1. A dangerous alliance.
2. A devoted advocate.
3. A doubtful acquisition.
4. A dour answer.

26:
1. He began by being faithful.
2. He became a victim of flattery.
3. He was broken by faithlessness.

28: 1–27

1. He failed to honour his inheritance.
2. He failed to honour his fellows.
3. He failed to honour his family.

33: 11–17

1. The way of rebellion.
2. The way of repentance.
3. The way of regeneration.

Ezra

1: 1-4
1. The Lord calls whom He will.
2. The Lord keeps His promise.
3. The Lord commends His people
4. The Lord commands His people.

1: 5-11
1. The Initiative shown—Grace.
2. The Inspiration known—Goodness.
3. The Injustice rectified—Gifts returned.

2: 1-67
1. Revealing the Lord's love of persons.
2. Revealing the Lord's compassion for strangers.
3. Revealing the Lord's concern for holiness.

2: 68-70
1. They were pioneers.
2. They were practical.
3. They were prophetic.

3: 1-7
1. Enthusiasm was high.
2. Enterprise was worthy.
3. Enemies were real.
4. Encouragement was forthcoming.

3: 8-13
1. Mercy was known in the rebuilding.
2. Music was made because of the rebuilding.
3. Memories were revived by the rebuilding.

4: 1-6
1. The authority for their refusal—Persian king.
2. The object of their refusal—pure religion.
3. The outcome of their refusal—persecution.

4: 7-24
1. Organized persecution—with us still.
2. Organized dishonesty—with us still.
3. Official opposition—with us still.
4. Ordered opportunity—with us still.

5: 1-5
1. Do we give up easily?
2. Do we respond to encouragement?
3. Do we rejoice in our convictions?

5: 6-17
1. The promise they did not keep.
2. The price they had paid.
3. The purpose they had in mind.
4. The permission they sought.

6: 1-12
1. Prayer is answered.
2. Provision is made.
3. Prayer is offered.
4. Purpose is served.

6: 13-15
1. The obedience the King commanded.
2. The obstruction removed.
3. The opportunity renewed.
4. The obedience that inspired them.

6: 16–22
1. A common act of praise.
2. A common acknowledgement of sin.
3. A common act of fellowship.

7: 1–10
1. His forbears were honourable.
2. His faith was inspired.
3. His fame was based on industry.

7: 11–26
1. The unexpected grace of the king.
2. The unexpected tolerance of the king.
3. The unexpected consideration of the king.
4. The unexpected command of the king.

7: 27–28
1. The acknowledgement of God.
2. The activity of God.
3. The assurance of God.

8: 1–21
1. The importance of persons.
2. The importance of purpose.
3. The inspired providence.
4. The instructed prayer.

8: 22–23
1. Is our experience of God personal?
2. Is our experience of God practical?
3. Is our experience of God prevailing?

8: 24–30
1. They were stewards of God's bounty.
2. They were set apart for God's service.
3. They were to safeguard God's gifts.

8: 31–36
1. Thankfulness for many mercies.
2. Thoughtfulness for weary travellers.
3. Thanksgiving for safe return home.

9: 1–15
1. When the light is brightest the shadows are deepest.
2. When the heart is saddest, the sympathy is strongest.
3. When the mercy is greatest, the sense of shame is greatest.

10: 1–17
1. They had broken faith—sin.
2. They now break up families—suffering.
3. They then preserved faith—salvation.

Nehemiah

1: 1–11
1. He was privileged but patriotic.
2. He was prayerful but practical.
3. He was penitent but claimed the promise.

2: 1–8
1. The compassion of a king.
2. The commission of a king.
3. The command of a king.

2 : 9–18
1. The end of travelling—Providence.
2. The beginning of a task—Purpose.
3. The secret of his triumph—Power.

2: 17–18
1. Are we concerned about the Church of God?
2. Are we committed to the Church of God?
3. Are we co-operating in the Church of God?

2: 19–20
1. The Church has her critics.
2. The Church has her King, too.
3. The Church has her convictions.

3: 1–32
1. A common purpose.
2. A common plan.
3. A common perseverance.

4: 1–8
1. Do we hinder the Lord's work?
2. Do we help the Lord's work?
3. Do we honour the Lord's work?

4: 9–14
1. Prayer—waiting upon God.
2. Prudence—watchfulness.
3. Personal responsibility.
4. Personal pride.

4: 15–23
1. The work of the Church—building up in faith.
2. The warfare of the Church—breaking down barriers to faith.
3. The wonder of the Church—buried but born again.

5: 1–13
1. The cry of the hungry.
2. The cry of the helpless.
3. The cry of the hopeless.
4. The response of the heart.

5: 14–19
1. His honesty.
2. His sense of duty.
3. His humanity.
4. His hospitality.
5. His humility.

6: 1–9
1. The stubbornness of evil.
2. The subtlety of evil.
3. The service of the Eternal.
4. The steadfastness of their endurance.
5. The strength that was given.

6: 10–14
1. He had something to hide.
2. He had something to say.
3. He had something to learn.
4. He had something to fear.

6: 15–7: 4
1. The challenge of triumph.
2. The charge of treason.
3. The compliment of trust.
4. The uncompleted task.

7: 5–7: 73
See EZRA Chap. 2.

8: 1–8
1. Is the Bible in demand today?
2. Is the Bible read today?
3. Is the Bible effective today?

8: 9–12
1. Gladness in the heart of God.
2. Sadness in the hearts of men.
3. Gifts to gladden the hearts of men.

8: 13–18
1. The Will of God—do we care?
2. The Will of God—do we co-operate?
3. The Will of God—do we consent to it?

9: 1–5a
1. Their sense of community was developing.
2. Their sense of commission was awakening.
3. Their need of confession was being born anew.

9: 5b–15
1. Worthy of praise for all time.
2. Worthy of praise from all men.
3. Worthy of praise for all mercies.

9: 16–25
1. The unforgotten past.
2. The unforgotten patience of the Lord.
3. The unforgotten providence of the Lord.

9: 26–31
1. The old, old story—sin.
2. The ever new story—the Saviour.
3. The everlasting story—salvation.

9: 32–38
1. The source of their confidence.
2. The secret of their confession.
3. The sorrow of their condition.
4. The sincerity of their contract.

10: 1–29
1. Powerful and powerless have a duty to God.
2. Rich and poor have their obligations.
3. Wise and unwise can turn to Him.
4. Old and young can find life in Him.

10: 30–39
1. Is our performance matching our profession?
2. Is our contribution a matter of conscience?
3. Is our churchmanship a matter of co-operation?

11: 1–2
1. They had the city but not the citizens.
2. They had the programme but not the power.
3. They had the leaders but not the led.

12: 27–47
1. Their religion brought them gladness.
2. Their religion brought them together.
3. Their religion brought them confidence.

13: 1–14
1. Reformation was first personal.
2. Reformation was then practical.
3. Reformation was providential.

13: 14, 22c, 31
1. Has God any favourites?
2. Have we any claim on God's favours?
3. Have we faith or fear?

13: 15-22

1. Was their reverence at fault?
2. Was their remembrance at fault?
3. Was their sense of responsibility at fault?
4. Was their relationship with others at fault?

13: 23-30

1. We can defy the laws of God.
2. We can deify the laxities of the great.
3. We can defile the holiest things in life.
4. We can be declared new again.

Esther

1: 1–12
1. The display of power.
2. The display of personality.
3. The display of passion.

1: 13–22
1. The cowardice of selfishness.
2. The craftiness of self-pride.
3. The contempt of the self-conscious.
4. The concern of self-love.

2: 1–11
1. The love they wanted to organize.
2. The love they could not organize.
3. The love he did not give.
4. The love he did not get.

2: 12–18
1. She was young but had a mind of her own.
2. She was young but had a way of her own.
3. She was young but not without wisdom.

2: 19–23
1. Divine purpose sometimes hidden from us.
2. Divine purpose, when revealed, commands obedience.
3. Divine purpose, when realized, finds opportunity.

3: 1–6
1. Does convention command our allegiance?
2. Does conviction cost us anything?
3. Does conscience command our obedience?

3: 7–15
1. Organised opposition to faith is not new.
2. Organised oppression of faith is not new.
3. Organised obedience to authority is not new.

4: 1–8
1. He was beyond caring.
2. He was beyond consolation.
3. He was beyond condemnation.

4: 9–17
1. The caution of faith.
2. The crisis of faith.
3. The challenge to faith.
4. The courage of faith.

5: 1–14
1. The purpose that gave her patience.
2. The courage that gave her calm.
3. The vision that gave her victory.

6: 1–5
1. Can we see divine purpose in little things?
2. Can we see divine purpose in forgotten things?
3. Can we see divine purpose in familiar things?

6: 6–14
1. We can promote the purpose of God without knowing it.
2. We can share in the purpose of God without knowing it.
3. We can submit to the purpose of God without knowing it.

7: 1–10
1. Racial hatred is with us yet.
2. Real humility is with us yet.
3. Royal honour is with us yet.

8: 1–8
1. Constancy has its reward.
2. Compassion has its right of way.
3. Conviction issues in right behaviour.

8: 9–14
1. The promise was kept.
2. The power was given.
3. The purpose was served.

8: 15–17
1. From humiliation to honour.
2. From terror to thanksgiving.
3. From resignation to recovery.

9: 1–10
1. The purpose of God will survive all shocks.
2. The purpose of God will be served by all sorts and conditions of men.
3. The purpose of God will not suffer defeat.

8: 11c, 9; 15–16
1. Temptation was great.
2. Trust was greater.
3. Triumph was greater still.

9: 11–19
1. Are we free from the spirit of retaliation?
2. Have we faith in the spirit of reconciliation?
3. Is our faith finding an outlet in remembrance?

9: 28
1. Providence of God operates through daily experience.
2. Patience of God is shown through daily experience.
3. Purpose of God is known in daily experience.

10: 1–3
1. Their talents were employed.
2. Their trust was encouraged.
3. Their triumph was enduring.

Job

1: 1–5
1. A man of piety.
2. A man of property.
3. A man of prominence.
4. A man of principle.

1: 6–12
1. Are we religious because it pays?
2. Are we religious because we are preserved from the evil of the world?
3. Are we religious because we are prosperous?

1: 13–22
1. Repeated sorrows to wear down his faith.
2. Reverence maintained despite his sorrows.
3. Reality reveals itself to him.
4. Rebellion is far from him.

2: 1–6
1. Are life's troubles sent?
2. Does trouble serve any purpose?
3. Does trouble search out our weak spots?

2: 7–10
1. The visitation.
2. The voice.
3. The vindication.
4. The victory.

2: 11–13
1. They came where he was.
2. They saw him as he was.
3. They stayed where he was.

3: 1–19
1. The explosion at last.
2. The explanation he seeks.
3. The experience he would know.

3: 20–26
1. Are we tired of life?
2. Are we afraid of life?
3. Are we restless in life?

4: 1–11
1. Do we practice what we preach?
2. Do we suffer because of our sin?
3. Do we not suffer because we are not sinners?

4: 12–21
1. What right have we to boast?
2. What right have we to complain?
3. What right have we to question?

5: 1–7
1. Suffering knows no exemptions.
2. Suffering knows no explanation.
3. Suffering is part of our experience.

5: 8–16
1. Do we take our troubles to the Lord?
2. Do we think greatly of the Lord?
3. Do we trust strongly in the Lord?

5: 17–27
1. If we are born to trouble, why not accept it?
2. If we are born to trouble, why not acknowledge its value?
3. If we are born to trouble, why be afraid of it?

6: 1–8

1. Do we have to carry more than we can manage?
2. Do we resent God's dealings with us?
3. Do we ever want to get away from it all?

6: 9–13

1. Man at the end of the trail: death.
2. Man at the end of his trust: darkness.
3. Man at the end of his tether: destiny.

6: 14–23

1. Condemnation brings no comfort.
2. Misunderstanding does not help misfortune.
3. Friendship can frustrate faith.

6: 24–30

1. Can we always plead ignorance of sin?
2. Can we always plead innocence of sin?
3. Can we always plead our integrity?

7: 1–6

1. Are we not familiar with the beginning of rebellion?
2. Are we not familiar with the beginning of restlessness?
3. Are we not familiar with the beginning of resignation?

7: 6–10

1. Movement but no motive.
2. Humiliation but no hope.
3. Tribulation but no tomorrow.

7: 11–21

1. Man makes his protest.
2. Man feels his perplexity.
3. Man would know the purpose.
4. Man seeks peace.

8: 1–7

1. Is sin the origin of adversity?
2. Is sinlessness the origin of prosperity?
3. Is suffering the origin of perplexity?

8: 8–22

1. Our heritage from the past.
2. Our helplessness in the present.
3. Our hope for the future.

9: 1–12

1. There are no easy answers.
2. There is no place for arrogance.
3. There is place for acceptance.

9: 13–24

1. The mystery of God's government of the world.
2. The misery of man's helplessness.
3. The mockery of man's hope,.
4. The morning of man's faith.

9: 25–35

1. If only we could forget!
2. If only we could be forgiven!
3. If only there were a mutual friend!

10: 1–7

1. He wants to know God's motive in letting him suffer.
2. He wants to know what God is like.
3. He wants to be sure God is to be trusted.

10: 8–22

1. He makes acknowledgement of God's providence.
2. He makes accusation regarding God's purpose.
3. He makes an appeal for the mercy of God.

11: 1–20

1. He lacked sympathy because he lacked knowledge.
2. He lacked sincerity because he thought he knew everything.
3. He lacked simplicity because he lacked spiritual understanding.

12: 1–25

1. Conventional answer does not help him.
2. Commonplace facts do not help him.
3. Conflict is the soul of life.

13: 1–19

1. He seeks not argument but access to God.
2. He seeks not platitudes but knowledge of God's purpose.
3. He seeks not favour but fairness from God.

13: 20–28

1. A prayer for the lightening of his burden.
2. A prayer for the lessening of his fears.
3. A prayer for light on his failure.
4. A prayer for light on the folly of his youth.

14: 1–6

1. Is life a blessing or a curse?
2. Is this life all, or is there another?
3. Is this life satisfying?

14: 7–22

1. The intimations of nature.
2. The uncertainty of the natural man.
3. The undying nature of man.

15: 1–16

1. Is it wrong to try to understand what is right?
2. Is it right to tolerate what is wrong?
3. Is it wrong to believe there is an answer?

15: 17–35

1. Does a bad man always have a bad conscience?
2. Does a bad man always come to a bad end?
3. Does a bad man always lose in the end?

16: 1–17

1. He finds no comfort in silence or speech.
2. He finds no comfort in his friends.
3. He finds no comfort in his thoughts of God.

16: 18–22

1. Is God indifferent to man's sorrow?
2. Is God less just than man?
3. Is God less real to the dead?

17: 1–16

1. When life mocks us—what then?
2. When light is denied us—what then?
3. When love fails us—what then?

18: 5–21

1. He was orthodox but intolerant.
2. He was arrogant and, therefore, unhelpful.
3. He was unimaginative and, therefore, unsympathetic.

19: 1–22

1. The loneliness of personal suffering.
2. The lingering conviction that God has His reasons.
3. The longing to be left alone.

19: 23–29

1. He believes the past revealed the providence of God.
2. He believes the present is revealing the punishment of God.
3. He believes the future will reveal the purpose of God.

20: 1–29

1. Is evil a permanent fact of life?
2. Is evil punished in this life?
3. Has evil a purpose in life?

21: 1–34

1. Does man's prosperity make him feel independent?
2. Is man's prosperity independent of character?
3. Is man's destiny determined by character?

22: 1–20

1. Does God take sides in human affairs?
2 Does God stand aside from human affairs?
3. Does God understand human affairs?

22: 21–30
1. Is our faith in God self-seeking?
2. Is our hope in God self-centred?
3. Is our love of God selfish?

23: 1–17
1. Can God be found?
2. Can the will of God be known?
3. Does God care?
4. Does God communicate Himself to man?

24: 1–12
1. Why doesn't God intervene?
2. Why does God permit injustice?
3. Why does God appear to be indifferent?

24: 13–25
1. Why are men wicked?
2. Why does God permit wickedness?
3. Why doesn't God punish the wicked?

25: 1–6
1. The holiness of God presented to man.
2. The helplessness of man in presence of God.
3. The hopefulness of man in presence of God.

26: 1–14
1. Do we understand the will of God towards man?
2. Do we understand the wisdom of God in the world?
3. Do we understand the ways of God with men?

27: 1–6
1. The complaint of a troubled man.
2. The character of a troubled man.
3. The claim of a troubled man.

27: 7–23
1. Do we question God's government of the world?
2. Do we make too much of our own suffering?
3. Do we give conventional answers to commonplace perplexities?

28: 1–28
1. Beyond our powers to find.
2. Beyond price.
3. Beyond praise.
4. Beyond proof.
5. Not beyond Providence to bestow it.

29: 1–25
1. Do we take our blessings for granted?
2. Do we touch the lives of others for good?
3. Do we treasure the confidence of others?

30: 1–31
1. When fortune fails—what then?
2. When faith falters—what then?
3. When one's fellows fall away—what then?

31: 1–40
1. Are we conscious of our goodness?
2. Are we proud of our goodness?
3. Are we satisfied with our goodness?
4. Are we saved by our goodness?

32: 1–10
1. The deference of youth.
2. The directness of youth.
3. The defiance of youth.

32: 11–22
1. Do words fail us sometimes?
2. Does wisdom fail us sometimes?
3. Does worship fail us sometimes?

D

33: 1–28
1. Does God speak through dreams?
2. Does God speak through distress of body?
3. Does God speak through the saints?
4. Does God speak through a Saviour?

33: 29–30
1. God does not stand apart from life.
2. God does not stand idle in life.
3. God does stoop to save in life.

34: 1–37
1. Do we love God for His own sake?
2. Do we love God because He is good?
3. Do we love God because He is just?
4. Do we love God because He is holy?

35: 1–16
1. Can we be accused of ingratitude?
2. Can we be accused of impatience?
3. Can we believe the Lord is indifferent?

36: 1–16
1. Is repentance the gateway to peace with God?
2. Is reconciliation its own reward?
3. Does rebellion get its own reward?
4. Do we rejoice when we suffer?

36: 17–33
1. Do we really trust God?
2. Do we really learn from our hardships?
3. Do we think greatly of God?

37: 1–24
1. The power revealed.
2. The preparation made.
3. The principle revealed.

38: 1–11
1. Is the world the result of chance or of divine creation?
2. Is the world haphazard or harmonious?
3. Is the world beyond control or under control?

38: 12–38
1. There is a limit to the industry of man.
2. There is a limit to the understanding of man.
3. There is a limit to the imagination of man.

38: 39–39: 30
1. Some created things suggest a purpose we do not grasp.
2. Some created things suggest a power we cannot control.
3. Some created things suggest a patience we cannot grasp.

40: 1–5–42: 2–6
1. The challenge he encountered.
2. The confession he made.
3. The confusion he experienced.
4. The conclusion to which he was led.

40: 6–41: 34
1. Are we too sure of ourselves?
2. Are we able to save ourselves?
3. Are we sure of God?

42: 7–17
1. Restless when thinking of his own suffering.
2. Reconciled to his lot when thinking of others.
3. Restored to self-respect among his friends.

Psalms (1—41)

BOOK I

1: 1-2
1. Happy is he who listens not to Evil.
2. Happy is he who thinks no Evil.
3. Happy is he who does no evil.
4. Happy is he who keeps righteousness ever before him.

1: 3
1. A Good man will be restful.
2. A Good man will have unfailing resources.
3. A Good man will be reliable.
4. A Good man's Reward will be sure.

1: 4-6
1. Godlessness is doomed to perish.
2. Godlessness is destined to be punished.
3. God delights in personal goodness.

2: 8
1. The Petition to God.
2. The Promise of God.
3. The Plan of God.

3: 1-4
1. Adversaries.
2. Advocate.
3. Answer.

3: 5-8
1. Decision.
2. Deliverance.
3. Defiance.
4. Dedication.

4: 1
1. The Boldness of Faith.
2. The Blessing of Remembered Mercies.
3. The Burden of present Evil.

4: 4-5
1. Adoration.
2. Meditation.
3. Temptation.
4. Direction.

4: 8
1. Confidence of the Psalmist.
2. Conviction of the Psalmist.
3. Contentment of the Psalmist.

5: 1-3
1. His Entreaty.
2. His Enthusiasm.
3. His Expectation.

5: 7
1. Attitude is thoughtful.
2. Approach is thankful.
3. Affirmation is with trembling.

5: 11
1. Providence.
2. Protection.
3. Praise.

6: 1, 2, 8, 9
1. Treatment he expected.
2. Treatment he asked for.
3. Treatment he received.

7: 8, 9
1. His Proclamation.
2. His Personal Prayer.
3. His Public Prayer.
4. His Perception.

8: 3, 4, 9
1. The World we see reveals Vastness.
2. The World we do not see reveals Value.
3. Both worlds speak with one voice.

75

9: 1

1. Worship.
2. Witness.
3. Wonder.

9: 3, 4a

1. Retreat of Evil when God is present.
2. Reckoning of Evil when God's Wrath is believed in.
3. Redemption from Evil when God is trusted.

9: 7–10

1. God rules.
2. God is righteous.
3. God is a Refuge.
4. God receives our Trust.

9: 12–18

1. The Cry of the humble is remembered.
2. The Claim of the Needy is remembered.
3. The Cause of the Downtrodden is remembered.

9: 16–20

1. Caught in their own cunning.
2. Consigned to endless confusion.
3. Condemned by their very condition

10: 11

1. Godless accuse God of having a bad memory.
2. Having a bad conscience.
3. Having a bad understanding.

10: 5b, 6

1. Scorns opposition—Arrogance.
2. Successful always—Pride.
3. Secure from Adversity—Blind.

11: 3, 4, 7

1. The Trial referred to.
2. The Truth implied.
3. The Trust encouraged.
4. The Triumph stated.

12: 1, 2, 7

1. Goodness is gone.
2. Godliness is going.
3. Greatness has departed.
4. God will provide and preserve.

13: 1–6

1. The Song of Distress.
2. The Song of Discovery.

14: 1–4

1. Atheism is folly.
2. Atheism fortifies no one.
3. Atheism is failure to face facts.

14: 7

1. Reformation must have religious foundation.
2. Restoration must have personal faith.
3. Rejoicing must reveal real feeling.

15: 1–5

1. The Challenge.
2. The Conditions.
3. The Consequence.

16: 1–3

1. Prayer for protection.
2. Prayer of Personal faith.
3. Prayer of personal poverty.
4. Prayer of Praise.

16: 5–6

1. His divine inheritance.
2. His daily experience.
3. His delightful confession.

16: 8, 9

1. Example of Faith.
2. Encouragement to Faith.
3. Enjoyment of Faith.

16: 11

1. Source of Revelation.
2. Certainty of Revelation.
3. Service of Revelation.

17: 5, 6
1. An acknowledgement of frailty.
2. An acknowledgement of Fear.
3. An act of Faith.
4. An appeal for favour.

17: 15
1. Personal Promise.
2. Personal Possession.
3. Personal Prophecy.

18: 2a
1. Defiance.
2. Defence.
3. Deliverance.

18: 16, 18b
1. God seeking us.
2. God saving us.
3. God supporting us.

18: 25, 26
God reveals His will to those who are
1. Merciful towards others.
2. Honourable before Him.
3. Pure within themselves.

18: 28
1. Assumes there is darkness.
2. Asserts there is light.
3. Announces victory of light over darkness.

18: 35
1. A shield of Salvation.
2. A Foundation for Fellowship.
3. A consideration of Encouragement.

18: 43b, c, 44a
1. A Lord.
2. A Leader.
3. A Loyalty.

19: 1–4
1. Seen in the skies.
2. Seen in the Seasons.
3. Seen in the Silences.
4. Seen in the Saviour.

19: 7–9
1. *The Law of the Lord.*
   (*a*) Complete—no substitutes.
   (*b*) Convincing—no uncertainty.
   (*c*) Correct—no comparison.
   (*d*) Clear—no compromise.
   (*e*) Clean—no faults.
   (*f*) Consistent—no contradictions.

20: 1–5
Prayer for
1. Divine Protection.
2. Divine Providence.
3. Divine Approval.
4. Divine Acceptance.

21: 3–4
1. Claim the blessing.
2. Commit yourself to Him.
3. Come for Life.

21: 13
1. Priority.
2. Power.
3. Praise.

22: 1–4, 6, 22
1. Confidence is shaken.
2. Conviction is unshaken.
3. Comparison humbles him.
4. Courage comes back to him.

22: 27–31
The Character of the Kingdom
1. Supernatural in scope.
2. Supernatural in source.
3. Supreme over all.
4. Succeeding generations shall know it.

23: 1
1. Personal in character.
2. Present in Power.
3. Providential in nature.

23: 2-3
1. We must be willing to be led.
2. We must be willing to be led away from main stream of life.
3. We must be willing to acknowledge our need of renewal.
4. We must be willing to acknowledge the demands of righteousness.

23: 4
1. Bad days will come.
2. Bold will be my faith.
3. Beside me stands the Lord.

23: 5
1. Guests of God's Provision.
2. Chosen for God's Purposes.
3. Equipped by God's Power.

23: 6
1. God's Goodness follows us.
2. God's Goodness never fails.
3. God's Goodness is our Final Home.

24: 1,2
1. This world is of divine Foundation.
2. This world offers divine Fellowship.
3. This world tells of divine Faithfulness.

24: 3-4
1. Possesses a clear conscience.
2. Is as honest as the day.
3. Possesses a proper sense of values.
4. Always keeps his word.

25: 4-5
1. Will of God can be known.
2. Purpose of God can be learnt.
3. Truth of God can be found.

25: 7
1. Forget my Past.
2. Forgive me now.
3. Fulfil Thy Promises.

25: 14
1. Fellowship.
2. Forgiveness.
3. Freedom from Fear.

25: 15-21
1. Bewilderment.
2. Loneliness.
3. Depression.
4. Distress.
5. Sin.
6. Shame.

26: 12
1. A Place of Rest.
2. A Place of Refreshment.
3. A Place of Revival.

27: 1
1. The Guidance of God.
2. The Grace of God.
3. Guardian Care of God.

27: 4
1. Desire is fervent.
2. Desire is for fellowship with God.
3. Desire is also for the Favour of God.

27: 7-9
1. Request to God.
2. Revelation of God.
3. Response of Man.
4. Reward remembered.

27: 14
1. Believe in your prayers.
2. Believe in yourself.
3. Believe in God's Trustworthiness.

28: 1
1. A Prayer is offered.
2. A Person is addressed.
3. A Painful alternative.

28: 9
1. A Prayer for Protection.
2. A Prayer for Prosperity.
3. A Prayer for Provision.

29
1. The Majesty of God.
2. The Manifestation of Power.
3. The Miracle of Grace.

30: 1–4
1. Help of God received.
2. Healing from God recognized.
3. Hope in God returned.
4. Holiness of God remembered.

30: 6–10
1. In Prosperity, I boasted of my strength.
2. In Adversity, I doubted my strength.
3. In Perplexity, I borrowed strength.

31: 1, 5
1. An Affirmation of Faith.
2. An Acknowledgement of Fear.
3. An Act of trusting fellowship.

31: 11
1. He was scorned by his enemies.
2. He was scoffed at by his neighbours.
3. He was a scandal to his friends.
4. He was shunned when out of doors, BUT He continued faithful.

32: 3–5
1. His confession was delayed.
2. His conscience was destroying his peace.
3. His condition was one of dryness.
4. His conversion.

33: 5–20
1. We praise God for His creation of the world.
2. We praise God for His control of the world.
3. We praise God for His Compassion for the world.

34: 8, 9
1. Make the Experiment.
2. Share the Experience.
3. Hope with Expectation.

34: 11, 12
1. Listen.
2. Learn.
3. Live.

34: 14
1. Repentance unto life.
2. Righteousness of life.
3. Reconciliation in life.

34: 18, 19
1. Strength in hours of darkness.
2. Succour in hours of depression.
3. Salvation in hours of distress.

36: 5–6
1. Compassion of God beyond our understanding.
2. Faithfulness of God beyond our grasp.
3. Goodness of God beyond our highest achievement.
4. Judgement of God beyond our deepest thought.

36: 9–10
1. Fellowship with God is vital to Life.
2. Fellowship with God brings Vision into Life.
3. Fellowship with God confers Value upon Life.

37: 3–7
1. Entrust your goodness to God.
2. Enjoy fellowship with God.
3. Expect Guidance from God.
4. Exercise reliance upon God.

37: 23–24
1. A good man's life is guided by God.
2. A good man's life gladdens the heart of God.
3. A good man's life is guarded by God.

37: 25
1. Retrospect. (looking back).
2. Recollection. (calling back).
3. Reproach does not shame him.

38
1. Physical ailment.
2. Mental anguish.
3. Personal Aspiration.
4. Personal Assurance.
5. Personal Affirmation.

39: 1–4

1. Restraint: prayer within himself.
2. Revolt: passion within himself.
3. Release: prayer beyond himself.

40: 1–3

1. God rewarded his patience.
2. God redeemed his perplexity.
3. God renewed his Praise.

40: 6–8

1. Not Sacrifices but Service.
2. Not Offerings but Obedience.
3. Not Duty but a Delight.

41: 1–9

1. Sickness.
2. Scandal.
3. Someone dear to him.
4. Saved and settled.

Psalms (42—72)
BOOK II

42: 1–2
1. Man's need for Refreshment.
2. Man's search for Reality.
3. Man's longing for Right Relationship with God.

42: 3, 4, 5
1. *Why the Tears?*
   Was it because of Sickness?
   Was it because of Sorrow?
   Was it because of Shame?
2. Religion had once been a Blessing.
3. *Why the Taunt?* 'Where is thy God'.
   Depression.
   Despair.
   Decision.

43: 3–4
1. A Petition from the Darkness.
2. A Place of Direction.
3. A Promise demanded.

43: 5(a–e)
1. Looking Inwards (*a & b*).
2. Looking Outward (*c*).
3. Looking Upward. (*d & e*).

44: 1–3
1. The Authority of the Past. (*v. 1a*).
2. The Achievements of the Past (*v. 1b, 2, 3a*).
3. The Acknowledgements of the Past. (*v. 3b*)

44: 20–21
1. A bold assertion (*v. 20a*).
2. A bad alternative (*v. 20b*).
3. A brave answer (*v. 21*).

45: 16–17
1. History is important—Toward Past.
2. Honour is more important—Toward Man.
3. Holiness is most important—Toward God.

46
The Secret of Confidence is
1. Not in Circumstances (*v. 2–3*).
2. Not in Social Stability (*v. 6*).
3. Not in Social Security (*v. 9*).
4. But in SALVATION of God (*v. 1*). (Shelter and Strength).

47: 8b
1. Our God is HOLY (holiness).
2. Our God is HOSPITABLE (sitteth).
3. Our God is at the HELM (throne).

48: 12–14
1. Our religion will stand Inspection (*v. 12*).
2. Our records will supply Inspiration. (*v. 13*).
3. Our resources will always be Invisible (*v. 14*)

49: 15
1. Fear of power of Death is natural to man.
2. Freedom from power of Death is natural to God.
3. Fellowship with God banishes that natural Fear.

49: 18, 19
1. Prosperity gives Pleasure.
2. Pride of Achievement brings Praise.
3. Prosperity passes away in Pity.

50: 14

What God asks for:
1. Praise   *What God gives:*
2. Promises   Security.
3. Prayer   Satisfaction.

50: 21–23
1. The Accusation (*v. 21*).
2. The Invitation (*v. 22*).
3. The Commendation (*v. 23*).

51: 1–5, 14
1. Remorse for sin (*v. 1, 2*).
2. Responsibility for sin (*v. 3, 4*).
3. Realisation of sin (*v. 5*).
4. Result of Forgiveness (*v. 14*).

51: 16, 17
1. Religion is not in Outward Observance but in Inner Obedience.
2. Religion is not in Outward Display but in Inner Discipline.
3. Religion is not in personal pride but in penitence of Spirit.

52: 6, 7, 8
1. The goodman is not without Understanding.
2. The goodman is not without a sense of Wonder.
3. The goodman is not without a sense of Gladness.
4. The goodman is not without a sense of Values.

55: 1–14
1. A man having difficulty with his FAITH (*v. 1–3*).
2. A man having difficulty with his FEELINGS (*v. 4–7*).
3. A man having difficulty with his FEARS (*v. 8–11*).
4. A man having difficulty with his FRIENDS (*v. 12–14*).
   BUT   (*v. 23c*).

56: 12–13
1. Psalmist is constrained to keep his promise (*v. 12a*).
2. Psalmist continues to offer his praise (*v. 12b*).
3. Psalmist comes with a second petition (*v. 13a*).
4. Psalmist commits himself to a holy purpose (*v. 13b*).

57: 1, 5
1. He seeks the Kindness of God (*v. 1a*).
2. He states his Confidence in God (*v. 1b*).
3. He stakes a great Claim for God (*v. 5*).

57: 7–10
1. The Proclamation (*v. 7a*).
2. The Promise (*v. 7b*).
3. The Performance (*v. 8, 9*).
4. The Power (*v. 10*).

58
The Mystery of Sin.
1. False Front—Deception (*v. 1, 2*).
2. False Start—Defect of character (*v. 3*).
3. False Growth—No Discipline (*v. 4*).
4. False Values—Darkness preferred to Light (*v. 8b*).
5. Final Word—Deliverance is with GOD (*v. 11*).

60:
God speaks sometimes through—
1. Defeat (*v. 1–3*).
2. Disgrace (*v. 4*).
3. Domination (*v. 6a– 8c*).
always through
4. Deliverance (*v. 11, 12*)

61: 5, 8
1. Heritage of Reverence (*v. 5b*).
2. Heritage of Remembrance (*recall v. 3, 5a*).
3. Heritage of Rededication (*v. 8*).

62: 1–2
1. The Practice of Prayer (*v. 1a*).
2. The Secret of Salvation (*v. 1b*).
3. The Cause of Confidence (*v. 2*).

62: 8–10
1. Source of our Convictions (*v. 8*).
2. Snare of Class Consciousness (*v. 9*).
3. Standards to be Commended (*v. 10*).

62: 11–12
3 Elements in O.T. Conception of God.
1. His Power (*v. 11*).
2. His Mercy (*v. 12a*).
3. His Justice (*v. 12b*).

63
1. The Search man makes—
   Thirst (*v. 1a*).
   Hunger (*v. 2a*).
   Prayer (*v. 4b*).
   Pursuit (*v. 8*).
2. The Satisfaction God offers—
   Praise (*v. 4a*).
   Provision (*v. 5*).
   Protection (*v. 7*).

65
1. Praise is offered.
2. Promise is made.
3. Prayer is made possible.

64: 7–10
An ancient comment on the Evildoer.
1. Retribution is promised (*v. 7, 8a*).
2. Retirement in Panic (*v. 8b*).
3. Return to Praise (*v. 9*).

65: 3
1. Confession of personal sin comes first.
2. Confession of People's Sin comes next.
3. Confession of Power of God to forgive comes last.

65: 4–13
1. The Worship of God (*v. 4a*).
2. The Work of God (*v. 5*).
3. The Witness to God (*v. 6–13*).

66: 5–20
1. Impressiveness of God's Power (*v. 5–7*).
2. Indications of God's Purpose (*v. 8–12*).
3. Inspiration of answered Prayers (*v. 16–20*).

67: 5–7
1. A Song for everyone (*v. 5*).
2. A Sign for everyone (*v. 6a*).
3. A Service for everyone (*v. 7b*).

68: 17–18
1. Symbols of Movement—God at Work.
2. Symbols of Majesty—God on High.
3. Symbols of Ministry—God Condescending.

68: 11
1. The People of God into Palestine.
2. The Word of God unto Prophets.
3. The Son of God unto Prepared Souls.

68: 34
1. Is our God big enough to direct Nations?
2. Is our God big enough to control Nature?
3. Is our God big enough to supply our Needs?

69: 1–3, 4–9, 30
1. A man who is overwhelmed (*v. 1–3*).
2. A man who is outnumbered (*v. 4*).
3. A man who is outcaste (*v. 5, 8, 9*).
4. A man who overcame (*v. 30*).

71: 16–18
1. Resolution (*v. 16a*).
2. Resources (*v. 16a*).
3. Recognition (*16b*).
4. Request (*v. 18*).

71: 20

1. An approach to the Lord (*v. 20a*).
2. An affliction from the Lord (*v. 20b*).
3. An awakening before the Lord (*20 c*).

72

1. Personality of the King. (*v. 1–7*).
2. Planting of the Kingdom (*v. 8–15*).
3. Prosperity of the Kingdom (*v. 16*).
4. Perpetual Praise of the King (*v. 17*).

Psalms (73—89)

BOOK III

73: 2–11, 16–17
1. A Common Complaint.
2. A Common Consequence.
3. A Common Conclusion.
4. A Comforting Consideration.

73: 25–26
1. The Cry from the heart.
2. The Call from on High.
3. The Confession of Hope.

73: 28
1. The Source of Contentment.
2. The Secret of Confidence.
3. The Soul of Communion.

74: 9
1. Old Standards gone.
2. Old Standard-Bearers gone.
3. Old Sureness gone.

75: 1–3
1. A return to Thanksgiving.
2. A reason for Testimony.
3. A renewal of Trust.

75: 9–10
1. Praise shall be my song.
2. Power of Evil shall be arrested.
3. Power of God shall be restored.

76: 1, 2
1. Revelation of God is proclaimed.
2. Reverence for God is practised.
3. Residence of God is published.

77: 3
1. Remembrance sometimes brings Remorse.
2. Remembrance sometimes brings Retribution.
3. Remembrance sometimes brings Recovery.

78: 2–4, 7
1. The Value of Tradition.
2. The Virtue of Testimony.
3. The Vision of Trust.

78: 19, 20, 25
1. The Question asked.
2. The Challenge stated.
3. The Charity shown.

78: 35–37
1. Instead of Worship they offered Words.
2. Instead of Witness they were found wanting.
3. Instead of Waiting upon God, they wavered.

78: 38–40
1. The Pardon of God.
2. The Providence of God.
3. The Patience of God.

78: 61, 72
1. The Method God used.
2. The Message God proclaimed.
3. The Movement God began.
4. The Miracle God performed.

80: 1, 2
1. Our Need of Guidance.
2. Our Need of Light.
3. Our Need of Power.

80: 18–19
1. The Promise.
2. The Privilege.
3. The Prayer.
4. The Praise.

81: 1–7
1. Is our Song lifeless?
2. Is our Saviour living?
3. Is our Salvation lasting?

81: 8–10
1. God speaks to all who listen.
2. God seeks those who listen.
3. God serves those who listen.

83: 1, 2, 17–18
1. The Appeal.
2. The Opposition.
3. The Opportunity.

84: 1, 2, 4
1. Where God dwells there is beauty.
2. Where God dwells He beckons.
3. Where God dwells there is Blessing.

84: 5–7
1. Resources to draw upon.
2. Refreshment to count upon.
3. Revelation to be sure of.

84: 11
1. God: the source of our Seeing.
2. God: the source of our Security.
3. God: the source of our Satisfaction.
4. God: the source of our Salvation.

85: 1–6
1. The Providences of the Past.
2. The Prayer of the Present.
3. The Perplexity of the People.
4. The Power and the Purpose.

85: 8
1. The Promise.
2. The Provision.
3. The Price.

86: 1–3
1. A man's cry.
2. A man's claim.
3. A man's confidence.
4. A man's confession.

86: 8, 9
1. Alone in Greatness.
2. Alone in Goodness.
3. Alone in Glory.

86: 16–17
1. He knew to whom to go.
2. He knew what had been done for him.
3. He knew that goodness tells.

87: 5
The Church of God embraces
1. Every class of persons.
2. Every country of persons.
3. Every communion of persons.

88: 3–8, 13
1. A Man deprived of Happiness.
2. A Man deprived of Health.
3. A Man deprived of Hope.
4. A Man deprived of Heaven.
5. A Man deprived of Hospitality.
6. A Man determined to Hold on.

89: 1, 2
1. Praise unbroken.
2. Provision unfailing.
3. Promise unchangeable.

89: 6–8, 13–14
1. The Lord is incomparable.
2. The Lord is inescapable.
3. The Lord is incorruptible.

89: 15–16

1. The Happiness of those who know.
2. The Hopefulness of those who serve.
3. The Heritage of those who believe.
4. The Honour of those who trust.

89: 33–34, 37

1. The Assurance that God's Love is never withheld.
2. The Assurance that God's Loyalty is never betrayed.
3. The Assurance that God's Light is never withdrawn.

89: 26

1. Worthy of our Love.
2. Worthy of our Worship.
3. Worthy of our Trust.

89: 49, 52

1. The Promise.
2. The Pity.
3. The Praise.

Psalms (90—106)
BOOK IV

90: 1
1. God, the abiding home of man.
2. God, the abiding home of every man.
3. God, the abiding home of every man always.

90: 4
1. Nothing is beyond His Knowledge.
2. Nothing is beyond His Care.
3. Nothing is beyond His Control.

90: 9b
1. How short a story?
2. What kind of story?
3. How will it end?

90: 12
1. Let us value the days we have.
2. Let us redeem the days we have.
3. Let us live one day at a time.

90: 14-15
1. The Morning of life can be satisfied.
2. The Afternoon of life can be encouraged.
3. The Evening of life can be gladdened.

90: 16-17
1. A prayer for Vision to see God at work.
2. A prayer that the Future may share that Vision.
3. A prayer for Prosperity in all our Undertakings.

91: 2
1. God: our secret hiding place.
2. God: our secret Strength.
3. God: our secret Hope.

91: 14-15
1. Encouragement when we confess Him.
2. Encouragement when we call upon Him.
3. Encouragement when in crisis.

92: 1-2
1. How fortunate we are to have God to turn to.
2. How fortunate we are to have Goodness to thank Him for.
3. How fortunate we are to have Gifts to bless Him for.

92: 5, 8
1. God is beyond our Knowledge.
2. God is beyond our Understanding.
3. God is beyond our Vision.

92: 12
1. Good man likened to a Tree that is Upright in growth.
2. Good man likened to a Tree that is deep rooted.
3. Good man likened to a Tree that is very fruitful.

93: 1
1. An Exclamation of Faith.
2. An Expression of Fear.
3. An Explanation of Fact.

93: 4

1. Mightier than Waters of Tribulation—ROUGH waters.
2. Mightier than Waters of Bitterness —DEEP waters.
3. Mightier than Waters of Repentance —SILENT waters.

94: 3–15

1. The Burden of Everyman.
2. The Blindness of Evil-doers.
3. The Blessing of Endurance.
4. The Boldness of Expectation.

94: 19

1. There is the Fear of Ill health.
2. There is the Fear of Loneliness.
3. There is the Fear of Anxiety concerning others.
4. There is the Fear of doing the Wrong thing.
5. There is the Fear of Criticism.

95: 8

1. Harden not your heart towards Him.
2. Harden not your heart towards His Ways.
3. Harden not your heart towards His Works.

96: 2–4

1. For every morning—the Lord's Providence.
2. For every nation—the Lord's Power.
3. For every people—the Lord's Preeminence.

96: 8

1. God is worthy of our Trust.
2. God is worthy of our Tribute.
3. God is worthy of our Testimony.

96: 10–13

1. Judgement there must be.
2. Joy there will be.
3. Justice will be done.

97: 1, 2

1. God rejoices the Multitudes.
2. God is wrapped in Mystery.
3. God reigns in Mercy.

97: 11, 12

1. Understanding is given to those who do right.
2. Happiness is given to those who love what is right.
3. Thanksgiving is given by those who know the source of what is right.

98

What God hath done:—
1. for all the world to see.
2. for all men to sing about.
3. for all nature to shout about.

99: 1–3

1. The Holiness of God that is proclaimed.
2. The Humility of man that is proper.
3. The Honour of God that is preserved.

100: 3

1. The Inheritance of Revelation.
2. The Initiative in Creation.
3. The Inspiration of His Protection.

100: 4–5

1. Come thankfully.
2. Come thoughtfully.
3. Come thoroughly convinced.

101

1. A Resolution as to his personal Conduct.
2. A Resolution as to his Company.
3. A Resolution as to public corruption.

102: 1–12

1. He wonders if God is unwilling.
2. He wants a reply urgently.
3. He worries to the uttermost.
4. He finds the world unfriendly.
5. He wins through and endures.

102: 14–18

1. They were unashamed of their traditions.
2. They were undaunted by the Future.
3. They were uncompromising in their convictions.
4. They were undertaking responsibility for the future.

102: 19–22

1. The Condescension of God.
2. The Compassion of God.
3. The Community of God.

102: 25–28

1. The Foundation of our Confidence.
2. The Fact of Change.
3. The Faith for Children of tomorrow.

103: 1, 2

1. The Call to Worship.
2. The Claims of Worship.
3. The Constraint of Worship.

103: 10–12

1. Beyond our deserving.
2. Beyond our discernment.
3. Beyond our disgrace.

103: 13–14

1. The Comparison drawn.
2. The Compassion shown.
3. The Consideration given.

103: 15–18

1. The Contrast that is obvious.
2. The Continuation of Mercy that is not obvious.
3. The Conditions of this Continuation—Obedience.

104

1. The Creator's Praise.
2. The Creator's Purpose.
3. The Creator's Pleasure.
4. The Creator's Providence.

105: 17

1. A Divine Mission.
2. A Despised Messenger.
3. A Dauntless Mediator.

105: 37

1. Forward despite hardship.
2. Reward through hardship.
3. Refreshed despite hardship.

105: 42–45

1. He Kept His Word.
2. He Completed His Work.
3. He Comforted them.
4. He Consecrated them.

106

1. Story of the Patience of God.
2. Story of the Passions of Men.
3. Story of the Provocation of God.
4. Story of the Pity of God.
5. Story of the Pain of God.

106: 14–15

1. The Greed of the multitudes.
2. The Grace they despised.
3. The Goodness of the Lord.
4. The Gall that became.

106: 21–46

Why they forgot:
1. Idolatry corrupted them.
2. Integrity deserted them.
3. Indecency overtook them.
4. Infirmity overwhelmed them.
5. Then: His Inheritance He restored to them.

Psalms (107—150)
BOOK V

107: 1–3
1. Worthy of our Praise.
2. Worthy of our Prayers.
3. Worthy of our Patience.

107: 4–7
1. Lives without Purpose.
2. Lives without Peace.
3. Lives without Power.
4. Lives made new through Prayer.

107: 8, 9, 16, 22, 32
1. The Goodness of God known in Divine Comfort.
2. The Goodness of God known in Divine Compassion.
3. The Goodness of God known in Divine Commemoration.
4. The Goodness of God known in Community of Praise.

107: 10–13
1. The Character of Unbelief.
2. The Consequences of Unbelief.
3. The Collapse of Unbelief.
4. The Compassion of the Lord.

107: 17–20
1. Some are sick because of Sin.
2. Some are sad because they are Scared.
3. Some are saved because a Saving Word is sent them.

107: 23–30
1. Nature speaks of God.
2. Nature celebrates God.
3. Nature serves the Will of God.

107: 33–41
1. Evil does not go unpunished.
2. Enterprise does not go unrewarded.
3. Endurance does not go unrecognised.

109: 4–5
1. The Contrariness of Life.
2. The Comfort in Life.
3. The Contradictions of Life.

110
1. The Christ of Supreme Authority.
2. The Christ of Power.
3. The Christ—Perfect in Purity.
4. The Christ—Perfect in Priesthood.
5. The Christ of Perseverance.

111: 1
1. Thanksgiving without Reservations.
2. Thanksgiving without Restraint.
3. Thanksgiving without Regret.

111: 4–6
1. God's Works are Permanent.
2. God's Works are Precious.
3. God has made Provision.
4. God keeps His Promises.
5. God shows forth His Power.

111: 8–9
1. The Laws of God do not change.
2. The Love of God does not change.
3. The Life of God does not change.

112: 6b, 7
1. A good man's Memory never fades.
2. A good man's Courage never fails.
3. A good man's Convictions never falter.

113: 5–9
1. The Condescension of the Lord.
2. The Compassion of the Lord.
3. The Conversion by the Lord.
4. The Contentment in the Lord.

114: 1–8
1. Behold—the Grace of God.
2. Behold—the Greatness of God.
3. Behold—the Glory of God.

115: 2–8, 12
1. The Accusation.
2. The Answer.
3. The Affliction.
4. The Assurance.

116: 3–9
1. The Suffering.
2. The Supplication.
3. The Salvation.

116: 12–19
1. A proper Question.
2. A proper Answer.
3. At the proper time. (*When*).
4. To the proper person (*To Whom*).
5. In the proper place (*Where*).

117
1. A Wonderful Invitation.
2. A Wonderful Inspiration.
3. A Wonderful Inheritance.

118: 8–13, 14
1. The Commendation he makes.
2. The Confidence he reveals.
3. The Complaint he makes.
4. The Conclusion he arrives at.

118: 19, 21
1. Request is made.
2. Response is given.
3. Redemption is known.

118: 22–23
1. Revelation refused.
2. Revelation rescued.
3. Revelation recognized.

119: 7–8
1. Readiness to acknowledge God's Will.
2. Realization of God's Will.
3. Recognition of God's Power.

119: 11
1. The World in which we live.
2. The Word by which we live.
3. The Witness I would give.

119: 13–16
1. The Proclamation of Faith.
2. The Prayer of Faith.
3. The Performance of Faith.

119: 18
1. By nature, we are blind.
2. By nature, God is Kind.
3. By Grace, we shall find.

119: 25
1. A Confession of helplessness.
2. A Cry for help.
3. A claim in hope.

119: 27–28
1. He asks for Understanding.
2. He gives an Undertaking.
3. He confesses he is Undone.
4. He pleads for Undergirding.

119: 41–42
1. He claims the Promise to Faith.
2. He claims the Power to be faithful.
3. He claims the Privilege of Faith.

119: 49, 52, 55
1. God's Remembrance—Basis of our Hope.
2. Our Remembrance—Basis of our Consolation.
3. Remembrance—Basis of our Loyalty.

119: 57–64

1. He makes a Promise.
2. He claims the Promise.
3. He considers his Plans.
4. He carries them out.
5. He contemplates the Past.
6. He confesses to Thankfulness.
7. He keeps good Company

119: 65, 66

1. He has been well-treated.
2. He wants to be well-balanced.
3. He wants to be well-informed.

119: 67, 68, 72

1. He has learnt his lesson.
2. He has learnt to believe in goodness of God.
3. He has learnt that Wisdom is better than Wealth.

119: 73–75

1. Personal Confession is made.
2. Personal Example is set.
3. Personal Experience is given (*shared*).

119: 81, 82, 83, 86

1. He longs for Peace.
2. He longs for Patience.
3. He longs for a sense of Purpose.
4. He longs for a sense of Power.

119: 89–91

1. God's Law does not change.
2. God's Love does not change.
3. God's World does not change.

119: 105–112

1. Declaration—Guidance of God is available.
2. Demand—Guidance must be obeyed.
3. Decision—Obedience is promised.

119: 126, 128

1. He expresses Impatience with God.
2. He expresses Indignation towards Men.
3. He claims Integrity within himself.

119: 129, 130, 133

1. Unexplainable—but they command Obedience.
2. Unfolded—they help clarify understanding.
3. Undertake for me, for I am uncertain.

119: 137–144

1. His conception of God's Law.
2. His concern for God's Law.
3. His conscientiousness in obeying God's Law.
4. His conviction for Life.

119: 145–152

1. Decision in Prayer.
2. Diligence in Prayer.
3. Delight in Prayer.

119: 165

1. Great Peace.
2. Great Loyalty.
3. Great Freedom.

120: 5

1. Banished from God.
2. Burdened with Godlessness.
3. In Bondage to Godlessness.

121: 1–2

1. Nature suggests Strength.
2. Need suggests Supply.
3. Never does Supply fail.

121: 3–8

1. The Lord is Untiring.
2. The Lord is Unresting.
3. The Lord is Understanding.
4. The Lord is Unchanging.

122: 1–4

1. A happy Memory.
2. A holy Memorial.
3. A heartfelt Ministry.

122: 6–9

1. The Church and our Prayers.
2. The Church and Prosperity.
3. The Church and her Purpose.

123

1. Petition to the Most High.
2. Perseverance towards the Most High.
3. Persecution for the Most High.

124

1. The Indebtedness he acknowledges.
2. The Insight he is given.
3. The Inspiration he experiences.

125

1. God is always trustworthy.
2. God is always trusting us.
3. God is always testing us.

126

1. They are surprised by Joy.
2. They sing for Joy.
3. They want to share their Joy.
4. They are sure of future Joy.

127

1. The Guardian Care of God.
2. The Guiding hand of God.
3. The Gracious Gifts of God.

128: 1–2

1. Reverence before God.
2. Right behaviour before God.
3. Reward from God's Bounty.
4. Rejoicing in God's Blessing.

130: 1–5

1. Prayer—the outburst of a broken soul.
2. Penalty—the fear of a broken soul.
3. Pardon—the hope of a broken soul.

131

1. He is discreet.
2. He is dependent.
3. He is dedicated.

132: 1–11

1. A King's Resolve is remembered.
2. A Kindly Religion is re-established.
3. A Kingly Redemption is recognised.

132: 12–18

1. Divine Conditions are imposed.
2. Divine Choice is made.
3. Divine Continuance is provided for.

133

1. Fellowship is fragrant.
2. Fellowship is fertilising.
3. Fellowship fulfils life.

135: 1–7

1. The Praise of God.
2. The Purpose of God.
3. The Power of God.

137

1. Remembrance overcomes them.
2. Request is made of them.
3. Resolution of loyalty.
4. Retribution—a warning.

138

1. Wholeheartedness in Worship.
2. Waiting in Wonder.
3. Witnessing worthily.
4. Working without wavering.

139: 1–6

1. He knows all.
2. He understands all.
3. He provides for all.

139: 7–12

1. God everlasting.
2. God everywhere.
3. God everyday.

139: 13–18

1. God—the Creator.
2. God—the Artist.
3. God—the Architect.

139: 19–22

1. The Stain on the World.
2. The Strife in the World.
3. The Stand we should take.

139: 23–24

1. A Prayer for right motives.
2. A Prayer for clean thoughts.
3. A Prayer for chaste desires.
4. A Prayer for worthy ambition.

140

1. The Confederacy of Evil.
2. The Conviction of Everyman.
3. The Conclusion of an Evil life.
4. The Consummation of a Good life.

141: 1–5

1. He is a suppliant for God's favour.
2. He offers his service towards others.
3. He is to speak no evil.
4. He is to do no evil.
5. He is to despise not the criticism of his friends.

142

1. His Distress.
2. His Depression.
3. His Deliverance.

143: 2–6

1. His fear.
2. His frailty.
3. His fight.

143: 7–10

1. His Dedication.
2. His prayer for Direction.
3. His prayer for Deliverance.
4. His prayer he may do his Duty.

144: 12–15

1. A Prayer for Family happiness.
2. A Prayer for a sufficiency of Food.
3. A Prayer for a Friendly world.
4. A Prayer for Faith in the Lord.

145: 3

1. Our God is Worthy.
2. Our God is worthy of our Witness.
3. Our God is worthy of our Wonder.

145: 13–20

1. The Majesty of God.
2. The Mercy of God.
3. The Manifestations of God.

146: 3–6

1. Helplessness in believing wrongly.
2. Happiness in believing God.
3. Hopefulness in believing God.

147: 2–4

1. The Work of God—the Church.
2. The Winning of the lost—the Challenge.
3. The Wonder of His Concern—Christian Action.
4. The Wonder of the Celestial World—Creation.

147: 7–20

1. God's Care for created things.
2. God's choice of a peculiar people.
3. God's correction of his people.

149: 6–9

1. A high call to Worship.
2. A high call to Witness.
3. A high call to Work.

150

1. A Call to Praise God.
2. A Concerto of Praise to God.
3. The Climax of Praise to God.

Proverbs

1: 1–7
1. The search for wisdom.
2. The secret of wisdom.
3. The scorn of wisdom.

1: 8–19
1. The value of a good home.
2. The virtue of honour.
3. The vanity of dishonour.

1: 20–33
1. Do we learn from the past?
2. Do we pay for our ignorance?
3. Do we profit from our insight?

2: 1–9
1. The way to wisdom.
2. The word of wisdom.
3. The work of wisdom.

2: 10–22
1. Wisdom is for life; it is not a luxury.
2. Wisdom lives in moral behaviour; not in mystery.
3. Wisdom brings self-respect; not shame.

3: 1–10
1. Is spiritual life real to us?
2. Is spiritual understanding alive in us?
3. Is spiritual principle strong in us?

3: 11–12
1. No discipline; no discipleship.
2. No hardship; no heroism.
3. No pain; no partnership.

3: 13–20
1. Is our sense of values scriptural?
2. Is our sense of values satisfying?
3. Is our sense of values steadfast?

3: 21–26
1. Heavenly light for earthly life.
2. Heavenly peace for earthly rest.
3. Heavenly strength for earthly strife.

3: 27–35
1. Is our morality practical?
2. Are our motives pure?
3. Is our meekness praiseworthy?

4: 1–9
1. Do we respect the gathered experience of the past?
2. Do we respond to the gathered experience of the past?
3. Do we rejoice in the gathered experience of the past?

4: 10–19
1. Direction is important.
2. Decision is imperative.
3. Destination is inevitable.

4: 20–27
1. Life needs altitude.
2. Life demands attention.
3. Life issues in an attitude.

5: 1–23
1. The recklessness confronting all men.
2. The remorse common to all men.
3. The result coming to all men.

6: 1–15

1. Embarrass no man.
2. Emulate the lowliest.
3. Eschew wickedness.

6: 16–19

1. Personal:
   (a) Pride.
   (b) Dishonesty.
   (c) Unworthy intentions.
   (d) Undisciplined mind.
2. Public:
   (e) Uncontrolled passions.
   (f) Uncontrolled tongue.
   (g) Irresponsible behaviour.

6: 20–35

1. Keep clean for Him.
2. Keep close to Him.
3. Keep clear by Him.

7: 1–27

1. Let us make up our minds about life.
2. Let us measure the motives of our lives.
3. Let us mind the morals of our lives.

8: 1–11

1. Do we want to understand the ways of God?
2. Can we understand the ways of God?
3. Can we underrate the wisdom of God?

8: 12–21

1. The proof of our religion—moral behaviour.
2. The purpose of our religion—restoration of broken relationship.
3. The power of religion is in its promises.

8: 22–36

1. Happy is he who seeks to understand life.
2. Happy is he who has found life.
3. Happy is he who does not refuse life.

9: 1–12

1. The hospitality of God.
2. The humility of God.
3. The hopefulness of God.

9: 13–18

1. Evil has its disciples.
2. Evil has its delights.
3. Evil has its deserts.

10: 12

1. Hatred disrupts society.
2. Hatred destroys the soul.
3. Love delivers society from evil.
4. Love delivers the soul from self.

10: 27–28

1. Does religion banish fears of the future?
2. Does irreligion bring fear of the future?
3. Does religion gladden the heart?
4. Does irreligion harden the heart?

11: 4

1. Riches—so uncertain.
2. Wrath—so unwelcome.
3. Righteousness—so unpopular.

11: 11

1. Citizens give character to a city.
2. Citizens determine the character of a city.
3. Citizens can destroy the character of a city.

11: 24

1. He who gives, gets.
2. He who goes out to give, gets more.
3. He who keeps, gets poor.

11: 26

1. Do we hoard God's gifts?
2. Do we hurt God's children by doing so?
3. Do we honour God by sharing His gifts?

12: 19

1. Truth can stand up to falsehood.
2. Truth can stand longer than falsehood.
3. Truth will still stand when falsehood fails.

13: 7-8

1. When riches turn to rags, what then?
2. When rags mean riches, what then?
3. When rags and riches depart, what then?

13: 12

1. The distinction of hope.
2. The disappointments of hope.
3. The discovery of hope.

13: 13-15

1. Irreverence gives no satisfaction.
2. Insight is satisfaction.
3. Inspiration brings satisfaction.
4. Ingratitude brings no satisfaction.

13: 24

1. What no-one likes—discipline.
2. What everyone needs—discipline.
3. What all may become—disciples.

14: 4

1. No toil—no triumph.
2. No partnership—no prosperity.
3. No responsibility—no result.

14: 10

1. Do we live alone?
2. Do we suffer alone?
3. Do we rejoice alone?

14: 12, 14

1. Life without guidance leads to darkness.
2. Life without God leads to death.
3. Life without good leads to damnation.
4. Life with God leads to deliverance.

14: 26-27

1. Reverence stabilizes life.
2. Reverence sanctifies life.
3. Reverence is the secret source of life.

14: 34

1. A nation's greatness—prosperity?
2. A nation's greatness—possessions?
3. A nation's greatness—personal integrity?

15: 1-2

1. Is our speech under control?
2. Is our speech making for strife or calm?
3. Is our speech converted.?

15: 11

1. Do we take God seriously?
2. Do we take godlessness seriously?
3. Do we take godliness seriously?

15: 16-17

1. Reverence can enrich our love of life.
2. Riches can embarrass our love of life.
3. Rejoicing can spring from love of life.

16: 2-4

1. Man proposes: plan.
2. God disposes: purpose.
3. Man prays: prayer.
4. God promises: providence.

16: 7

1. Reverence for the Lord.
2. Respect for one's fellow men.
3. Reconciliation between men.

16: 32-33

1. Forbearance better than fight.
2. Self-control better than conquest of others.
3. Life is uncertain but Love is in control.

17: 17
1. True friendship never wearies.
2. True friendship never wears out.
3. True friendship never wavers.

17: 22
1. Gladness is wholesome.
2. Gladness brings healing.
3. Gloom brings hurt.

18: 10
1. Is God trustworthy?
2. Is God trusted?
3. Is God our trustee?

18: 24
1. Has friendship led us into disappointment?
2. Has friendship taught us to distinguish?
3. Has friendship led us into discovery?

19: 17
1. A kindness is shown.
2. A kindness is received.
3. A kindness is returned.

19: 23
1. Reverence for God leads to a larger life.
2. Reverence for God leads to a satisfying life.
3. Reverence for God leads to confidence in life.

20: 4
1. Are we pulling our weight in life?
2. Are we paying our way in life?
3. Are we paying for our waywardness?

20: 9
1. Beyond the best of us.
2. Beyond any of us.
3. By Grace alone.

20: 27
1. Conscience: is it welcome?
2. Conscience: is it working?
3. Conscience: is it witnessing?

21: 3
1. Honour within.
2. Honesty without.
3. Hypocrisy (*without either*).

21: 4
1. Self-centredness is sin.
2. Self-importance is sin.
3. Self-advertisement is sin.

21: 30
1. Does God have His way with us?
2. Does God overrule our plans?
3. Does God overtake our rebellion?

22: 1–2
1. What do others value most highly in us?
2. What do we value most highly from them?
3. What do we and they share with everyone?

22: 6
1. What we all need—instruction.
2. What we all deserve—discipline.
3. What we all remember—both.

22: 17–21
1. The necessary approach.
2. The obvious advantage.
3. The desired assurance.
4. The ready answer.

22: 28
1. They indicated ownership.
2. They invited obedience.
3. They were easily observed.

24: 19–20
1. Worry not.
2. Envy not.
3. Fear not.

25: 1–7
1. The proclamation: mystery.
2. The pursuit: mastery.
3. The preparation: meekness.

25: 11–12

1. The right word at the right time.
2. The right word in the right ear.
3. The right word from the right person.

25: 21–22

1. Mercy—have we tried it?
2. Magnanimity—do we believe it?
3. Merit—shall we deserve it?

25: 25

1. That would be surprising.
2. That would be satisfying.
3. That would be strengthening.

27: 1

1. Is our dependence upon God daily?
2. Is our deference before God daily?
3. Is our debt to God a daily one?

27: 8

1. Have we cut adrift from God?
2. Have we lost our way in life?
3. Have we lost the desire to get back to God?

27: 17

1. Why be lonely?
2. Why not share our love?
3. Why not enjoy life?

28: 13

1. Unconfessed sin brings no peace.
2. Unconfessed sin brings no pardon.
3. Confessed sin alone releases power.

29: 18

1. No revelation: no religion.
2. No religion: no righteousness.
3. No righteousness: no restraint.

30: 1–4

1. What do we really know?
2. What do we think we know?
3. What do we want to know?

30: 5–6

1. Our God is faithful.
2. Our God fortifies the faithful.
3. Our God's final word has been given.

30: 7–9

1. Consider the honesty of this man.
2. Consider the humility of this man.
3. Consider the honour of this man.

30: 11–14

1. No respect for older folk.
2. No respect for truth about themselves.
3. No respect for knowledge.
4. No respect for gentleness.

30: 18–31

1. Are we losing our sense of the wonder of life?
2. Are we losing our sense of the unexpectedness of life?
3. Are we losing our sense of providence in life?
4. Are we losing our sense of the uncertainty of life?

Ecclesiastes

1: 1–11
1. The monotony of existence.
2. The meaning of existence.
3. The message of existence.

1: 12–18
1. How aimless are our lives?
2. How aimless is our knowledge?
3. How aimless is our experience?

2: 1–11
1. So full of self—so empty of satisfaction.
2. So full of pride—so empty of purpose.
3. So full of possessions—so empty of peace of mind.

2: 12–17
1. Can we not improve upon the past?
2. Can we not instruct the present?
3. Can we not inspire the future?

2: 18–26
1. There are injustices in every man's life.
2. There is inspiration for every man's life.
3. There are inequalities in every man's life.
4. There is an inheritance for every man's life.

3: 1–9
1. Is life planned?
2. Is my life planned?
3. Is my life profitable?

3: 10–11
1. There is a Master.
2. There is a master-plan.
3. There is mystery.

3: 12–15
1. God is unchanging in purpose.
2. God is unchanging in patience.
3. God is unchanging in power.

3: 16–17
1. Wickedness in high places.
2. Wickedness in holy places.
3. Watchfulness in the holy place.

3: 18–22
1. Is man just flesh and bone?
2. Is man destined to oblivion?
3. Is man sure only of the present?

4: 1–6
1. The perplexity of human life.
2. The perversity of human behaviour.
3. The peace of humble acceptance.

4: 7–12
1. The vanity of unshared prosperity.
2. The virtue of shared prosperity.
3. The value of shared prosperity.

4:13–16
1. The faith in what we can become.
2. The fickleness of human nature.
3. The finality of human striving.

5: 1–3
1. The need for reverence before God.
2. The need for restraint before God.
3. The need for responsibility before God.

5: 4–7

1. How real is our religion?
2. How real is our repentance?
3. How real is our reverence?

5: 8–9

1. We are not to lose our assurance in life.
2. We are not to forget the final authority in life.
3. We are not to forget that God is involved in life.

5: 10–17

1. The love of wealth does not bring satisfaction.
2. The love of wealth does not bring serenity.
3. The love of wealth does not bring security.

5: 18–20

1. The recognition of God—Giver of all good.
2. The responsibility before God—from Whom our gifts come.
3. The realization—God is in control.

6: 1–6

1. Is God the author of our frustrated hopes?
2. Can God transform our frustrated hopes?
3. Will God, finally, frustrate our hopes?

6: 7–12

1. There is a hunger common to us all.
2. There is a hunger our labour cannot satisfy.
3. There is a hunger the world cannot satisfy.

7: 1–6

1. Does personal honour count any more?
2. Does personal hardship commend itself any more?
3. Does personal humility concern us any more?

7: 7–10

1. Is there a time for silence?
2. Is patience a virtue?
3. Were the old days better?

7: 11–14

1. Which enriches life, wisdom or wealth?
2. Which enlarges life, prosperity or adversity?
3. Which encourages life, arrogance or acceptance?

7: 15–18

1. Godliness in excess can burn itself out.
2. Godlessness in excess can keep on burning.
3. Godfearing men balance their duties and their devotion.

7: 19–22

1. Our real strength is within, not without.
2. Our real salvation · is within, not without.
3. Our real sincerity is within, not without.

7: 23–29

1. The resolution he made.
2. The reality he sought.
3. The rock on which he stumbled.
4. The reason he offered.

8: 1–8

1. Does our ignorance keep us humble?
2. Does our obedience keep us unafraid?
3. Does our patience keep us waiting?
4. Does this battle keep us fighting?

8: 8

1. Our wisdom concerning death is little enough.
2. Our warfare with death is lawful enough.
3. Our weapons facing death are limited enough.

8: 9–13
1. He was observant and lived close to life.
2. He was oppressed because of man's inhumanity to man.
3. He was optimistic because of man's reverence for God.

8: 14–17
1. The anomalies of life.
2. The activities of life.
3. The answer of life.

9: 1–3
1. The discovery he made.
2. The doubt he expresses.
3. The danger he fears.

9: 4–10
1. The encouragement—life, however humble, is sweet.
2. The experience—life, however humble, can be satisfying.
3. The enterprise—life, however humble, calls for active service.

9: 11–18
1. The need for reverence.
2. The need for readiness.
3. The need for resources.

10: 1–7
1. The details that matter.
2. The deference that matters.
3. The dignity that matters.

11: 1–2
1. The risk faith must take.
2. The response faith may expect.
3. The responsibility faith must accept.

11: 3–6
1. We need, not caution, but courage.
2. We need not knowledge alone but confidence, also.
3. We need not certainty alone but also co-operation.

11: 7–10
1. Make the most of life.
2. Seek the best in life.
3. Serve the highest in life.

12: 1–5
1. Let us bring our enthusiasm to the Lord.
2. Let us bring our enterprise to the Lord.
3. Let us bring our uncertainties to the Lord.
4. Let us bring our strength to the Lord.

12: 5–8
1. Is life worth living?
2. Is death the end?
3. Is the future safe?

12: 11
1. The Word is a stimulus to thought.
2. The Word is a challenge to action.
3. The Word is a call to remembrance.

12: 13–14
1. Reverence for the character of God.
2. Respect for the power of God.
3. Righteousness in the presence of God.
4. Remembrance of the justice of God.

Song of Solomon

1: 1–4
1. The Love of God—beyond what we already know.
2. The Love of God—beyond what we deserve.
3. The Love of God—beyond our expectations.

1: 5–6
1. Is the Church different from the world?
2. Is the Church indebted to the world?
3. Has the Church neglected her own spiritual life?

1: 7–8
1. Are we seeking the Lord?
2. Are we following the Lord?
3. Are we finding the Lord?

1: 9–17
1. Is our reverence worthy of the Love revealed?
2. Is our response worthy of the Love declared?
3. Is our religion worthy of life?

2: 1–4
1. The love of which we are unworthy.
2. The love in which we find our worth.
3. The love by which we are reconciled.
4. The love by which we return home.

2: 5–7
1. The Love desired by the simple.
2. The Love that supports.
3. The Love that satisfies.

2: 8–9
1. The Lord God has come to our world.
2. The Lord God has provided for our world.
3. The Lord God would dwell with us.

2: 10–14
1. The call of the Lord.
2. The call to begin again with the Lord.
3. The call to confidence in the Lord.

2: 15–17
1. Do we put temptation in the way of the young?
2. Do we laugh at their faith?
3. Do we inspire their confidence?

3: 1–4
1. The dark night of the soul.
2. The diligent search of the soul.
3. The discovery of the soul.

3: 6–11
1. The method of His coming—unexpected.
2. The majesty of His coming—unexampled.
3. The meaning of His coming—life unfinished without it.

4: 1–7
1. The tribute.
2. The tenderness.
3. The thanksgiving.

4: 8–12
1. How great was our danger.
2. How great is our deliverer.
3. How great is our debt.

4: 15–5: 1
1. In Him are unfailing resources.
2. In Him is unfailing refreshment.
3. In Him is unfailing rejoicing.

5: 2–6
1. Do we respond when He calls?
2. Do we make excuses when He calls?
3. Do we repent of our refusals?

5: 7–9
1. The Church has not escaped persecution.
2. The Church has never forsaken her Lord.
3. The Church has never surrendered her Lord.

5: 10–16
1. In Him we find health.
2. In Him we find holiness.
3. In Him we find wholesomeness.

6: 1–3
1. We sometimes lose the vision.
2. We sometimes must venture again.
3. We sometimes must renew our vows.

6: 4b
1. The Church acknowledges a Master.
2. The Church is on the march.
3. The Church is fulfilling a mission.

6: 8–9
1. There are many Communions but only one Church.
2. There are many competitors but only one Christ.
3. There are many companions but only One abiding.

6: 10–13
1. The unrealized in life—the patience of God.
2. The unexpected in life—the providence of God.
3. The unavoidable in life—the purpose of God.

7: 1–13
1. The sacredness of marriage.
2. The sacrament of the body.
3. The satisfaction in marriage.

8: 1–2
1. Is our love of the Lord big enough?
2. Is our love of the Lord big enough to defy convention?
3. Is our love of the Lord big enough to inspire conviction?

8: 5–6a
1. Have we found Someone on whom to lean?
2. Have we forgotten the day when first we loved and lived?
3. Have we found faith that falters not?

8: 6b–7
1. The mystery of the love of God.
2. The mastery of the love of God.
3. The majesty of the love of God.
4. The miracle of the love of God.

8: 8–9
1. Are we concerned about the undeveloped?
2. Are we encouraging the undeveloped?
3. Are we enemies of the undeveloped?

8: 10
1. Is the Church true to herself?
2. Is the Church true to her Lord?
3. Is the Church triumphant in the Lord?

E

8: 11–12

1. He knew power but no peace.
2. He knew success but no satisfaction.
3. They were poor but precious to each other.

8: 13–14

1. Are we witnessing to the right people?
2. Are we witnessing in the right place?
3. Are we witnessing at the right time?

Isaiah

1: 8
Is this the Church of our day?
1. Overshadowed (As a cottage).
2. Overrun (as a lodge).
3. Overwhelmed (as a besieged city).

1: 18
The Challenge of Conversion.
1. Call to Think.
2. Call to Think impossible can happen.
3. Call to Think incredible will happen.

2: 5
'God is Light'.
1. Unfailing, always available.
2. Unchangeable, always reliable.
3. Unquenchable, always burning.

2: 3
1. Invitation—our Worship to offer.
2. Instruction—His Wisdom to learn.
3. Inspiration—His Work to do.

2: 7–8
1. Possessions in which they trust (*v. 7a*).
2. Power of which they boast (*v. 7b*).
3. Poverty of which Idols are symbolic (*v. 8*).

3: 5
'What happens when Religion is ignored'.
1. Confusion in the Nation's life.
2. Confusion in Local Community life.
3. Confusion in the Home (*see. 6, 7*).

4: 6
The Church in every Age.
1. A Place of Refreshment.
2. A Place of Rest.
3. A Place of Reward.

5: 7
The Church Perfect and Imperfect.
1. The Church is here to be Fruitful. But what does the Lord find?
2. Instead of WISDOM—FOLLY
   Instead of GOODNESS—GODLESSNESS.

5: 20–23
'On whom the Wrath of God falls':
1. On those without Moral Principles (*v. 20*).
2. On those without Mental Perspective (*v. 21*).
3. On those without Spiritual Profession (*v. 22–23*).

6: 5
1. Confession.
2. Compassion.
3. Conviction.

6: 1–8
The Birth of a Soul on Fire.
1. Conversion for Isaiah had a definite HISTORY.
2. Conversion for Isaiah had a definite character—Sense of HOLINESS of GOD.
3. Conversion for Isaiah had a purpose —to reveal HIGHEST to him.
4. Conversion for Isaiah had a Message of HUMILITY.
5. Conversion for Isaiah gave him a heightened sense of HEARING.

7: 9b
'*A Glimpse into Mystery of Faith*'.
1. Faith is always Personal (Yes).
2. Faith is a Way of Prosperity (Surely).
3. Faith is a highway to Permanence (Established).

7: 10–14
'*Working His Purpose out*'.
1. An Opportunity refused (Ask).
2. Oppression revealed (Weary).
3. An Offer renewed (Therefore).

7: 14
'*The Incarnation prophesied*'.
1. The Mystery of His Birth—Behold.
2. The Miracle of His Birth—Virgin.
3. The Meaning of His Birth—Immanuel.

8: 19, 20
Advice in Adversity.
1. Refuse to consult Mediums and Ghosts.
2. Regard the Living—not the Dead.
3. Resolve to consult the Lord—His Message and Witness.

9: 2, 6a
1. Hopelessness transformed to HOPE (*v. 2a*).
2. Uncertainty transformed to CERTAINTY (*v. 2b*).
   WHY
3. God's Purpose made Plain—Child.
   God's Person made Positive—Son.

9: 6b
1. Here is WISDOM unchanged.
2. Here is POWER unfailing.
3. Here is LOVE unchanging.
4. Here is HOPE unquenchable.

10: 1–3
Warning of Judgement to come.
A. *Condemnation* of those guilty of:
   CRUELTY
   OPPRESSION
   COVETOUSNESS
   AVARICE

B. *Consideration*
   1. No argument will save you (*v. 1*).
   2. No advice to fall back on (*v. 2b*).
   3. No abundance of possessions to take with you (*v. 3c*).
C. *Conclusion* (*v. 4b*).

10: 21–22; 11: 1–2
The Manner of His Coming.
1. His Ancestry. Remnant of Jacob (*10, v. 21–22*).
2. His Approach. A Revelation (*11, v. 1*).
3. His Anointing. The Spirit of the Lord (*11, v. 2*).

11: 6–9
When Christ Comes.
1. The Impossible comes to pass.
2. The Incredible becomes a fact.
3. The Inhumanity of men will cease.
4. The Invisible will be seen to be real.

12: 4
1. Praise.
2. Proclamation.
3. Profession.

13: 6–8
1. Destruction.
2. (*a*) Desolation.
   (*b*) Despair.

13: 19
1. The Pinnacle of human achievement.
2. The Pride of a nation.
3. The Poverty that is prophesied.

14: 1, 2
1. Their national status is restored.
2. Their national shame is redeemed.
3. Their national strength is renewed.

14: 4–7
1. The Peace that is now promised.
2. The Punishment now powerless.
3. The Praise now poured forth.

14: 12–15, 22–23
1. The Nameless Ambition.
2. The Nemesis of worldly Ambition.
3. The Necessary Answer.

14: 24–27
1. God's Purpose for the World will not be denied.
2. God's Plan for the world will not be defied.
3. God's Praise in the world cannot be doubted.

14: 31–32
1. The Cry of Astonishment.
2. The Crux of the Answer.
3. The Church of the Assurance.

15: 6
1. Refreshment has gone.
2. Reserves have gone.
3. Resources have gone.
4. Rejoicing has gone.

17: 10, 6, 7, 8
1. Unfaithful in their Worship of God (v. 10).
2. Unfruitful in their work for God (v. 6).
3. Undismayed—they wait upon God again (v. 7).
4. Unashamed—they denounce false Gods (v. 8).

19: 1
1. Nature Subject to His Control.
2. Nature Serves His Purpose.
3. Nature Symbolizes His Power.

19: 19–20
1. God at life's Centre.
2. God at life's Circumference.
3. God—life's Salvation.

19: 24, 25
1. A one-sided Alliance.
2. A wonderful Ambassador.
3. A well-earned Approval.

21: 9b, 10
1. Freedom has come.
2. Fallen are the false gods.
3. Fear frightens no longer.

21: 12
1. Faith has its Guardians.
2. Faith faces Facts.
3. Faith has Patience.

22: 22–23
1. The authority which is exchanged.
2. The authority which is exercised.
3. The authority which is established.
4. The authority which is the Emblem of Salvation.

24
1. No Planting without Ploughing (v. 1).
2. No Sunshine without Shadow (v. 4).
3. No Law without Lawlessness (v. 5).
4. No Order without Disorder (v. 10).
5. No Justice without Judgement (v. 21–23).

25: 1
1. A profession of Personal Faith.
2. A Promise to promote God's Interests.
3. A Promise to praise His name in so doing.
4. The Performances of God proclaimed.

25: 8
1. Resurrection promised.
2. Repentance made possible.
3. Redemption prophesied.

26: 3–4
1. The Lord's Protection is Personal.
2. The Lord's Protection is Perfect.
3. The Lord's Protection is Permanent.

26: 13
1. Recognition of One Lord.
2. Remorse for the Past.
3. Resolution for the Future.

28: 16
1. A proved Foundation.
2. A precious Foundation.
3. A permanent Foundation.

31: 5
1. Defence—Shelter.
2. Deliverance—Safety.
3. Destiny—Security.

33: 2
1. Unseen but real.
2. Unhurried but timely.
3. Unbroken but ready for action.

33: 8
1. Defied the Moral Law.
2. Denied Social Obligations.
3. Destroyed personal duties.

35: 3
1. Encourage the Weary—Physically tired.
2. Encourage the Weak-knees—Morally Weak.
3. Encourage the Wondering—Spiritually bewildered.
   By what means?
1. Word of Enabling.
2. Word of Endless Emphasis.

35: 5–10
1. The High Note of Miracle.
2. The High Way of Holiness.
3. The High Hope of Gladness.

37: 3
1. Day of Distress.
2. Day of Disruption.
3. Day of Disgrace.

37: 14
1. A Problem presents itself.
2. A Problem is faced squarely.
3. A Problem is prayed over.

38: 5
1. A Fervent Prayer is heard.
2. A Full Answer is granted.
3. A Final Deliverance is promised.

38: 16
1. Reliance upon God.
2. Refreshment in God.
3. Revival from God.

38: 17
1. Disappointment.
2. Deliverance.
3. Discovery.

39: 1, 2, 6; 37: 1, 2
1. Pride goes before a Fall.
2. Perversity mocks our Plans.
3. Prayer redeems from Panic.

40: 1, 2
1. Lift up your hearts.
2. Let the people sing.
3. Linger not on the past.

40: 6–8
1. The Command of God.
2. The Compassion he draws.
3. The Conclusion he arrives at.
4. The Comfort he promises.

40: 9–11
1. The Lord's Concern.
2. The Lord's Control.
3. The Lord's Consideration.
4. The Lord's Compassion.

40: 28–31
1. The Majesty of God's Being.
2. The Mastery of God's Power.
3. The Maximum of God's Help.

41: 8
1. The Servant of God's Purpose.
2. The Select One of God's Privilege.
3. The Son of God's Providence.

41: 10
1. The Comfort of the Fact of God.
2. The Challenge to Faith in God.
3. The Consequence of Faith in God.

42: 1
1. Christ—The Praise of God.
   —The Power of God.
   —The Purpose of God.

42: 2
1. The Character of Christ.
2. The Compassion of Christ.
3. The Conviction of Christ.

42: 8, 9
1. A Prophet is forthright.
2. A Prophecy is fulfilled.
3. A Prophecy is foretold.

42: 14–17
1. The Patience of God.
2. The Plan of God.
3. The Paradox of God.
4. The Punishment of God.

43: 2–4
1. A Companion in Sorrow.
2. Courage in Adversity.
3. Confidence in Affliction.
4. Conviction of Divine Love and Care.

43: 10–12
1. One God we Worship.
2. One Lord we serve.
3. One Lord who saves.

43: 18–19, 20–21
1. Looking back—Discouragement.
2. Looking up—Encouragement.
3. Looking forward—Enthronement.

43: 27
1. Our Inheritance is sinful. .
2. Our Instructors have not escaped.
3. Our Institutions have not escaped.

44: 28
1. The man God called.
2. The city God encouraged.
3. The Church God created.

45: 17
1. Salvation is Divine not Human.
2. Salvation is Permanent not Passing.
3. Salvation is Honourable not Dishonourable.

45: 22–25
1. The CALL of God
2. The CHALLENGE of God
3. The Campaign of God

} unto SALVATION

46: 9
1. God is *Infinite* therefore no one else is God.
2. God is *Incomparable* therefore no one like Him.
3. God is an *Interpreter* therefore He declares end and beginning; ancient prophecies to events to come.

47: 10, 11
1. Arrogance of Wickedness.
2. *Result of Arrogance.*
   Ignorance of Evil Consequence.
   Incompetent in dealing with it.
   Unprepared to avoid it.

48: 21
The Lord was:
1. Faithful to His Promises.
2. Furnished the Necessities of life.
   1. Leadership—Guidance.
   2. Refreshment—Assuaged Thirst.

48: 1
1. Known as Israelites.
2. Speak as Israelites.
3. Worship as Israelites but not in sincerity or honesty.

49: 6
The Prophet's broader conception of Israel's DESTINY.
1. Nationalism must GO.
2. New Nation must COME.
3. Larger Need must be MET.

49: 14–15
1. The Complaint.
2. The Comparison.
3. The Comfort.

50: 7

1. Doctrine.
2. Decision.
3. Determination.
4. Discovery.

51: 3

1. The Triumph of the Lord.
2. The Transformation by the Lord.
3. The Tribute to the Lord.

51: 12

1. Unfailing Resources of Encouragement.
2. Useless Fears of Enemies.
3. Unnatural forgetfulness of Essentials.

52: 10

1. The Fact of Revelation.
2. The Field of Revelation.
3. The Future of Revelation.

53: 5

The Accuracy of Prophecy concerning the PASSION

1. Wounded = cf Matt.27. *v. 35.*
2. Bruised = cf Matt. 27. *v. 29, 30.*
3. Chastised = John 19. *v. 1.*
4. Blows (stripes) = cf John 19. *v. 34.*

53: 6

1. The SIN that UNITES us.
2. The SINS that SEPARATE us.
3. The SON who SAVES us.

53: 12

1. The Passion of our Lord.
2. The Priesthood of our Lord.
3. The Prosperity of our Lord. (Missions, Expansion, etc.).

54: 7-8

1. Forsaken (*v. 7a*).
2. Forgiven (*v. 7b*).
3. Darkness (*v. 8a*).
4. Deliverance (*v. 8b*).

54: 10

1. Catastrophe may come.
2. Kindness of God will remain.
3. Covenant will stand.

54: 2

1. Missionary Vision—Enlarge the place.
2. Missionary Venture—spare not . . . stakes.
3. Missionary Victory—thou shalt break forth, etc.

55: 1

1. The Paradox of Paradise.
2. The Price of Peace.
3. The Parable of Prosperity.

55: 6

1. *The Warning.*
   The Lord is not always AVAILABLE.
   The Lord is not always ACCESSIBLE.
2. *The Way Home.*
   Man must REPENT of SIN.
   Man must RETURN to SAVIOUR.
3. *The Welcome.*
   The Lord will show (1) PITY.
   The Lord will extend (2) PARDON.

55: 8, 9, 11

1. The Contrast (*v. 8*).
2. The Comparison (*v. 9*).
3. The Consummation (*v. 11*).

57: 15

1. The Boldness of the Prophet.
2. The Benediction of the Prophecy.
3. The Bounty of the Promise.

57: 20

1. The Ungodly are never STILL.
2. The Ungodly are never SILENT.
3. The Ungodly are never SATISFIED.

58: 1, 3, 4, 6, 8

1. Declaration of God (*v. 1a*).
2. Denunciation by God (*v. 1b*) Optional? Covered by (*v. 1*).
3. Dismay of Faithful (*v. 3*).
4. Disharmony among Faithful (*v. 4*).
5. The DESIGN of the Lord (*v. 6, 7, 8*).

58: 9

1. *The Challenge of the Promise.*
   (*a*) Answer.
   (*b*) Assurance.
2. *The Conditions of the Promise.*
   (*a*) No oppression
   (*b*) No malice ⎬ Negative.

   (*c*) Compassion
   (*d*) Comfort ⎬ Positive.
3. *The Consequences of the Promise.*
   (*a*) Encouragement.
   (*b*) Enlightenment.
   (*c*) Enablement.

58: 12

The Privilege of Posterity.
1. Reconstruction.
2. Revival.
3. Renewal—(*a*) Society, (*b*) Homes.

59: 1, 2

1. A Prophet's Exclamation.
2. A Plain Explanation.
3. A Patient Examination.

59: 8

Description of Ungodly Man.
1. Ignorance is his.
2. Injustice is his.
3. Inconsiderate is he.
4. Inevitable Inheritance.

59: 16

1. Divine Inspection.
2. Divine Insight.
3. Divine Initiative.

59: 20–21

1. The Coming of the Lord.
2. The Conquest by the Lord.
3. The Contract of the Lord.

60: 1–3

The Story of the Gospel.
1. Dawn—Christmas.
2. Darkness—Good Friday.
3. Deliverance—Easter Day.

60: 4

1. Devotion ('lift up').
2. Duty ('roundabout').
3. Discovery ('and see').

60: 11

The Call to the Church.
1. Gates open! In Welcome and In Wonder.
2. Gates open continually! In Glory of the Day and In Gloom of Night.
3. Gates open continually to Glory of God. (*v. 13b*).

60: 19

A Parable from Nature.
As the
1. Sun gave Light.
2. Sun gave Heat.
3. Sun gave Direction.

So the Lord gives
1. Illumination to MINDS.
2. Warmth to HEARTS.
3. DIRECTION to the WILL.

61: 1

1. The Climax of Prophecy.
2. The Charter Proclaimed.
3. The Christ Promised.

61: 4

1. Rebuild ancient ruins—Religion.
2. Revive ancient standards—Morals.
3. Restore family life—Personal Relations.

61: 10

1. Praise is a Privilege.
2. Praise is Personal.
3. Praise is a Pilgrimage.
4. Praise is a Profession of Thanksgiving.

61: 11
Parable of Power of God.
1. Renewal of Nature—Wild & Cultivated.
2. Revival of Nation's thought.
3. Resurrection of Righteousness and Praise.

62: 10–11
1. Welcome to returning Exiles.
2. Way opened up for them.
3. Warning to them all.
   'Thy Salvation Cometh.'

63: 16
The Claim of an Exile returning.
1. No Ancestry to boast of.
2. No Nationality to be proud of.
3. No Doubts to be ashamed of.

63: 19; 64: 1–4
1. Confession (*v. 63, 19a*).
2. Complaint (*v. 63, 19b, 19c*).
3. Compassion (*v. 64, 1–3*).
4. Conviction (*v. 64, 4*).

64: 6
The Burden of True Confession.
1. We are Undesirable.
2. We are Undeserving.
3. We are Uncertain.
4. We are Unstable.

64: 8
An Approach to Prayer.
1. Acknowledgement of God as Personal.
2. Admission of ourselves as 'Earthly'.
3. Acceptance of God as Creator-Craftsman.

65: 1
God's Attitude to our Prayers.
1. Waiting to Reply to us.
2. Wanting to Reveal Himself.
3. Waiting to be Recognised.

65: 17, 19
The Glory of the Church is that it is the OBJECT of
1. a HOLY Command—Our Duty (*v. 18a*).
2. a HOLY Creation—Design (*v. 18b*).
3. a HOLY Confidence—Decision (*v. 19*).

65: 24–25
Encouragements to PRAYER.
1. Ready to answer.
2. Responsive to our Prayers.
3. Realisation—miracles can happen, impossible can come to pass.

66: 1, 2
1. Divine Utterance—Thus saith.
2. Divine Authority—Heaven is my Throne.
3. Divine Choice—Earth my Footstool.
   Bible speaks.
   Bible speaks with authority.
   Bible speaks with authority to all men.

66: 18
The overruling Providence of God.
1. We cannot hide from God.
2. We cannot hinder His Triumph.
3. We cannot halt the coming of His Kingdom.

Jeremiah

1: 7-8
1. You have a Master.
2. You will be given a Message.
3. You will achieve Mastery.

1: 9-10
1. Initiation.
2. Inspiration.
3. Instruction.

1: 16
1. Irreligion (forsaken true God).
2. Idolatry (false objects of reverence).
3. Invention (making their own gods).

1: 19
1. Expect to be opposed.
2. Believe you will overcome.
3. Claim the Lord's Promise to overrule.

2: 4-13
1. The Protest through the prophet of God.
2. The Pleading through the prophet of God.
3. The Proclamation through the prophet of God.

2: 19
1. Wickedness brings its own punishment.
2. Neglect of God brings its own penalty.
3. Irreverence also brings its own penalty.

2: 26-28
1. A Vain Appeal.
2. A Valuable Warning.
3. A Vacant Heaven.

2: 31-32
1. Consider the Provision for our daily needs—has God failed?
2. Consider our Provision for other's needs—has man failed?
3. Consider the Parable provided for us here.

3: 7
1. The Patience of God.
2. The Pleading of God.
3. The Pain of God.

3: 12-13
1. The Command of the Lord.
2. The Call of the Lord.
3. The Compassion of the Lord.
4. The Confession we must make.

3: 23
1. A right Decision.
2. A real Admission.
3. A royal Salvation.

4: 21-22
1. Weary of the sights and sounds of war.
2. Worried by the stupidity of the Godless.
3. Bewildered by the sinfulness of his countrymen.

4: 23–25

1. Disorder on the earth.
2. Darkness in Heaven.
3. Doubt of Fundamentals.
4. Disappointment at the failures of men.

5: 20–23

1. Divine Commission to announce.
2. Divine Challenge to arrest attention.
3. Divine Craftsmanship to attest claim.
4. Divine Comment.

5: 30–31

1. Messengers are false prophets.
2. Ministers are feeble pastors.
3. Members fondly approve of this.
4. Misgiving concerning the future.

6: 27

1. Church is a Tower:
   To look out on the world.
   To look to for direction.
   To look beyond and above the world's standards.
2. Church is a Fortress:
   To provide shelter.
   To provide nourishment.
   To provide community life.

7: 3–7

1. Useless repetition condemned.
2. Unworthy lives must be acknowledged.
3. Unjust behaviour must cease.
4. Unnecessary sacrifices must stop.
5. Unwise attachments undesirable.
6. Unless these are repented of, there is no true religion.

7: 28

1. Disobedient to God: Self-centred.
2. Disinclined to learn: Self-satisfied.
3. Disabled in Truthfulness: Self-righteous.

8: 19–22

1. Is there no comfort in religion?
2. Is there no comfort in ritual?
3. Is there no comfort in prosperity?
4. Is there no comfort in Nature?

9: 23–24

1. The failure of
   (a) Earthly wisdom.
   (b) Earthly power.
   (c) Earthly wealth.
2. The Faith that inspires:
   (a) Conviction of Love of God.
   (b) Conviction of Justice of God.
   (c) Conviction of Goodness of God.
3. The Fact that matters.

10: 12

1. Earth—Symbol of Power: Coal, radium, gold, etc.
2. World—Symbol of Purpose: Order of nature, etc.
3. Heavens—Symbol of Perfection: Ideals, Paradise, etc.

10: 23–24

1. Our Destiny is not in our hands.
2. Our Direction is not in our hands.
3. Our Disciplines are not all human: some are Divine.

11: 9a, 10–11

1. Retreat to the Past.
2. Rebellion in the Present.
3. Retribution in the Future.

12: 1–4

1. The Prophet's Plea.
2. The Prophet's Problem.
3. The Prophet's Protest.

13: 8–11

1. The Punishment of Self-satisfaction.
2. The Plight of Self-righteousness.
3. The Paralysis of Self-deception.

13: 23, 24, 27

1. The Challenge.
2. The Contrast.
3. The apparent Conclusion.
4. The final Cry.

14: 7–9
1. Condemnation.
2. Confession.
3. Confusion.
4. Consternation.
5. Compassion.

14: 19–21
1. People are bewildered.
2. People are broken-hearted.
3. People are blameworthy.
4. People beseech the Lord to remember His covenant.

15: 15–21
1. Admission of defeat.
2. Statement of his defence.
3. Cry of Despondency.
4. Decree of the Lord.
5. Deliverance by the Lord.

16: 16–17
1. Patience.
2. Plan.
3. Perception.

17: 4
1. Cut off from fellowship with God.
2. Caught up in false, uncertain values.
3. Character is always being put to the test.

17: 7–8
1. Trust brings peace because it it honours the Lord.
2. Trust brings Peace because it harnesses hidden powers.
3. Trust brings peace because its harvest never fails.

17: 9
1. How easily we deceive ourselves.
2. How early we know how to sin.
3. How empty is our knowledge of ourselves.

17: 14–16
1. Broken but not beyond repair.
2. Sinful but not beyond redemption.
3. Scorned but not beyond reconciliation.

18: 15–17
1. When Prayer is neglected, ritual is useless.
2. When prayer is neglected, tradition is useless.
3. When prayer is neglected, pride is useless.
4. When prayer is neglected, God becomes unreal.

19: 14–15
1. Went where the people were.
2. Spoke for God without fear.
3. Made God's Judgement clear.

20: 8–10
1. Silent when he ought to speak.
2. Selfish when he ought to serve.
3. Scared when he ought to be strong.
4. Sceptical when he ought to be sure.

21: 8–9
1. Declaration made.
2. Decision means death if he remains.
3. Decision means deliverance if he goes.
   Deliverance is not without its disciplines.

22: 20–21
1. Lebanon: symbol of Beauty.
   symbol of Wealth.
   symbol of Prosperity.
   and yet rebellious.

23: 4
1. They are satisfied.
2. They are strong.
3. They are steadfast.

23: 5–6
1. A Man of royal ancestry.
2. A Monarch of ability.
3. A Master of Law and Order.
4. A Mediator of Salvation.

23: 16
1. They speak to flatter.
2. They declare Fancies not Facts.
3. They speak without authority.

23: 30–32
1. Those who borrow their Messages.
2. Those who have no real Mission.
3. Those who confuse meanings.

24: 1–10
1. The Problem presented.
2. The Providence promised.
3. The Penalty prophesied.

25: 7
1. The Lord accused them of Pride.
2. The Lord suffers their Provocation.
3. The Lord reminds them of the Penalty.

26: 12, 14–15
1. The Truth of God must be declared.
2. The Truth of God demands a decision.
3. The Truth of God can be dangerous.

26: 24
The Lord has His disciples.
1. In all generations.
2. In all classes of Society.
3. In all kinds of circumstances.

27: 5, 6, 11
1. Power of God revealed in Creation.
2. Purpose of God revealed in choice of Babylon.
3. Promises of God revealed in Charity towards Jews.

28: 1, 3, 15
1. A False Prophet; therefore he made
2. False promises; and was guilty of
3. False Performance.

29: 4–7
1. Get something constructive to do.
2. Maintain normal domestic life.
3. Think of others.
(An ancient prescription for Depression).

29: 14
1. He will reveal Himself.
2. He will restore their freedom.
3. He will revive their national life.
4. He will return them home.

29: 32
1. No more Falsehoods.
2. No more Followers.
3. No more Future.

30: 1, 2, 3
1. Compulsion felt by prophet.
2. Commission given to the prophet.
3. Compassion known by the prophet.

30: 17
1. The Lord will restore Health.
2. The Lord will grant Healing.
3. The Lord will reestablish Holiness.

31: 7
1. Good News to publish.
2. Good Lord to praise.
3. Godly people to preserve.

31: 19–20
1. Correction by the Lord.
2. Contrition before the Lord.
3. Condemnation by himself.
4. Compassion of the Lord.

31: 21
1. A Highway suggests a sense of Direction.
2. A Highway suggests Determination.
3. A Highway suggests a sense of Destiny.

31: 31–34

1. After years of failure, Israel given another chance.
2. After years of Ritual, religion to become spiritual.
3. After years of Privilege, religion to be the possession of the people.

31: 34

1. The Comprehensiveness of Forgiveness.
2. The Compassion of Forgiveness.
3. The Completeness of Forgiveness.

32: 22–23b

1. A Promise kept.
2. A Promised land entered.
3. A Promise broken.

32: 26–27

1. I am a God who is personal.
2. I am a God who is everpresent.
3. I am a God perfect in power.

32: 33–35

1. Pride ⎫
2. Idolatry ⎬ Ancient and modern
3. Cruelty ⎭ evils.

33: 3

1. Invitation to Prayer.
2. Inspiration of Prayer.
3. Insight that comes through Prayer.

33: 4–7

1. Chastisement.
2. Forgiveness.
3. Restoration.

33: 20, 22, 26

1. A Challenge made.
2. A Covenant recalled.
3. A Comparison drawn.
4. A Conquest announced.

35: 5–8, 19

1. Temptation in the present.
2. Tradition from the past.
3. Triumph in the future.

36: 28, 32c

1. Conscience will not be beaten.
2. Conscience will not be shaken.
3. Conscience grows as we try to silence it.

37: 3

1. Appeal to a prophet they usually despise.
2. Ask for prayers they usually neglect.
3. Abandon the pride they usually make so much of.

37: 17, 19, 21

1. The Cowardice of Pride.
2. The Quest of a Prince.
3. The Question of a Prophet.
4. The Confession of a Prince.

38: 4–6

1. A false accusation; bad for morale.
2. A faithless adviser; bad for morality.
3. A foul act; bad for memory.

38: 8–13

A study in Black.
1. The Compassion of Ebedmelech.
2. The Courage of Ebedmelech.
3. The Conquest of Ebedmelech.

38: 11

1. Nothing is too old if it meets present need.
2. Nothing is too worn if it can be used again.
3. Nothing is cast away if it can be brought into service again.
so
1. Gospel is old but meets present need.
2. Gospel is well-worn but not worn out.
3. Gospel is cast away by many but continues to bring God to man.

38: 14–15, 19–20

1. A Monarch consults a Man of God.
2. A Monarch is challenged by a Man of God.
3. A Monarch confesses to a Man of God.
4. A Monarch is comforted by a Man of God, but ONLY ON CONDITIONS.

40: 11, 12

1. Suffering strengthens the bond of sympathy.
2. Sympathy stimulates the desire to serve.
3. Service for others softens our own suffering.

41: 4–8

1. Faithful in adversity.
2. Faithless approach.
3. False advice.
4. Foul Act.
5. Final Appeal.

42: 21–22

1. Purpose of God:
   that we should know Him.
   that we should obey Him.
2. Plight of Man:
   because of disobedience he contends with
   (a) War and Strife.
   (b) Hunger of all kinds.
   (c) Disease.

43: 8

1. Jeremiah still listening for Voice of God.
2. He still leads the people.
3. He still loves the people even though they have distrusted him.

44: 28

1. Promise of Deliverance to a Few.
2. Preserved for Destiny of the Jew.
3. Pledged to decide the false from the True.

47: 6–7

1. A Profession of Panic.
2. A Petition for Peace.
3. A Purpose proclaimed.

50: 4, 5

1. The Promise to the Faithful.
2. The Persecution of the Faithful.
3. The Purpose of the Faithful.
4. The Perseverance of the Faithful.
5. The Permanence of the Faithful.

51: 10

1. Faith rewarded.
2. Fellowship restored.
3. Failure rebuked.

51: 50

1. Divine Encouragement.
2. Divine Entreaty.
3. Divine Enterprise.

Lamentations

1: 1–3
1. Honoured but now humbled.
2. Favoured but faithless.
3. Privileged but powerless.

1: 4–5
1. Does God share the sorrows of His children?
2. Does God inflict the sorrows of His children?
3. Does God permit the suffering of His children?

1: 6–8
1. Does the Church disappoint?
2. Does the Church dwell on the past too much?
3. Does the Church delight in God or man?

1: 9
1. Is the Church unfaithful?
2. Is the Church unthinking?
3. Is the Church unexpectant?

1: 9c–11
1. An acknowledgement of defeat.
2. An acknowledgement of despair.
3. An acknowledgement of the deliverer.

1: 12–13
1. Are we guilty of indifference towards the Church?
2. Are we guilty of ignorance concerning the Church?
3. Are we guilty of ingratitude in the Church?

1: 14–16
1. Can God inflict punishment?
2. Can God break down all our resistance?
3. Can God deprive us of all comfort?

1: 17–19
1. Is there always an answer to prayer?
2. Is there any escape from deserved punishment?
3. Is there any excuse for pride?
4. Is there any encouragement left to us?

1: 20–22
1. How sensitive is our conscience toward God?
2. How sincere is our confession before God?
3. How sure is our conviction of God?

2: 1–6
1. Can we deal with the reverses of life?
2. Can we deal with the rejection of love?
3. Can we deal with the riddle of life?

2: 7–14
1. Is the Church under the judgement of God?
2. Is the Church practising the justice of God?
3. Is the Church justifying her existence before God?

2: 15–22

1. What the world expected—Rejection.
2. What the world did not expect—Righteousness at work.
3. What the world did not experience—Resurrection of Faith.

3: 1–21

1. He accepts responsibility for human sin.
2. He accepts the reality of human bondage.
3. He accepts the rejection of human pride.
4. He advocates the renewal of hope.

3: 22–24

1. The gospel of hope.
2. The ground of hope.
3. The greatness of hope.

3: 25–30

1. The goodness of God—source of our confidence.
2. The goodness of God—source of our courage.
3. The goodness of God—source of our confession.

3: 31–33

1. The Word of hope.
2. The Word of healing.
3. The Word from the heart of God.

3: 34–36

1. Aggression is not of God.
2. Abuse of justice is not of God.
3. Absence of honesty is not of God.

3: 37–39

1. Do we believe this is God's world?
2. Do we believe there is but one God?
3. Do we believe God is just?

3: 40–42

1. Looking inwards—honesty.
2. Looking upwards—hope.
3. Looking downwards—humility.

3: 43–51

1. Does God meet rebellion with retaliation?
2. Does God meet prayer with persecution?
3. Does God meet penitence with pardon?

3: 52–66

1. The chastisement of the Lord.
2. The cry to the Lord.
3. The compassion of the Lord.
4. The commitment to the Lord.

4: 1–10

1. Materialism was common.
2. Morals were corrupt.
3. Manners were coarse.

4: 11–16

1. Privileges were abused.
2. Power was misused.
3. People were misled.

4: 17–20

1. For salvation they looked in the wrong place.
2. For salvation they looked to the wrong person.
3. For salvation they looked in the wrong direction.

4: 21–22

1. Those who inflict suffering must expect it.
2. Those who endure suffering can rejoice in it.
3. Those who have sinned can be redeemed.

5: 1-18

1. They were made prayerful through suffering.
2. They were made penitent through shame.
3. They were made perfect through suffering.

5: 19-22

1. God does not change—is that our conviction?
2. God does chastise us—is that our experience?
3. God must change us—is that our confession?

Ezekiel

1: 1–3
1. A day to be remembered.
2. A day of revelation.
3. A day of reinforcement.

1: 4–5
1. The power of God.
2. The purity of God.
3. The personality of God.

1: 6–9
1. The unspeakable glory of God.
2. The unyielding strength of God.
3. The unchanging purpose of God.

1: 10–14
1. The reason of God.
2. The royalty of God.
3. The resignation of God.
4. The redemption of God.

1: 15–21
1. The perfection of God.
2. The purpose of God.
3. The power of God.
4. The plan of God.

1: 22–28
1. The Authority he recognized.
2. The Majesty he acknowledged.
3. The Beauty that overwhelmed him.

2: 1–10
1. Commissioned to declare the reality of God.
2. Commissioned to declare the revelation of God's Will.
3. Commissioned to denounce the rebellion of God's chosen.
4. Commissioned to declare the righteousness of God.

3: 1–11
1. Message is given him.
2. Method must be his own.
3. Mission is to his own people.

3: 12–15
1. The overwhelming sense of constraint.
2. The awesome sense of conviction.
3. The anxious sense of compassion.

3: 16–21
1. Responsibility he must accept.
2. Righteousness he must proclaim.
3. Responsibility of which he is relieved.

3: 22–27
1. How does God speak to man?
2. Why does God speak to man?
3. When does God speak to man?

4: 1–17
1. Silent but serving the Lord.
2. Humiliated but honouring the Lord.
3. Disciplined but diligent before the Lord.

5: 1–4
1. Disobedience issues in physical distress.
2. Disobedience issues in spiritual death.
3. Disobedience issues in moral despair.
4. Disobedience evokes divine mercy towards a harassed few.

5: 5–13
1. Privileged but proud.
2. Honoured but now humiliated.
3. Wicked and now subject to wrath.

5: 14–17

1. The greatness that was Jerusalem.
2. The God who was jealous of His name.
3. The gift that was a judgement.

6: 1–14

1. The common malady—idolatry.
2. The common mentality—ingratitude.
3. The common misery—ignominy.
4. The uncommon mercy—intervention.

7: 1–9

1. The collapse of a nation.
2. The cause of that collapse.
3. The conviction that will come.

7: 10–22

1. All are involved in the fact of sin.
2. None can escape the consequence of sin.
3. All are involved in the futility of sin.
4. None can escape the folly of sin.

7: 24

1. ' Social revolution.
2. Moral revolution.
3. Spiritual revolution.

7: 23–27

1. Disobedience calls for discipline.
2. Confusion cries out for comfort.
3. Values must be vindicated.

8: 1–18

1. God comes in glory.
2. God acted in grace.
3. God cast out by His own people.
4. God cast away His own people.

9: 1–11

1. Sorrow for sin.
2. Sacrifice demanded.
3. Salvation (in the cross).
4. Sorrow for his brethren.
5. Sorrow for God.

10: 1–22

1. Devastation of the holy city.
2. Departure of the Holy God.
3. Decisiveness of the holy wrath of God.

11: 1–13

1. The indolence of the self-satisfied.
2. The indictment of the self-satisfied.
3. The intervention of the Lord.
4. The intercession of the prophet.

11: 14–17

1. The claim.
2. The condescension.
3. The change of circumstances.

11: 18–21

1. Repentance.
2. Reformation.
3. Regeneration.
4. Righteousness.

11: 22–25

1. God moves in a mysterious way.
2. God speaks to those who listen.
3. God serves those who wait upon Him.

12: 1–16

1. The inability to understand the work of God.
2. Their indifference towards the work of God.
3. The instruction in the work of God.
4. The inspired few who are chosen.

12: 17–28

1. A famine of the Word of God—always with us.
2. A fact to be accepted—God has spoken.
3. A faith to be realized—God still speaks.

13: 1–9

1. The frustrations of truth.
2. The flattery of falsehood.
3. The failure of faithlessness.

13: 10–16

1. How strong are the defences of evil?
2. How strong is the deception of evil?
3. How certain is the destruction of evil?

13: 17–23

1. War on superstition.
2. War on sacrilege.
3. War on selfishness.

14: 1–11

1. Is there mockery in our approach to God?
2. Is there meekness in our approach to God?
3. The mercy of God's approach to us.

14: 12–23

1. Repentance must be personal.
2. Righteousness must be personal.
3. Redemption will be personal.

15: 1–8

1. They had been untrue to themselves.
2. They had been unfaithful to their training.
3. They had been unfruitful in their trust.

16: 1–14

1. The lonely guest of God.
2. The loving conquest of God.
3. The living grace of God.

16: 15–29

1. They were guilty of ingratitude.
2. They were guilty of iniquity.
3. They were guilty of idolatry.

16: 30–43

1. The heartbreak of the Lord.
2. The heresy of His people.
3. The helplessness of His people.
4. The hope held out to them.

16: 44–52

1. Comparison did not favour them.
2. Contrast did not flatter them.
3. Condemnation did not escape them.

16: 53–63

1. Can God overrule our sin?
2. Can God overshadow our shame?
3. Can God overlook our sin and our shame?

17: 1–24

1. The collapse of pride.
2. The capture of a people.
3. The counsel of panic.
4. The coming of a prince.

18: 1–32

1. Not heredity but the heart.
2. Not retribution but restoration.
3. Not repentance only but righteousness, also.

19: 1–14

1. The consequences of disobedience.
2. The collapse of a dynasty.
3. The cause of dismay.

20: 1–26

1. The persistence of man's disobedience.
2. The patience of God's discipline.
3. The pattern of God's displeasure.

20: 27–32

1. Do we not blaspheme the Lord today?
2. Do we not bear false witness today?
3. Do we not break faith today?

20: 33–44

1. God is working His purpose out.
2. God offers man personal encounter with Himself.
3. God, in mercy, awaits our penitence.

20: 45–49

1. Does God work through natural events?
2. Does God work through human experiences?
3. Does God work through human enquiry?

21: 1-7

1. Judgement is forthcoming.
2. Judgement is to be feared.
3. Judgement will be final.

21: 8-27

1. The wages of sin is death.
2. The way of salvation is death to self.
3. The word of salvation is deliverance.

21: 28-32

1. Vengeance is mine, saith the Lord.
2. Visitation is merciful, saith the Lord.
3. Vow is mine, saith the Lord.

22: 1-5

1. Can we sin alone?
2. Can we save ourselves?
3. Can we survive alone?

22: 6-16

1. Social corruption.
2. Religious corruption.
3. Moral corruption.
4. Communal corruption.
5. Consequent condemnation.

22: 17-22

1. No longer serving His purpose.
2. No longer deserving His patience.
3. No longer seeking His pardon.

22: 23-31

1. Injustice.
2. Idolatry.
3. Insincerity.
4. Ignorance.

23: 1-49

1. Is God indifferent to evil?
2. Is God incapable of dealing with evil?
3. Is God idle concerning evil?

24: 1-14

1. The punishment in parable form.
2. The purification in parable form.
3. The pardon that was denied.

24: 15-27

1. The retribution demanded of them.
2. The repentance denied them.
3. The release denied them.
4. The reason demonstrated them.

25: 1-7

1. Have we profited from the religion of others?
2. Have we promoted the religion of others?
3. Have we protected the religion of others?

25: 8-11

1. Has God worked to no purpose?
2. Does God withhold His powers?
3. Does God impose penalties?

25: 12-14

1. It is not for man to exercise the privileges of God.
2. It is not for man to question the power of God.
3. It is not for man to doubt the promises of God.

25: 15-17

1. Does the spirit of vengeance dwell with us still?
2. Does God visit nations with judgement today?
3. Does God overrule human wickedness?

26: 1-21

1. The manner of God's judgement.
2. The means God uses.
3. The message God intended.

27: 1-36

1. They were over-confident.
2. They would be overtaken.
3. They would be overwhelmed.

28: 1-10

1. He claimed all honour.
2. He scorned all humility.
3. He died without honour.

28: 11–19
1. Outwardly divine.
2. Inwardly human.
3. Ultimately humbled.

28: 20–26
1. The purpose revealed through their rebellion.
2. The purpose revealed through their reproof.
3. The purpose revealed in the promised restoration.

29: 1–12
1. The arrogance of power.
2. The abuse of friendship.
3. The abasement of national prestige.

29: 13–16
1. The hour of their return.
2. The habitation of their return.
3. The humiliation of their return.

29: 17–21
1. Remembrance.
2. Recompense.
3. Recovery.

30: 1–19
1. Judgement will be universal.
2. Judgement will be unexpected.
3. Judgement will be upright.

30: 20–26
1. The man God humbled.
2. The man God honoured.
3. The message God proclaimed.

31: 1–14
1. The earthly glory.
2. The earthly glory that departed.
3. The earthly glory that was deserted.

31: 15–18
1. The pride that was humbled.
2. The power that was destroyed.
3. The purpose that was proclaimed.

32: 1–16
1. The visitation will be severe.
2. The visibility will be poor.
3. The vanquished will be alarmed.
4. The victory will be complete.

32: 17–32
1. The violence of nations against the Lord's people.
2. The Verdict of the Lord.
3. The vanity of opposition to the Lord.

33: 1–9
1. Our responsibility before the Lord is personal.
2. Our responsibility before our fellows is personal.
3. Our responsibility for ourselves is personal.

33: 10–11
1. Despair produced by a sense of guilt.
2. Discovery proclaimed by the prophet.
3. Deliverance promised through the prophet.

33: 12–16
1. Repentance is encouraged.
2. Righteousness is encouraged.
3. Restitution is encouraged.

33: 17–20
1. Not our riches but our rags.
2. Not our record but our repentance.
3. Not our reasoning but our righteousness.

33: 21–33
1. Have we anything that was not given?
2. Have we any right to the Kingdom?
3. Have we any righteousness of which to boast?
4. Have we responded to the Word of God?

34: 1–10
1. Leadership had been faithless.
2. Leadership had been a failure.
3. Leadership had been false.

34: 11–16
1. Redemption is God's initiative.
2. Reconciliation is God's promise.
3. Restoration is God's prerogative.

34: 17–24
1. The humiliation they had experienced.
2. The honour they would know.
3. The hospitality they would share.
4. The heritage they would enter upon.

34: 25–31
1. Is God the source of our confidence?
2. Is God the source of our courage?
3. Is God the source of our character?
4. Is God the source of our convictions?

35: 1–15
1. The purpose in the punishment.
2. The revelation in the ruins.
3. The will in the word.

36: 1–15
1. From shame to satisfaction.
2. From rejection to restoration.
3. From poverty to power.

36: 16–23
1. Careless of the Lord's commands.
2. Captive at the Lord's will.
3. Careless of the Lord's character.
4. Called to witness the Lord's work.

36: 24–27
1. Brought home.
2. Forgiven.
3. Born again.
4. Free to serve.

36: 28
1. Restoration to freedom.
2. Restoration to faith.
3. Restoration to fellowship.

36: 29–32
1. The Grace of God purifying.
2. The Grace of God providing.
3. The Grace of God bringing to penitence.

36: 33–38
1. After forgiveness—fruitfulness.
2. After barrenness—beauty.
3. After contempt—conviction.
4. After request—response.

37: 1–6
1. The chaos of faithlessness.
2. The challenge to faith.
3. The compassion that faileth not.

37: 7–14
1. The restoration of the nation.
2. The resurrection of faith.
3. The response to faith.
4. The reason for the response.

37: 15–23
1. Reunion—symbol of the Guidance of God.
2. Repentance—symbol of the Grace of God.
3. Regeneration—symbol of the Glory of God.

37: 24
1. Recognition of one leader in the restored community.
2. Responsibility of one leader towards the community.
3. Right behaviour in the restored community.

37: 25–28
1. Restoration will bless them.
2. Reconciliation will be theirs.
3. Religion will be central.

38: 1–16
1. Does God use His enemies to test His friends?
2. Does God permit evil to take advantage of good?
3. Does God permit suffering that His purpose be revealed?

38: 17-23
1. Do we believe in the wrath of God?
2. Do we believe in the reign of God?
3. Do we believe in the royalty of God?

39: 1-10
1. The adversaries of God most high.
2. The activity of God most high.
3. The acknowledgement of God most high.

39: 11-29
1. God intervenes in history.
2. God interprets history.
3. God inspires history.

40: 1-4
1. He is bidden to look.
2. He is bidden to learn.
3. He is bidden to live.
4. He is bidden to love.

40: 5-27
1. Is God interested in details?
2. Does God employ intermediaries?
3. Does God inspire man's handiwork?

40: 28-38
1. Building was symmetrical.
2. Building was sensible.
3. Building was serviceable.

40: 39-41: 4
1. It was thoroughly furnished.
2. It was thoughtfully furnished.
3. It was triumphantly furnished.

41: 15-26
1. Symbolic of the presence of God.
2. Symbolic of the providence of God.
3. Symbolic of the personality of God.

42: 1-14
1. Suggestive of a divine purpose.
2. Suggestive of a divine plan.
3. Suggestive of a divine providence.

42: 15-20
1. Symbolic of their growing knowledge of God.
2. Symbolic of their growing concern for godliness.
3. Symbolic of the growing cleavage between the holy and the unholy.

43: 1-4
1. After repentance—restoration to fellowship.
2. After restoration—revelation to faith.
3. After revelation—remembrance of fact.
4. After remembrance—reverence in fear.

43: 5-12
1. Suggestive of the presence of God.
2. Suggestive of the personal nature of God.
3. Suggestive of the passion of God.
4. Suggestive of the pain of God.
5. Suggestive of the purpose of God.

43: 13-27
1. How costly is our worship?
2. What confession do we make in worship?
3. What compassion does worship arouse in us?

44: 1-3
1. When God comes, life is different.
2. When God comes, He demands decision.
3. When God comes, He brings deliverance.

44: 4-14
1. Are we too familiar with God?
2. Are we too careless about God's house?
3. Are we content to serve God humbly?

44: 15–3
1. Chosen for privilege.
2. Equipped for privilege.
3. Conscious of privilege.
4. Conscience of the people.
5. Content with their portion.

45: 1–8
1. Has God a place in our lives?
2. Has God a plan for our lives?
3. Has God power in our lives?

45: 9–12
1. No oppression must be countenanced.
2. No disorder will be permitted.
3. No injustice will be allowed.
4. No dishonesty will be tolerated.

45: 13–17
1. Are we in debt to God?
2. Are we disobedient before God?
3. Are we delighting in God?

45: 18–25
1. Is our commemoration regular?
2. Is our commemoration one of rejoicing?
3. Is our commemoration regulated?

46: 1–12
1. Can we separate worship and work?
2. Can we separate faith and fellowship?
3. Can we separate master and man?

46: 13–18
1. Do we remember only in emergencies?
2. Do we realize our inheritance?
3. Do we receive our just deserts?

46: 19–24
1. The condescension of the Lord.
2. The concern of the Lord.
3. The compassion of the Lord.

47: 1–12
1. The source of blessing.
2. The scale of blessing.
3. The salvation in the blessing.
4. The steadfastness of the blessing.

47: 13–48: 7
1. God and social justice.
2. God and personal worth.
3. God and social relationships.

48: 8–29
1. Public worship no longer central.
2. Personal worth no longer central.
3. Personal word no longer central.

48: 30–35
1. Some come to the Lord through hardship.
2. Some come to the Lord when young.
3. Some come to the Lord in the middle years of life.
4. Some come to the Lord when evening's shadow falls.
5. All will mingle in the presence of the Lord.

Daniel

1: 1–2
1. The Peril to which they were exposed.
2. The Permission that was granted.
3. The Punishment they deserved.
4. The Protection they were denied.

1: 3–16
1. The Compliment implied.
2. The Compromise tempting them.
3. The Courage they showed.
4. The Challenge they threw down.
5. The Conduct that won through.

1: 18–21
1. Exiles from Promised Land but not from the Promise.
2. Examples in their Exile.
3. Excelled all standards in Exile.

2: 1–16
1. Custom dies hard.
2. Craftiness at work.
3. Calm in Crisis.

2: 17–19
1. A Problem shared.
2. A Prayer offered.
3. A Privilege is known.

2: 20–23
1. Prayer.
2. Praise.
3. Purpose.

2: 24
1. His Concern for others.
2. His Concern for Custom.
3. His Concern for Authority.

2: 27–49
1. The Evangelist in Exile.
2. His Enterprise in Exile.
3. His Enabling in Exile.
4. His Enlightenment of the King.
5. His Encouragement of his friends.

2: 35–36
1. The Fact of Idolatry.
2. The Folly of Idolatry.
3. The Fate of Idolatry.

2: 47
1. In Nature—the Secret of Power.
2. In Christ—the Secret of Personality.
3. In Church—the Secret of Purpose.

2: 49
1. The Reward of Faithfulness.
2. The Request of a Faithful Friend.
3. The Royalty of Faith.

3: 1–3
1. The Arrogance of a King.
2. The Advertisement of a King.
3. The Apostasy of a King.

3: 8–18
1. The Watchers.
2. The Warning.
3. The Witness.

3: 16–18
1. The Fellowship stands united.
2. The Fellowship speaks unitedly.
3. The Fellowship is steadfast.

3: 21–25
1. Bound but not beaten.
2. Tortured but still testifying.
3. Abandoned to Flames but Abounding in Faith.

3: 26–27
1. Unafraid.
2. Untouched.
3. Unrepentant.

4: 20–27
1. The Sin of Pride.
2. The Blindness of Pride.
3. The Selfishness of Pride.

4: 29–33
1. The Pride that flatters.
2. The Poverty that frightens.
3. The Pride that falters.

5: 6–7
1. A troubled conscience.
2. A transfigured countenance.
3. A terrified Cry.

5: 24–28
1. The Messenger of God.
2. The Message from God.
3. Meekness before God.

6: 4–23
1. Aggravated by his success.
2. Attacked at his strongest point.
3. Angry because of his sincerity.
4. Ashamed of his timidity (the king).
5. Awed by his discovery (the king).

6: 14–23
1. Friend in Need.
2. Faith in Deed.
3. Faith in his creed.

7: 1–4
1. Symbol of Struggle.
2. Symbol of Strength.
3. Symbol of Speed.
4. Symbol of Soul.

7: 1–8
1. The Confusion here represented.
2. The Contrast here described.
3. The Consummation here predicted.

7: 9–12
1. Judgement established.
2. Judgement dispensed.
3. Judgement tempered with Mercy.

7: 13–14
1. Not of human origin.
2. Not of human authority.
3. Not of human order.

7: 15–27
1. Enlightenment on the Vision.
2. Encounter in the Vision.
3. Encouragement from the Vision.

8: 1–14
1. The Fact of Aggression.
2. The Failure of Aggression.
3. The Fact of Apostasy.
4. The Fact of Assurance.

9: 1–15
1. His Approach is humble.
2. His Acknowledgement of Sin, with shame.
3. His Assurance of Forgiveness.

9: 16–19
1. The Burden of his Prayer.
2. The Basis of his Prayer.
3. The Battle-cries of his Prayer.

9: 20–23
1. His Intercession for others in their difficulties.
2. His Insight into his own.
3. His Inheritance.

9: 24
1. The Plan of God in Redemption.
2. The Prophecy of the Redeemer.
3. The Pardon in the Redemption.

10: 1, 12, 19
1. The Revelation to Faith.
2. The Response to Faith.
3. The Resurrection of Faith.

DANIEL

10: 21

1. The Truth revealed.
2. The Truth recognized.
3. The Truth recorded.
4. The Truth that is relevant.

11: 31–35

1. Strangers to God in their Prosperity.
2. Struggling for God in their Poverty.
2. Sure of God in their Persecution.

11: 45; 12: 1

1. The Inevitable End.
2. The Inspired Entry.
3. The Inheritance entered upon.

12: 8–13

1. The Problem confronting him.
2. The Portion allotted him.
3. The Patience demanded of him.
4. The Promise given to him.

Hosea

1: 1–2
1. Called to Serve.
2. Called to Suffer.
3. Called to Save.

1: 4, 6, 9
1. The Punishment they deserved.
2. The Providence they have defied.
3. The Privilege they have forfeited.

1: 7
1. Not what was expected.
2. Not the result expected.
3. Not the method expected.

1: 10–11; 2: 1
1. Posterity is assured.
2. Promise is given.
3. Prosperity is promised.

2: 2–4
1. Not beyond Praying for.
2. Not beyond Penitence.
3. Not unworthy of Punishment.

2: 5
1. Guilty of Infidelity.
2. Guilty of Ingratitude.
3. Guilty of Idolatry.

2: 6–8
1. Discipline is necessary.
2. Discovery is made.
3. Darkness is banished.

2: 9–15
1. What we take for granted.
2. What we are offered—the gospel.
3. What we are promised—the grace of hope.

2: 16–18
1. Fellowship is restored.
2. Faith is restored.
3. Freedom is restored.

2: 19–23
1. The Initiative is of God.
2. The Insight God gives.
3. The Interest God shows.
4. The Inheritance God shares.

3: 1–3
1. The Command given.
2. The Comparison drawn.
3. The Compassion shown.
4. The Contract agreed upon.

3: 4–5
1. The Punishment imposed upon them.
2. The Privileges denied them.
3. The Purpose of it all.

4: 1–4
1. The Condemnation.
2. The Causes.
3. The Character of the people.
4. The Consequences.
5. The Concern that is absent.

4: 5–10
1. The Doom of Dishonesty.
2. The Darkness of Ignorance.
3. The Discharge of Infidelity.
4. The Disgrace of Iniquity.

4: 12–14
1. The Tragedy of False Gods.
2. The Tyranny of False Gods.
3. The Truth of False Gods.

4: 17–19

1. The People are beyond hope.
2. The People are beyond Help.
3. The People are beyond Honour.

5: 1–6

1. He charges them with Apostasy.
2. He accuses them of Arrogance.
3. He warns them of coming Afflictions.

5: 15; 6: 1–3

1. The Patience of God.
2. The Penitence of the People.
3. The Perseverance Promised.

6: 4–6

1. Out of the heart not out of hand.
2. From the heart not from the hand.
3. With the heart not with the hand.

7: 1–2

1. Good exposes Evil.
2. Truth exposes Falsehood.
3. Holiness exposes Sin.

7: 7b

1. Irreligion—cause of moral rebellion.
2. Irreligion—cause of personal restlessness.
3. Irreligion—cause of national wretchedness.

7: 8

1. Disappointing.
2. Disagreeable.
3. Disastrous.

7: 9–10

1. Unexpected hardship.
2. Unsuspected decline.
3. Unrepentant hearts.

7: 11–16

1. Their Rebellion brings Retribution.
2. Their Rebellion brings no Reward.
3. Their Repentance brings no Renewal.

8: 4–6

1. Idolatry brings no satisfaction.
2. Idolatry brings no salvation.
3. Idolatry brings no sanity.

8: 7–10

1. They did not live responsibly.
2. They did not expect retribution.
3. They would not repent.

8: 11–14

1. Evil unashamed leads to greater Evil.
2. Enlightenment has been given but is unrecognised.
3. Insincere is their worship—Insecure will be their lot.
4. Infidelity is their Sin—Infirmity awaits them.

9: 3–8

1. Is the Work of the Lord to be in vain?
2. Is the Worship of the Lord to be in vain?
3. Is the Will of the Lord to be in vain?
4. Is the Witness to the Lord to be in vain?

9: 10

1. The Pleasure of the Lord.
2. The Pain of the Lord.
3. The Punishment of the Lord.

9: 17

1. Prediction is made.
2. Privileges have been abused.
3. Persecution will be experienced.

10: 1–4

1. Worldly Prosperity can lead to spiritual Poverty.
2. They mix Principles and Profanity.
3. They will be Punished when they are not Prepared for it.

10: 5–11

1. The False religion that failed them.
2. The False religion that shamed them.
3. The False religion that enslaved them.

10: 12
1. Their lives should be honest.
2. Their lives should be humble.
3. Their lives should be holy.
4. Their lives should be happy.

10: 13–15
1. What a man sows, that he reaps.
2. What a man trusts, that he serves.
3. What a man lives by, that determines his destiny.

11: 1–4
1. The Love that was seeking.
2. The Love that was sinned against.
3. The Love that served.
4. The Love that was scorned.

11: 8–9
1. The Cry in the heart of the Lord.
2. The Crisis in the heart of the Lord.
3. The Compassion in the heart of the Lord.
4. The Conscience in the heart of the Lord.

11: 12; 12: 1
1. They have no Sincerity before the Lord.
2. There is no Substance to their Gods.
3. They have no sensibility to the Lord's Leading.

12: 2–6
1. Rebellion cannot go unpunished.
2. Recall the Mercies of the Past.
3. Repent whilst there is time.
4. Regeneration is your deep need.

12: 8–9
1. The Peril of Self-Satisfaction.
2. The Peril of Self-Righteousness.
3. The Peril of Self-Delusion.
4. The Peril of Self-Will.

12: 10
1. The Lord speaks through human Voices.
2. The Lord speaks through human Values.
3. The Lord speaks through human Virtues.

13: 1–3
1. Irreligion—cause of decay.
2. Idolatry—caused by decay.
3. Ignorance—cause of their final doom.

13: 4–6
1. In time of struggle, they feared God.
2. In time of Success, they feared no God.
3. At all times, there is but one God.

13: 9–10
1. Retribution had to be.
2. Refuge is still free.
3. Redemption is in Me.

13: 14
1. A Glorious Conviction.
2. A glorious Compassion.
3. A glorious Counter-blast of Faith.

13: 15
By way of Parable.
1. The Wind of Destruction.
2. The Word of Destiny.
3. The Water that Disappears.
4. The Wealth that Dwindles.

14: 1–4
1. The Plea.
2. The Prayer.
3. The Perception.
4. The Pardon.

F

14: 5a

1. The Lord's Blessing comes in Silence.
2. The Lord's Blessing comes in Secret.
3. The Lord's Blessing comes to Save.

14: 6

1. The Church of the Redeemed will be Visible.
2. The Church of the Redeemed will be valuable.
3. The Church of the Redeemed will be Vigorous.

14: 5b

1. The Redeemed shall prosper.
2. The Redeemed shall be purified.
3. The Redeemed shall be perfected.

14: 7–8

1. Repentance, there must be.
2. Revival, there will be.
3. Resurrection, there will be, too.

Joel

1: 1–12
1. The Messenger—His call.
2. The Method—Its character.
3. The Message—Its completeness.

1: 1–7
1. The Urgency.
2. The Unveiling.
3. The Unbelief.

1: 8–12
1. Let your Repentance be real.
2. Let true Religion return to you.
3. Let your sense of Responsibility be renewed.

1: 13–15
1. The Renewal of the Ministry.
2. The Revival of the Means of Grace.
3. The Return of the Lord.

1: 16–20
1. Despair is affirmed.
2. Dependence upon God acknowledged.
3. Deliverance from God is prayed for.

2: 1–3
1. The Call to realize our Danger.
2. The Call to Dedication.
3. The Call to realize the Difference.

2: 4–11
1. Is the Church organizing for attack?
2. Is the Church overcoming?
3. Is the Church obedient to her Lord?

2: 12–14
1. Even now, Repentance is open to them.
2. Even now, Reconciliation is offered them.
3. Even now, Restoration is possible.

2: 17
1. Do we pray in Emergencies only?
2. Do we profess to be Examples of Faith?
3. Do we proclaim the Excellence of our Lord?

2: 18–21
1. The Prerogative of the Lord.
2. The Provision of the Lord.
3. The Providence of the Lord.
4. The Promise of the Lord.

2: 22–26
1. Renewal of Nature.
2. Regeneration of human nature.
3. Restoration of broken fellowship.
4. Rejoicing within the fellowship.

2: 27
1. The Awakening unto Salvation.
2. The Authority for our Salvation.
3. The Assurance of Salvation.

2: 28–29
1. The Pledge of the Holy Spirit.
2. The Power of the Holy Spirit.
3. The Possession of the Holy Spirit.
4. The Plenitude of the Holy Spirit.

2: 28–29
1. The Gift of the Holy Spirit.
2. The Grace of the Holy Spirit.
3. The Glory of the Holy Spirit.

2: 30–32

1. Signs of Judgement.
2. Certainty of Judgement.
3. Salvation from Judgement.

3: 1–13

1. Rebellion brings Retribution.
2. Discipline demands Decision.
3. Crisis calls for Co-operation.

3: 14

1. The Valley of Unexpectedness.
2. The Valley of Uncertainty.
3. The Valley of Unpreparedness.
4. The Valley of Urgent Decision

3: 18–21

1. The Grace that is boundless.
2. The Gospel that is born.
3. The Glory that blesses.

Amos

1: 1–2
1. The Man God chose.
2. The Message God gave.
3. The Miracle God performed.

1: 3–2: 16
1. Rebellion brings Desolation.
2. Retribution knows no distinction.
3. Righteousness demands Discipline.

3: 1–2
1. They had been delivered but had forgotten their Duty.
2. They had been chosen but had not accepted the Challenge.
3. They were the more privileged and deserved the greater punishment.

3: 3–8
1. Their Rebellion had been Deliberate.
2. Their Rebellion had been defiant.
3. Their Rebellion had led to disaster.
4. Their Rebellion had called forth a divine Declaration.

3: 9–15
1. No Sense of Responsibility.
2. No Escape from Retribution.
3. No Excuse for Unrighteousness.

4: 1–3
1. Their Cruelty is condemned.
2. Their Characters are condemned.
3. Their Call is coming.

4: 4–5
1. Parade but no Performance.
2. Ritual but no Righteousness.
3. Gifts but no Goodness.
4. Freewill Offering but no Faith.

4: 6–13
1. Warning but no work of Repentance.
2. Wickedness but no word of Regret.
3. Waste but no Waiting upon God.
4. Sown the Wind—now reap the Whirlwind.

5: 1–5
1. The Infidelity that has brought them low.
2. The Ignorance that keeps them down.
3. The Invitation that is offered them.
4. The Instruction that is given them.

5: 7, 10–15
1. They are unjust.
2. They are unworthy.
3. They are unsatisfied.
4. They are unbelieving.
5. They are urgently called to repent.

5: 16–24
1. None are exempt from Sorrow.
2. None can escape Suffering.
3. No excuse for Self-righteousness.
4. No Substitute for moral Steadfastness.

141

5: 25-27
1. Ritual the Lord does not require.
2. Rebellion the Lord will not ignore.
3. Righteousness calls for Discipline.

6: 1-6
1. Is the Church trusting in a false sense of Security?
2. Is the Churchman better than the unchurched?
3. Is the Church putting first things first?

6: 7-14
1. The Pride that goes before a Fall.
2. The Preservation of the Faith.
3. The Purity of the Faith.
4. The Penalty of Faithlessness.

7: 1-6
1. The Insight given.
2. The Intercession made.
3. The Intervention forthcoming.

7: 7-9
1. The Steadfast Lord.
2. The Standard of the Lord.
3. The Striving of the Lord.

7: 10-17
1. Priestly Jealousy at work.
2. Prophet justifies his work.
3. Promised Judgement.

8: 1-2
1. The Sign.
2. The Significance.
3. The Signature withdrawn.

8: 4-14; 9: 8
1. The Works of Wickedness.
2. The Word of Warning.
3. The Word they will want.
4. The Word that will fail them.
5. The Word that awaits them.

9: 1-8
1. No escape from Judgement.
2. No exemption from Responsibility.
3. No exemption from the all-embracing Mercy.

9: 9-12
1. The Discipline.
2. The Discovery.
3. The Dedication.

9: 13-15
1. The Abundance.
2. The Atonement.
3. The Assurance.

Obadiah

1–14

1. No Evil beyond the Judgement of God.
2. No Earthly Wisdom beyond the Judgement of God.
3. No Earthly Enemy beyond the Judgement of God.

15–17

1. What we give, we get.
2. What we receive, we are responsible for.
3. What we value, we venture for.

18–21

1. Religion will be reestablished.
2. Rebellion will be put down.
3. Right relationships will be restored.

Jonah

1: 1–4
1. The Order received.
2. The Offence committed.
3. The Obedience he did not give.
4. The Opposition he did not expect.

1: 5–10
1. The Measures they took.
2. The Mistake Jonah made.
3. The Mercy they sought.
4. The Meaning they wanted to know.

1: 11–16
1. Big enough to accept responsibility.
2. Big enough to learn.
3. Big enough to bow to Will of God.
4. Big enough to offer thanksgiving.

1: 17; 2: 10
1. The Discipline imposed.
2. The Darkness experienced.
3. The Deliverance known.

2: 1–9
1. The Reason for his Petition.
2. The Record of his experience.
3. The Resurrection to life.

3: 1–10
1. The Patience of God.
2. The Preaching for God.
3. The Penitence before God.

4:
1. The Wounded Pride of Jonah.
2. The Wonderful Patience of the Lord.
3. The Watchful Provision of the Lord.
4. The Wailing Prophet.
5. The Wondrous Compassion of the Lord.

Micah

1: 1–9
1. The Authority for his message—Revelation.
2. The Aim of his message—Repentance.
3. The Application of his message—Remorse.
4. The Alarm in his message—Resolution.

1: 5
1. Persecution of the Poor.
2. Wickedness of the Wealthy.
3. Luxury of the Lazy.

1: 10–16
1. Did they learn from history?
2. Did they scorn holiness?
3. Did they hope for help?

2: 1–4
1. Prophet condemns abuse of Power.
2. Prophet condemns abuse of Privilege.
3. Prophet condemns abuse of Persons.

2: 4–6
1. Retribution awaits Greed.
2. Reproof awaits godlessness.
3. Respectability not Godliness.

2: 7–11
1. They misread the Purpose of God.
2. They misruled the People of God.
3. They misunderstood the Prophets of God.

2: 12–13
1. The Promise of God.
2. The People of God.
3. The Plan of God.

3: 1–4
1. They are without conscience.
2. They make a Convenience of God.
3. They must pay for their Crimes.

3: 5–7
1. Corruption in the name of religion.
2. Consequences that follow.
3. Confusion is their reward.

3: 8
1. He claims Power has been given him.
2. He claims wisdom has been given him.
3. He claims Courage has been given him.

3: 9–12
1. No honour among them.
2. No humility among them.
3. No honesty among them.
4. No happiness for them.

4: 1–5
1. God—central in the world's Wisdom.
2. God—central in the world's Wellbeing.
3. God—central in the world's Worship.

4: 6–8
1. A Plan for the Future.
2. A Providence for the Future.
3. A Promise for the Future.

4: 9–10

1. When the Foundations crumble —what then?
2. When the Fight is most severe —what then?
3. When Faith is most tested—what then?
4. Then, the Faithfulness of God is known.

4: 11–13

1. The Church and her Adversaries.
2. The Church and her Advocate.
3. The Church and her Advance.

5: 2

1. The Saviour's Coming to us.
2. The Saviour's Commitment for us.
3. The Saviour's Communion with the Father, eternally.

5: 3–4

1. First, the Discipline.
2. Then, the Distinction.
3. Then the Discovery.

5: 5–9

1. The Promise of God's Providence.
2. The Promise of God's Protection.
3. The Promise of God's Power.
4. The Promise of God's Purpose.

5: 10–15

1. Weapons of War or the Will of God?
2. Organization or Obedience to the Will of God?
3. Organized Fear or Faith in the Will of God?

6: 1–5

1. The Pleading of God in the Present.
2. The Pleasure of God in the Past.
3. The Purpose of God in the Future.

6: 6–8

1. Religion—a right attitude towards God.
2. Religion—a right attitude towards men.
3. Religion—a right attitude towards ourselves.

6: 9–16

1. The Scandal of their Behaviour.
2. The Shadow on their Behaviour.
3. The Scorn of their Brethren.

7: 1–7

1. The Collapse of Society.
2. The Cruelty within Society.
3. The Corruption within Society.
4. The Contention within Society.
5. The Cure—complete Change of heart.

7: 8–10

1. The Believer's Confidence.
2. The Believer's Contrition.
3. The Believer's Comfort.
4. The Believer's Challenge.

7: 11–13

1. The Re-establishment of the Church.
2. The Reaching out of the Church.
3. The Reality of Challenge to the Church.

7: 14–15

1. A Prayer that Privilege may return.
2. A Prayer that Prosperity may return.
3. A Prayer that Promises may be renewed.

7: 16–17

1. When will nations realize their Poverty?
2. When will nations realize their Pride?
3. When will nations be truly Penitent?

7: 18–20

1. The Fact of the Loving-kindness of God.
2. Our Faith in the Loving-kindness of God.
3. Our Forgiveness in the Loving-kindness of God.
4. The Forebearance of the Loving-kindness of God.

Nahum

1: 1-6
1. God is not indifferent.
2. God is not impatient.
3. God is not incompetent.
4. God is in control.

1: 7-8
1. This enlarges our Faith.
2. This encourages our Faith.
3. This enlightens our Faith.
4. This exalts our Faith.

1: 9-15
1. The Supremacy of the Purpose of God.
2. The Certainty of the Pardon of God.
3. The Certainty of the Promises of God.

2: 1
1. Wickedness has its day.
2. Warfare is certain.
3. Wisdom dictates Watchfulness.

2: 3-8
1. It was conquered because of Confusion.
2. It was defeated because it was demoralized.
3. It was brought to ruins because no Resources were left.

2: 9-13
1. Glory has departed.
2. Greed has its judgement day.
3. God has acted.

3: 1-13
1. Wickedness comes back on itself.
2. Wickedness covers itself with shame.
3. Wickedness cannot comfort itself.

3: 14-19
1. Resistance is useless.
2. Restoration is impossible.
3. Rejoicing is inevitable.

Habakkuk

1: 1–4
1. Unsolved Problem.
2. Unanswered Prayer.
3. Unwearying Persecution.
4. Unsearchable Providence.

1: 5, 6, 11
1. The Incredible comes to pass (*v. 5a*).
2. The Initiative is of God (*v. 5b*).
3. The Instrument is of His appointment (*v. 6*).
4. The Ignorance revealed (*v. 11*).

1: 12
1. The Contrast (See 1: 11) (*12a*).
2. The Conviction (*v. 12b*).
3. The Conclusion (*v. 12c*).

1: 13–16
1. The Holiness of God proclaimed (*v. 13a*).
2. The Helplessness of Man confessed (*v. 14*).
3. The Silence of God perplexes (*v. 13b*).
4. The Stupidity of Man described (*v. 16*).

2: 2–4
1. Altitude—Get away from problem.
2. Attitude—Wait upon the Lord.
3. Answer—The Lord is Faithful.

2: 4
1. Pride has no Future (*v. 4a*).
2. Providence honours Faith (*v. 4b*).
   (*a*) Faith that waits.
   (*b*) Faith that worships.
   (*c*) Faith that works.

2: 14
1. The Presumption (there is evil).
2. The Prophecy (there will be knowledge of God's Will).
3. The Possession (as the waters cover the sea).

2: 20
1. Sublime Confidence is here.
2. Silent Confession is here.
3. Silence is called for here.

3: 2
1. He accepts God's Will with penitence.
2. He appeals to God's Power for an outpouring.
3. He advocates God's Mercy in punishment.

3: 9b
1. Providence is Personal. 'Thou'.
2. The Way of Providence. 'Rivers' for our Good.
3. The Way of People. 'Barriers' for our Evil.

3: 17–19
1. A Catalogue of Failure.
2. A Confession of Faith.
3. A Conviction of God's Faithfulness.

Zephaniah

1: 1–2
1. A man of royal descent.
2. A man of royal duty.
3. A man with royal declaration.

1: 3–6
1. He declares Judgement awaits Infidelity.
2. He declares Judgement awaits Neglect.
3. He declares Judgement awaits Indifference.

1: 7–13
1. He sounds the alarm.
2. He senses approaching destiny.
3. He serves notice on the arrogant.

1: 14–18
1. Victory will come.
2. Victims there must be.
3. Vows must be kept.
4. Values must be preserved.

2: 1–7
1. Does God favour the faithful?
2. Can God transform a community?
3. Does God remember His children?

2: 8–11
1. The Privilege of the Faithful.
2. The Pride of the Fallen.
3. The Promise for the Future.

2: 12–15
1. Worldly prosperity does not last.
2. Worldly Power does not last.
3. Worldly Privileges do not last.

3: 1–2
Hindrances to fellowship with God:
1. Self-will.
2. Self-satisfaction.
3. Self-contentedness.
4. Self-centredness.

3: 3–4
1. The Institutions are unworthy.
2. The Instructors are unworthy.
3. The Interpreters are unworthy.

3: 5–9
1. Justice of God is not withheld.
2. Patience of God is not withheld.
3. Purpose of God is not withdrawn.

3: 9–13
1. They shall worship but one God.
2. They shall wonder at the Mercy of God.
3. They shall awaken to the work of God in their midst.

3: 14–20
1. The Promise of Rejoicing.
2. The Promise of Reconciliation.
3. The Promise of Redemption.
4. The Promise of Responsibility.

Haggai

1: 1–9
1. He recalls God's Word to him.
2. He recalls God's People to their Duty.
3. He recalls God's Pleasure towards them.
4. He recalls God's Provision for them.

1: 9–11
1. When Claims of God are forgotten, disappointment comes.
2. When Claims of God are forgotten, disillusionment comes.
3. When Claims of God are forgotten, discovery is made.

1: 12–15
1. They returned to Reverence for God.
2. They returned to Rebuilding for God.
3. They were reassured concerning God.

2: 1–7
1. Building is smaller but the Blessing is the same.
2. Building must continue for the Blessing remains.
3. Building will continue for the Blessing will continue.

2: 9
1. They who builded were few but enthusiastic.
2. They who builded were poor but energetic.
3. They had suffered but had survived.
4. They were obedient and heard the Promise.

2: 10–19
1. Unworthiness in the Past deserved punishment.
2. Unwillingness in the past produced selfish pride.
3. Unexpectedly, the Word of Pardon.

2: 20–23
1. Does God act in History?
2. Does God affect History?
3. Does God direct History?

Zechariah

1: 1–6
1. The Trials they had known.
2. The Test they had failed.
3. Truth they must know.
4. The Turn-round they must make.

1: 7–21
1. God's Concern is for all His people.
2. God's Condemnation is upon all evil.
3. God's Consolation is for all.
4. God confirms His Covenant.

2: 1–5
1. Prophetic of the Church to be rebuilt.
2. Prophetic of the Church without barriers.
3. Prophetic of the Church and her new Baptism.

2: 6–13
1. A Word to those in exile—Come Home.
2. Another Word to those in exile—Confide in Me.
3. A further Word to those in exile—Come and See.
4. A Final Word to those in exile—Come unto Me.

3: 1–5
1. Chosen.
2. Changed.
3. Crowned.
4. Comforted.

3: 6–7
1. The Conditions of Service.
2. The Call to serve.
3. The Companionship to share.

3: 8–10
1. The Promise of the Saviour.
2. The Perfection of the Saviour.
3. The Preciousness of the Saviour.
4. The Permanence of the Saviour.
5. The Pardoning Saviour.

4: 1–6a; 10b–14
1. Light—Symbol of Salvation—Gospel.
2. Oil—Symbol of Supply—Grace.
3. Trees—Symbol of Source—God.

4: 6b–10a
1. The Lord's Undertaking for us.
2. The Lord's Encouragement.
3. The Lord's Enterprise.
4. The Lord's Enlightenment.

5: 1–4
1. Sin is universal.
2. Sin finds us out.
3. Sin calls for a settlement.

5: 5–11
1. Their Sin has been covered—Message of Salvation.
2. Their Sin has been carried away—Mediator of Salvation.
3. Their Sin has been concealed—Mystery of Salvation.

6: 1–8
1. God seeks Justice for all peoples.
2. God serves Judgement upon all peoples.
3. God deals Justly with all peoples.

151

6: 9–15
1. No Kingdom without a King.
2. No King without a crown.
3. No Crown without a cross.

7: 1–14
1. The Lord calls for Righteousness not ritual alone.
2. The Lord calls for Faithfulness not fasting alone.
3. The Lord calls for Compassion not for self-commendation.

8: 1–3
1. The Lord's Passion for His People.
2. The Lord's Presence with His People.
3. The Lord's Privilege for His People.

8: 4–6
1. When the Lord is present, there is Contentment.
2. When the Lord is present, there is Freedom.
3. When the Lord is Present there is Expectancy.

8: 7–8
1. The Grace of God in Salvation.
2. The Goodness of God in the Sanctuary.
3. The Glory of God in Service.

8: 9–13
1. The Alienation in the Past.
2. The Amendment in the Present.
3. The Anticipation for the Future.
4. The Assurance for all time.

8: 14–17
1. The Mercy that forgives.
2. The Mercy that comforts.
3. The Mercy that invites co-operation.

8: 18–23
1. The Rejoicing of a ransomed people.
2. The Reconciliation of a ransomed people.
3. The Reputation of a ransomed people.

9: 1–8
1. The Purpose of God will prevail.
2. The Pride of man will perish.
3. The Purifying of man will be proclaimed.
4. The Protection of God is promised.

9: 9–10
1. The Majesty of the King.
2. The Methods of the King.
3. The Mastery of the King.

9: 11–14
1. The Contract God will honour.
2. The Conversion God will bless.
3. The Confirmation God will give.
4. The Confidence God will share.

9: 15–17
1. The Faithful are preserved by the Lord.
2. The Faithful are precious to the Lord.
3. The Faithful are promised the Lord's Blessing.

10: 1–5
1. The Appeal to trust the Goodness of God.
2. The Alarm because of the Enemies of God.
3. The Attack upon the Enemies of God.
4. The Advocacy of the Power of God.

10: 6–12
1. Their Sin is forgiven and forgotten —Mercy.
2. Their strength, fortified and multiplied—Grace.
3. They may be far away but still are in fellowship—Love.
4. They are now favoured and free—Loving-kindness.

11: 7
1. A God-given Mission.
2. Goodwill towards those without.
3. Good relations within.

12: 1–9

1. The Omnipotence of God.
2. The Opportunity of the Church.
3. The Offence of the Church.
4. The Outcome for the Church.

12: 10–14

1. The Prediction of the Lord who suffered—Redemption.
2. The Purifying of the Believer's sorrow—Remorse.
3. The Personal challenge of the Believer's sorrow—Repentance.

13: 1–6

1. After the sorrow, the Cleansing.
2. After the Cleansing—the clear conscience.
3. After the self-seeking—the self-examination.

13: 7–9

1. The Passion of the Lord.
2. The Persecution of the Lord's Disciples.
3. The Purification of the Lord's Disciples.
4. The Perfecting of the Lord's Disciples.

14: 1–3

1. Does God interrupt human affairs?
2. Does God intervene in life of the Church?
3. Does God intercede on behalf of the Church?

14: 4–8

1. The Lord acts.
2. The Lord comes.
3. The Lord gives.
4. The Lord blesses.

14: 9–11

1. Man shall acknowledge one God only.
2. Man shall worship one God only.
3. Man shall find Salvation in one God only.

14: 12–15

1. Justice demands Judgement.
2. Truth demands Tribute.
3. Worship demands Witness.

14: 20–21

1, Sacredness in small duties.
2. Sacredness in secular things.
3· Sincerity in Service.

Malachi

1: 1–6
1. The Love they did not recognize.
2. The Love they did not respect.
3. The Love they did not return.

1: 7–9
1. Is our worship worthy?
2. Is our witness worthy?
3. Is our work worthy?

1: 10–14
1. Professionalism destroys Sincerity.
2. Pagans display Sincerity.
3. Privilege demands Sincerity.
4. Promise declared with Certainty.

2: 1–9
1. Corruption calls for condemnation.
2. Deceit calls for Discipline.
3. Reconciliation calls for Righteousness.

2: 10–12
1. The Relationship of which they are reminded.
2. The Responsibility they are forgetting.
3. The Rebellion of which they are accused.

2: 13–16
1. Sentiment no substitute for Sincerity.
2. Personal Pride no substitute for Purpose of God.
3. Worldliness no substitute for Watchfulness.

2: 17–3: 1
1. The Questions men ask.
2. The Courier men will know.
3. The Christ men will behold.

3: 2–6
1. The Challenge of Judgement.
2. The Church and her Judgement.
3. The Consolation in Judgement.

3: 7–12
1. The Divine Invitation.
2. The Divine Initiative.
3. The Divine Integrity.

3: 13–18
1. A Perplexity we all share.
2. A Providence we all share.
3. A Position we all can take up.
4. A Prayer we all can make.

4: 1–3
1. The Promise of Doom.
2. The Promise of Dawn.
3. The Promise of Deliverance.

4: 4–6
1. The Ministry of Remembrance.
2. The Miracle of Reconciliation with God.
3. The Message of Restored relationships with men.

NEW TESTAMENT

Matthew

1: 1–17
1. In Christ, Social barriers disappear.
2. In Christ, Sex differences cease to dominate.
3. In Christ, Saint and Sinner find a Saviour.

1: 17
1. From Insignificance to Greatness.
2. From Greatness to Shame.
3. From Shame to Glory.

1: 18–20
1. The Creative Moment.
2. The Chosen Method.
3. The Challenging Miracle.

1: 21–23
1. The Appearing of the Son of God.
2. The Appointment of the Son of God.
3. The Acceptance of the Son of God.

2: 1–2
1. The Coming of Christ.
2. The Coming of the Magi.
3. The Challenge they imply.
4. The Confession they would make.

2: 3–10
1. The Reaction of Suspicion.
2. The Reaction of Superiority.
3. The Reaction of Glad Surrender.

2: 11–12
1. They came to see for themselves.
2. They saw Him.
3. They were conquered.
4. They were cautious.

2: 11
1. Their Acknowledgement of Jesus as Master.
2. Their Acknowledgement of Jesus as Mediator.
3. Their Acknowledgement of Jesus as the Man of Sorrows.

2: 13
1. The Persecution begins.
2. The Providence bestowed.
3. The Patience shown.

2: 19–23
1. The Shadowed Years.
2. The Shadowed Land.
3. The Shadowed Home.

2: 23
1. Nazareth: the hidden years.
2. Nazareth: the hidden fears.
3. Nazareth: the hidden tears.

3: 1–12
1. The Herald of the Gospel.
2. The Heroism of the Herald.
3. The Humility of the Herald.

3: 7–9
1. Unashamed of his task.
2. Uncompromising in his attitude.
3. Unafraid of his enemies.

3: 10–12
1. The Weakness of Tradition—Self-satisfaction.
2. The Witness to Truth—Self-abasement.
3. The Work of Truth—Self-surrender.

3: 13–17

1. The Psychological Moment.
2. The Saviour's Meekness.
3. The Solemnizing Memory.

4: 1–2

1. The Moment of Testing.
2. The Meaning of the Testing.
3. The Method of the Testing.

4: 3–11

1. Tempted to express His Power Selfishly.
2. Tempted to express His Power Sensationally.
3. Tempted in a way even more Subtle.

4: 12–17

1. From the Wilderness into the World.
2. From Security to Struggle.
3. From Prayer to Proclamation.

4: 18–22

1. The Companionship He sought.
2. The Call He extended.
3. The Character of those who responded.
4. The Consequences to the world.

4: 18c

1. The Fisherman knows what Patience is needed.
2. The Fisherman knows what Partnership means.
3. The Fisherman knows how Painstaking his Preparation must be.
4. The Fisherman knows how Prompt in action he must be.
5. The Fisherman knows he must Put himself out of sight.

4: 23–25

1. He came to encourage Understanding of God.
2. He came to banish uncertainty about God.
3. He came to deliver the underprivileged unto God.

5: 1–2

1. For whom intended—Christian believers.
2. By whom inspired—Christ.
3. By whom inherited—the Church.

5: 3

1. Not the Cowardly but the Courageous.
2. Not the Self-conscious but the Self-critical.
3. Not the Deluded but those Destitute of Power.

5: 4

1. Happy are they whose hearts bleed for the Sorrow of others.
2. Happy are they whose hearts burn for the Sin of the world.
3. Happy are they who are heartbroken for their own sin.

5: 5

1. Happy is he who knows the measure of his ignorance.
2. Happy is he who acknowledges his human frailty.
3. Happy is he whose life is centred in God.

5: 6

1. Happy is he desperately eager to be right with God.
2. Happy is he desperately eager to be right with his fellows.
3. Happy is he who is desperately eager to be right with himself.

5: 7

1. Happy is he who understands.
2. Happy is he who stands alongside us.
3. Happy is he who stands for us.

5: 8

1. Happy is he whose motives are free from selfishness.
2. Happy is he whose motives are free from self-approval.
3. Happy is he whose motives are inspired by loving-kindness.

5: 9

1. Happy is he who breaks down barriers.
2. Happy is he who makes friends of enemies.
3. Happy is he who makes life more tolerable for others.

5: 10-12

1. Happy is he who suffers because of Christian Love.
2. Happy is he who suffers because of Christian Loyalty.
3. Happy is he who suffers because of his Christian Life.

5: 13

1. The Christian is essentially different from the world.
2. The Christian is essential to the world.
3. The Christian must enter into the life of the world.

5: 14-26

1. The Compliment—we are to be like Christ.
2. The Comparison—we are to be seen to be like Christ.
3. The Command—we are to shine for Christ.

5: 17-18

1. The Divine Law that cannot change.
2. The Divine Law that comes to life in Christ.
3. The Divine Law that challenges us today.

5: 19-20

1. His respect for the Divine Law.
2. His reverence for human life.
3. His royal law for life.

5: 21-22

1. The Authorities they quoted.
2. The Authority who was questioned.
3. The Authentic principle illustrated.

5: 23-26

1. Not outward act but inner attitude.
2. Not the religious rite but right relationships.
3. Not the justice of our cause but the charity of our hearts.

5: 27-30

1. Not outward deed only but inner disobedience.
2. Not Sick-nursing but surgery.
3. Not Sins but Sin.

5: 31-32

1. The Old world and women.
2. The New world and women.
3. The Eternal word and women.

5: 33-37

1. The Old Attitude towards a Promise.
2. The New Approach towards a Promise.
3. The New Principle concerning a Promise.

5: 38-41

1. The Law of Retaliation—has it disappeared?
2. The Law of Right-relationships—do we believe it?
3. The Love that never Retreats—have we tried it?

5: 42

1. The Love we should show.
2. The Love shown us.
3. The Love borrowed from us.

5: 43-48

1. The Love that overcomes hatred.
2. The Love that overwhelms hostility.
3. The Love that overflows in prayer.
4. The Love that has no respect for persons.

6: 1-4

1. The Practice of Giving.
2. The Principle of Giving.
3. The Pattern of Giving.

6: 4

1. Christian reward is limited to Christians.
2. Christian reward is unlimited in satisfaction.
3. Christian reward is unlimited in Service.
4. Christian reward is unlimited fellowship with Christ.

6: 5–8

1. Parade of Piety is condemned.
2. Prayer in private is commended.
3. Providence and our Petitions.

6: 9a

1. Prayer for Disciples' use.
2. Prayer demanding Disciplined use.
3. Prayer for Daily use.

6: 9b

1. The Fellowship it suggests.
2. The Faith it encourages.
3. The Force it emphasizes.

6: 10

1. The Object of our Reverence.
2. The Object of our Redemption.
3. The Object of all Righteousness.

6: 11

1. Emphasizes our Daily Dependence.
2. Emphasizes our Duty to less fortunate folk.
3. Emphasizes need for Diligent partnership with God.

6: 12, 14–15

1. The Statement concerning Forgiveness.
2. The Standard of Forgiveness.
3. The Solemn Summary of Forgiveness.

6: 12, 14–15

1. The Principle stated.
2. The Promise made.
3. The Penalty incurred.

6: 13

1. A heritage we all share.
2. A hope we all can share.
3. A Helper we all can share.

6: 16–18

1. Fasting is good as a Discipline for all.
2. Fasting is good for Disciples of the Lord.
3. Fasting is good for Discovery.

6: 19–21

1. The World we see—a good Investment.
2. The world we do not see—a better Investment.
3. The world we cannot see—the best Investment.

6: 22–23

1. Barriers to Vision:—
   (a) Self-Love.
   (b) Self-righteousness.
   (c) Self-consciousness.

6: 24

1. The Ultimatum of the Lord.
2. The Utmost for the Lord.
3. The Urgency of the Lord.

6: 25–32

1. Worrying is unobservant.
2. Worrying is useless.
3. Worrying is unbelieving.
4. Worrying is unworthy.

6: 33–34

The Antidote to Worry:—
1. A Worthy Powerful Interest.
2. A Worthy Permanent Interest.
3. A Working Plan for daily living.

7: 1–5

1. No-one is good enough.
2. No-one knows enough.
3. No-one is impartial enough.

7: 6

1. Some cannot understand the Gospel.
2. Some will not accept the Gospel.
3. Some are convinced not by words but by Gospel witness.

7: 11

1. The Encouragement to Prayer.
2. The Everlasting Yea to Prayer.
3. The Eternal Wisdom in answers to Prayer.

7: 12

1. What we most desire we should give to others.
2. What we greatly enjoy we should share with others.
3. What we have received we should want others to possess.

7: 13–14

1. The Way of the Disciple.
2. The Way of Discipline.
3. The Way of Discovery.

7: 15–20

1. Disguised as religion.
2. Demonstration of true religion.
3. Demand of true religion.

7: 21–23

1. Not the offering of ritual but the obedience of the heart.
2. Not our achievements but the acceptance of His Will.
3. Not the flattery we offer but the faithfulness we show.

7: 24–27

1. Do we listen carefully?
2. Do we live thoughtfully?
3. Do we labour faithfully?

8: 1–4

1. The Approach of the Leper—Confidence.
2. The Attention of Jesus—Compassion.
3. The Achievement of the Leper—Cure.
4. The Advocacy of Jesus—Caution and Correction.

8: 5–13

1. The unusual Concern of a soldier.
2. The immediate Compassion of the Lord.
3. The utter confidence of the soldier.
4. The utmost Confession of the Lord.
5. The urgent Command of the Lord.
6. The unusual Cure of the Servant.

8: 14–15

1. The Lord was no stranger in that home.
2. The Lord was no stranger to sickness.
3. The Lord was no stranger to service.

8: 16–17

1. The End of the Day but not of His Loving-kindness.
2. The End of the Day but not of His Healing Power.
3. The End of the Day but not of His Patience.

8: 18–22

1. The Magnetism of Christ Jesus.
2. The Meaning the Scribe must know.
3. The Message they both must learn.

8: 23–27

1. Their Turmoil—His Trust.
2. Their Distress—His Disappointment.
3. His Control—their Calm restored.
4. His Action—their Astonishment.

8: 28–34

1. The Supreme Control of Jesus.
2. The Sad Condition of the Men.
3. The Selfishness of the Villagers.
4. The Soul of the Story.

9: 1–8

1. His Opportunity—their Faith.
2. His Opponents—their faulty faith.
3. His Objective—their Forgiveness.

9: 9
1. The Lord saw Matthew—Discovery.
2. The Lord called Matthew—Destiny.
3. The Lord conquered Matthew—Dedication.

9: 10–13
1. His Love was all-inclusive—theirs was exclusive.
2. His Way was kindly—theirs was condemnatory.
3. His Mission was to Heal and Help—theirs was to hinder and hurt.

9: 14–15
1. The Question.
2. The Contrast.
3. The Cross.

9: 16–17
1. Towards the Old—a gentle heart.
2. Towards the New—a glad heart.
3. Towards the Old and the New—a grateful heart.

9: 18–31
1. Had he tried everything else?
2. Had she given up trying?
3. Had they tried and failed?

9: 18–19, 23–26
1. His motive in coming to Jesus.
2. The Miracle of his coming to Jesus.
3. The Miracle that came to pass because of Jesus.

9: 20–22
1. He gave a hearing to one sick woman.
2. He gave healing to one sick woman.
3. He brought Heaven to one sick woman.

9: 27–31
1. They were blind but nevertheless followed.
2. They understood not but did have Faith.
3. They believed and their blindness fell from them.

9: 28
1. Not the Crowd but the Cottage.
2. Not the Enthusiasm alone but also the Encounter.
3. Not the world without but the Witness within.

9: 32–34
1. The unfailing Resources of the Lord.
2. The unashamed Rejoicing of the crowds.
3. The unworthy reaction of the Pharisees.

9: 35
1. The Message.
2. The Mission.
3. The Miracle.

9: 36–38
1. Are we less bewildered today?
2. Are we less believing today?
3. Are we less bold today?

10: 1–4
1. Their Call.
2. Their Equipment.
3. Their Character.

10: 2–4
1. Chosen.
2. Challenged.
3. Contrasted.

10: 5–6
1. Their Manpower was limited.
2. Their knowledge was limited.
3. Their Objective must be limited.

10: 7–8
1. The Word they must preach.
2. The Works they must do.
3. The Wealth they must share.

10: 9–10
1. They were to travel light.
2. They were to count on liberality.
3. They were to serve the Lord.

10: 11–15
1. The Opportunity they give.
2. The Opportunity that seldom returns.
3. The Opportunity that determines Destiny.

10: 16–22
1. The Dangers promised them.
2. The Defence promised them.
3. The Deliverance promised them.

10: 23
1. Don't give in but get out.
2. Don't give in but look up.
3. Don't give in but look around.

10: 24–25
1. Not exempt from strife.
2. Not excluded from strength.
3. Not exempt from Slander.

10: 26–31
1. Have confidence in your Message.
2. Have confidence in your Master.
3. Have confidence in your Ministry.

10 : 32
1. We confess Christ when we love Him.
2. We confess Christ when we learn from Him.
3. We confess Christ when we labour for Him.
4. We confess Christ when we long for His Return.

10: 33
1. We deny Christ when we are ashamed of Him.
2. We deny Christ when we accept the world's standards.
3. We deny Christ when we appear to be Christian and are not.

10: 34–39
1. The Truth that disturbs.
2. The Trial that comes.
3. The Test that decides.
4. The Triumph that awaits.

10: 40
1. The Revelation of the Love of God.
2. The Recipient of that Love.
3. The Retelling of that Love.

10: 41–42
1. Hospitality to the Word has its reward.
2. Hospitality to the Worker has its reward.
3. Hospitality to the Witness has its reward.
4. Hospitality to the Waifs of the World has its reward.

11: 1–6
1. The Fear that was expressed.
2. The Facts that were made known.
3. The Faith that was invited.

11: 7–11
1. Did they think John the Baptist was unimportant?
2. Did they expect someone unworkmanlike?
3. Did they realize John the Baptist was incomparable?
4. Yet John the Baptist did not know the fullness of the Love of God in Christ.

11: 12–15
1. The Enthusiasm of the Faithful.
2. The Eagerness of the Faithful.
3. The Enlightenment concerning John.
4. The Earnestness of the Lord.

11: 16–19
1. The Ways of Men—Contrary.
2. The Way of John—Curious.
3. The Way of the Lord—challenging.
4. The Wisdom of the Lord—justified by results.

11: 20–24

1. They were self-contained—they wanted nothing.
2. They were self-satisfied—they wanted things as they were.
3. They were self-righteous—they wanted nothing new.
4. They were self-condemned—they wanted nothing to do.

11: 25–27

1. Not Resentment but Rejoicing
2. Not Riches but Revelation.
3. Personal but not Private.

11: 28

1. The Invitation.
2. The Insight.
3. The Instruction.
4. The Illumination.

12: 1–8

1. Not the Maintenance of Law but of Life.
2. Not the Ministry of Legalism but of Love.
3. Not the Miseries of Men but the Master they should serve.

12: 9–14

1. The Handicap of the Man.
2. The Hatred of the Authorities.
3. The Happiness restored.

12: 14–21

1. The Gathering Storm.
2. The Great Serenity.
3. The Glorious Service of the Saviour.

12: 18–21

1. The Spirit of Grace.
2. The Silence of Grace.
3. The Service of Grace.

12: 22–28

1. The Attitude of the Spectators.
2. The Approach of the Cynics.
3. The Answer of the Saviour.
4. The Assurance of the Saviour.

12: 30

1. Are we serious about Christ?
2. Are we certain about Christ?
3. Are we serving Christ?

12: 31–33

1. The Fact of Sin.
2. The Forgiveness of Sin.
3. The Unforgiveable Sin.

12: 34–37

1. Words are Revelations.
2. Words are Responsibilities.
3. Words are Remembered.

12: 38–42

1. The Sign they would not read.
2. The Sign they could not read.
3. The Sign that condemned them.

12: 43–45

1. The Nature of Wickedness.
2. The Need for Watchfulness.
3. The Need for Work.

12: 46–50

1. The Fellowship of His family—slow to understand.
2. The Fellowship of His friends—quick to condemn.
3. The Fellowship of the Faithful—abiding.

13: 1–9, 18–23

1. Ground is hard—Minds are closed.
2. Ground is stony—Minds are shallow.
3. Ground is thorny—Minds are preoccupied.
4. Ground is good—Minds are prepared.

13: 23

1. The Privilege of Listening.
2. The Privilege of Learning.
3. The Privilege of Loving.

13: 10–17

1. Secret of Christ is known to Christian Insight.
2. Secret of Knowledge is revealed to constant Industry.
3. Secret of Faith is revealed to Child-like in heart.

13: 24–30, 36–43

1. Are we good gardeners?
2. Are we charitable in our judgements?
3. Are we convinced of Judgement?

13: 31–32

1. The Enterprise of the Church of God.
2. The Expansion of the Church of God.
3. The Encouragement of the Church of God.

13: 33

1. The Work of God is sometimes Secret.
2. The Work of God is sometimes Silent.
3. The Work of God is always sure.

13: 44

1. The Discovery of God's Will.
2. The Delight in God's Will.
3. The Dedication to God's Will.

13: 45–46

1. The Objective—God's Will be done.
2. The Opportunity—to do God's Will.
3. The Obedience—to do God's Will.

13: 47–50

1. The Outreach of the Church.
2. The Outsider and the Church.
3. The Outcome for the Church.

13: 51–53

1. You have understood Me.
2. You must now undertake for Me.
3. You must bring all your talents, old and new, into my Service.

13: 54–58

1. The Word of Healing.
2. The Word of Hostility.
3. The Word of Helplessness.

14: 1–12

1. The Fear of a troubled conscience.
2. The Folly of a troubled Coward.
4. The Fury of Cowardice.
4. The Faithfulness of Companions.

14: 13–14

1. The Master's Distress.
2. The Master's Discipline.
3. The Master's Diligence.

14: 15–21

1. Nature alone cannot satisfy our deepest hunger.
2. Human Nature alone cannot satisfy our deepest hunger.
3. Divine Nature alone satisfies deepest hunger.

14: 22–33

1. Alone with God.
2. Alarm of His brethren.
3. Alongside His brethren.
4. All for His brethren.
5. All from His brethren.

14: 34–36

1. Saved to Serve.
2. Salvation is sought.
3. Salvation is found.

15: 1–9

1. The Pursuit of the Authorities.
2. The Pettiness of their charges.
3. The False Piety they encourage.
4. The Poverty of their religion.
5. The Prophecy that condemned them.

15: 10–20

1. True religion—Obedience not Orthodoxy.
2. True religion—Righteousness not ritual.
3. True religion—not proud achievement but right personal attitudes.

15: 21–28

1 Christ and territorial barriers— crossed.
2. Christ and physical barriers—cured.
3. Christ and personal barriers— conquered.

15: 29–31

1. The Maintenance of the Gospel— Expansion.
2. The Ministry of Grace—Extension.
3. The Manifestation of Glory— Excellence.

15: 32–39

1. The Master and human need.
2. The Master and human doubt.
3. The Master and human satisfaction.

16: 1–4

1. What they wanted—a spectacular sign.
2. What they lacked—understanding.
3. What they were given—reminder of God's sign in Christ.

16: 5–12

1. The Warning.
2. The Worry.
3. The Wonder.
4. The Warfare.

16: 13–16

1. The Place of Decision.
2. The Purpose of Decision.
3. The Personal Decision.

16: 16–18

1. The Affirmation concerning the Lord.
2. The Approval by the Lord.
3. The Assurance of the Lord.
4. The Appointment by the Lord.

16: 19

1. The Revelation given.
2. The Responsibility bestowed.
3. The Resolution required.

16: 20

1. The Lord was not ready.
2. They were not ready.
3. The world was not ready.

16: 21

1. The Obedience He would render.
2. The Offering He would make.
3. The Obstacle He would overcome.

16: 22–23

1. The Resentment.
2. The Reply.
3. The Reason.

16: 24–25

1. The Personal Call.
2. The Private Challenge.
3. The Promised Consequence.

16: 26

1. The Peril of Prosperity.
2. The Price of Personal Power.
3. The Peril to Personality.

16: 27–28

1. The Promised Return.
2. The Promised Reward.
3. The Promised Realization.

17: 1–8

1. The Hunger for Fellowship—Real.
2. The Hour of Fellowship—Radiant.
3. The Happiness of Fellowship— Remembrance.
4. The Heart of Fellowship—the Redeemer.

17: 1–8

1. Countenance was changed in Prayer.
2. Continuity of Message was confirmed in Prayer.
3. Courage to continue was given in Prayer.

17: 9–13

1. The Need for Caution.
2. The Need for Conviction.
3. The Need for Correction.

17: 9, 14–16

1. From the fact of Fellowship to the Fact of one's Fellows.
2. From Prayer to Performance.
3. From Servant to Saviour.

17: 17–20

1. Disappointed with His Disciples.
2. Diligent in Distress.
3. Deals with their Difficulties.

17: 22–23

1. He shares His Secret.
2. He shares His Certainty.
3. He shares their Sorrow.

17: 24–27

1. The Lord's Concern for Custom.
2. The Lord's Concern for the Kingdom.
3. The Lord's Concern for His Companions.

18: 1–4

1. Not the Worldly Wise and Proud.
2. Not the Wealthy and Proud.
3. Not the Wicked and Proud.
4. But the Wonder and Trust of a child.

18: 5–7

1. Welcome the Child—Welcome Christ.
2. Wilfully obstruct the child—wilfully offend Christ.
3. Wrongly instruct the child—ordained to perdition.

18: 8–10

1. Does our Loyalty hurt?
2. Does our Love hurt?
3. Does our Looking hurt?

18: 11

1. The Proclamation He makes.
2. The Purpose of it.
3. The Persons addressed.

18: 12–14

1. The Love of the Shepherd is personal.
2. The Love of the Shepherd is persevering.
3. The Love of the Shepherd is precious.
4. The Love of the Shepherd is a pattern of the Love of God.

18: 15–19

1. Interview with person concerned.
2. Intervention of trusted friends.
3. Inspiration of the Fellowship.
4. Injury to the Fellowship.

18: 19–20

1. We must be objective, not self-centred.
2. We must be sure of our objective in prayer.
3. We must be sure of God's willingness to satisfy.
4. We must be sure God is with us in life.

18: 20

1. True Faithfulness in Worship.
2. True Freedom in Worship.
3. True Fulfilment in Worship.

18: 21–35

1. The Question concerning Forgiveness.
2. The Cost of Forgiveness.
3. The Call to Forgive.

19: 1

1. The Teaching to His disciples.
2. The Trail for His disciples.
3. The Triumph before His disciples.

19: 1–11

1. The Interest shown.
2. The Ideal for mankind.
3. The Infirmity of mankind.
4. The Individual and mankind.
5. The Inspiration for mankind.

19: 12
1. Some are born lame.
2. Some are made lame.
3. Some choose to be lame, yet all can serve the Lord.

19: 13–15
1. His attraction for them.
2. His attitude towards them.
3. His approval of them.

19: 16–22
1. The Self-Introduction.
2. The Searching Invitation.
3. The Stubborn Insistence.
4. The Sudden Instruction.
5. The Self challenged.

19: 23–26
1. Riches encourage Pride of Place. . .
2. Riches encourage Pride of Possessions.
3. Riches encourage Pride of Personal Worth.
4. Riches can be converted.

19: 27–30
1. An unfortunate question but no Rebuke.
2. An unforgettable quest and its reward.
3. The uttermost quest and its reward.
4. The utterly surprising.

20: 1–16
1. A Welcome awaits those early in the service of the Lord.
2. A Welcome awaits those late in the service of the Lord.
3. Reward is determined by Love not by Law.
4. Reward is determined, also, by Humility, not by honours.

20: 17–19
1. The Resolution of the Lord.
2. The Repetition by the Lord.
3. The Resurrection of the Lord.

20: 20–23
1. The uninstructed request.
2. The unrelenting requirement.
3. The unknown reward.

20: 24–28
1. The Opportunity to speak.
2. The Overturned standards of value.
3. The Overcoming Saviour.
4. The Overwhelming Salvation.

20: 30–34
1. Partners in Darkness.
2. Partners in Discouragement.
3. Partners in Determination.
4. Partners in Discipleship.

21: 1–11
1. The Fulfilment of His own Planning.
2. The Fulfilment of Prophecy.
3. The Fulfilment of People's Prayers.

21: 1–11
1. The Determination He shows.
2. The Demand He makes.
3. The Deliverance He offers.

21: 12–14
1. When Christ comes in, Injustice goes out.
2. When Christ comes in, Dishonesty goes out.
3. When Christ comes in, Barriers disappear.
4. When Christ comes in, Miracles happen.

21: 15–17
1. The Anger of the Professionals.
2. The Acclamation of the Children.
3. The Approval of the Lord.

21: 18–20
1. Display.
2. Disappointment.
3. Disappearance.

21: 21–22
1. The Qualification—Believing Faith.
2. The Conquest—Burdens Buried.
3. The Courage—Burdens bravely borne.

21: 23–27
1. Their Concern for authority.
2. Their Cowardice before His authority.
3. His Courage concerning authority.

21: 28–32
1. Wayward but won over at last.
2. Well-behaved but not well-intentioned.
3. Wicked but welcomed.
4. Warned but wayward still.

21: 33–34
1. The Plan of God.
2. The Provision of God.
3. The Purpose of God.

21: 35–41
1. The Prophets of God.
2. The Pre-eminence of the Son.
3. The Punishment of God.

21: 42–46
1. Privileged but producing nothing.
2. Condemned but crowned at last.
3. Resist Him and Rejoice not.
4. Challenge and Choice.

22: 1–10
1. What we are offered in Christ.
2. What excuses we make when we refuse.
3. What we miss when we refuse.
4. What we find when we accept.

22: 11–14
1. We are the Guests of God, in worship.
2. Have we the Garments of Reverence, Repentance and Rejoicing, in our worship?
3. Have we received the Gospel or rejected it?

22: 15–22
1. Their Purpose in coming to Him.
2. His Prudence in answering them.
3. The Principle He gave them.

22: 23–33
1. Their thoughts about marriage were earthbound.
2. Their thoughts about God were earthbound.
3. Their thoughts of Resurrection were earthbound, too.

22: 34–40
1. What we all want to know.
2. What we all have learnt.
3. What we all will not do.

22: 41–46
1. His Concern to know.
2. Their Confusion.
3. His Claim to be the Son of God.

23: 1–12
1. He commends obedience to Principles of the Law.
2. He condemns ostentation in Life.
3. He calls for Love towards God, the Father.
4. He Claims Leadership for Himself.
5. He commends Lowliness in others.

23: 13
1. The Hypocrisy they practised.
2. The Hindrances they put in the way.
3. The Happiness they denied others.

23: 14
1. They rob the poor.
2. They relish their piety.
3. Their reward is a greater punishment.

23: 15
1. The campaign in which they engage.
2. The convert they win.
3. The condemnation they impose.

23: 16–22
1. How honest are we?
2. How humble are we?
3. How honourable are we?

23: 23–24
1. They are fussy in small duties.
2. They are faithless in larger duties.
3. They are foolish in leadership.

23: 25–28
1. They are outwardly faultless.
2. They are inwardly foul.
3. They are always faithless.

23: 29–33
1. A Show of Piety.
2. The Shadow of the Past.
3. The Shame of the Past.
4. The Shadow in the Present.

23: 24–36
1. History condemned them.
2. History challenges us.
3. History judges us.

23: 37–39
1. The Broken Heart.
2. The Broken Heroes.
3. The Broken Hope.
4. The Broken Heritage.
5. The Blessed Hope.

24: 1–2
1. When Christ goes out, the world comes in.
2. When Christian values disappear, worldly values reappear.
3. When Christian worship ceases, worship of lesser things begins.

24: 3, 14, 27–28
1. The Secret of His Return.
2. The Salvation offered before His Return.
3. The Suddenness of His Return.
4. The Certainty of His Return.

24: 4, 5, 11–13, 23–26
1. We must be alert to Deception.
2. We must refuse to be daunted.
3. We must be diligent.

24: 6–8, 29–31
1. Has God departed from His world?
2. Does God encourage His world?
3. Does God discipline His world?
4. Has God disclosed His last word to the world?

24: 9–10
1. The Christian and Persecution.
2. The Christian and His Principles.
3. The Christian and the Pattern of his life.
4. The Christian and Public Life.

24: 15–22
1. The Collapse of Ungodliness.
2. The Chaos of Unrighteousness.
3. The Call to Understanding.

24: 32–35
1. The Word to the Wise.
2. The Word to the Worldly.
3. The Word of Witness.

24: 36–41
1. A Matter in the Providence of God.
2. A Matter for Preparation by men.
3. A Matter for Prayer.

24: 42–51
1. We are to be disciplined in Watchfulness.
2. We are to be diligent in our Work.
3. We have no day to Waste.

25: 1–13
1. The Last moment may be too late.
2. The Lost opportunity may never return.
3. The Love-Offering of Life must be our own, not another's.

25: 14–30

1. Our Gifts are different.
2. Our Gifts should be cultivated.
3. Our Gifts are our Judgement.
4. Our Gifts are our opportunity.

25: 31–46

1. Here is something we can all do.
2. Here is something we can all do for its own sake.
3. Here is something we can all do which turns out to be done to Him.

25: 31–46

1. The Day.
2. The Division.
3. The Duty—done or undone?

26: 1–5

1. The Cross and the Courage.
2. The Contrast—Passover and Passion.
3. The Cowardice of the Authorities.

26: 6–13

1. The Love that knew no Bounds.
2. The Love that knew no Bonds.
3. The Love that knew no Barrier.

26: 14–16

1. The Companions he dishonoured.
2. The Christ he would humble.
3. The Contract they agreed upon.

26: 17–19

1. The Place they would know.
2. The Plan He shared with them.
3. The Preparation they completed.

26: 20–25

1. The Love that blessed them.
2. The Love that bled for them.
3. The Love that betrayed Him.
4. The Love that burnt within Him.

26: 26–30

1. The Symbolism of Faith.
2. The Signature of Faith.
3. The Supremacy of Faith.

26: 31–35

1. The Price of Loyalty.
2. The Preciousness of Loyalty.
3. The Pride of Loyalty.
4. The Prophecy of Loyalty (forgotten).

26: 36–46

1. The Place of Crisis.
2. The Prayer of Commitment.
3. The Partner's Collapse.
4. The Place of Contrast.
5. The Plan of Campaign.

26: 47–50

1. Truth and Tradition.
2. Tribute and Treachery.
3. Trust and Terror.

26: 51–56

1. Have you forgotten my Prayers?
2. Have you forgotten the Power of God?
3. Would you frustrate the Purpose of God?

26: 57, 59–66

1. The Calm of Jesus.
2. The Claim of Jesus.
3. The Confidence of Jesus.
4. The Condemnation of Jesus.

26: 67–68

1. As then, so now, Christ challenges Doubt.
2. As then, so now, Christ calls for Disciples.
3. As then, so now, Christ calls for Decision.

26: 58, 69–75

1. The Desperation of a loving heart.
2. The Confusion of a loving heart.
3. The Break-down of a loving heart.

27: 3–10

1. Regret but no Recall.
2. Remorse but no Restitution.
3. Remembrance but no Rejoicing.

G

27: 1, 2, 11–23
1. Jesus questioned but in command.
2. Jesus sacrificed but silent.
3. Jesus judged but Himself Judgement.

27: 11–24
1. Pilate: warned but weak.
2. Pilate: unwilling but unable to say No.
3. Pilate: confused and cowardly.

27: 24–25
1. Too soiled ever to be clean.
2. Too involved to be innocent.
3. Too ironic to be irrelevant.
   (Destruction of Jerusalem and Deliverance through Christ's Atoning Death).

27: 32
1. Did he resent carrying the Cross?
2. Did he afterwards remember the Cross?
3. Did he not rejoice in the Cross?

27: 26–35
1. The Humiliation.
2. The Heedlessness.
3. The Horror.
4. The Hospitality of Relief.
5. The Hospitality of Heaven.

27: 35–37
1. They knew not who He was.
2. They knew not what they were doing.
3. They knew not what He was doing.

27: 38
1. He was born to save sinners.
2. He lived amongst sinners.
3. He died between sinners.

27: 39–44
1. Was He tempted to misuse His Powers?
2. Was He tempted to think of Himself?
3. Was He tempted to contradict Himself?
4. Was He tempted to abuse His position?

27: 45–46, 50
1. The world covers its eyes.
2. The Word comforts His soul.
3. The Work is completed.

27: 47–49
1. The Mystery.
2. The Mercy.
3. The Misunderstanding.

27: 51–56
1. Darkness between God and Man is lifted.
2. Death is conquered.
3. Discipleship begins for one man.
4. Devotion stands unafraid.

27: 57–60
1. The Man whose hatred was conquered.
2. The man who humbled himself.
3. The man who honoured the Lord.

27: 61
1. Love devotedly stands by in life.
2. Love devotedly steadfast in death.
3. Love seeking still to help.

27: 62–66
1. The Fear that troubled them.
2. The Fact that transformed the world.
3. The Fact that cannot be denied.

28: 1–6
1. Love's Vigil.
2. Love's Vision.
3. Love's Victory.

28: 6–8
1. The Mystery of His Resurrection.
2. Their Mission because of His Resurrection.
3. The Miracle of their Rejoicing.

28: 9–10
1. In Obedience we discover who Jesus is.
2. In Obedience we discover our Strength.
3. In Obedience we discover our Reward.

28: 11-15

1. The Disturbance they encountered.
2. The Dishonesty they encouraged.
3. The Disgrace they expected.
4. The Discovery they were denied.

28: 16-20

1. The Christ who came to them.
2. The Confidence He shared with them.
3. The Commission He gave them.
4. The Companionship He promised them.

Mark

1: 1–3
1. The world needed a Divine Word.
2. The Way needed a Divine Son.
3. The Work needed a Divine Warrant.

1: 5–8
1. John arouses their Sense of Sin.
2. John is armed with Sincerity.
3. John announces the Saviour.

1: 9–13
1. The Background.
2. The Baptism.
3. The Blessing.
4. The Battle.

1: 14–15
1. Jesus accepts a Challenge.
2. Jesus proclaims a Kingdom.
3. Jesus pleads for Conversion.

1: 17
1. Christ calls us to Sacrifice.
2. Christ calls us to Service.
3. Christ's call confers Strength.

1: 19–20
1. The Temptation that confronted them.
2. The Tribute they paid Him.
3. The Torch they lighted.

1: 21, 22, 23, 25
1. Jesus respected Traditions of the Past.
2. Jesus revealed Truth as never before.
3. Jesus rescued a man from Torment.

1: 29–31
1. The Disciples' Concern.
2. The Saviour's Compassion.
3. The Woman's Conduct.

1: 32–34
1. Darkness of many Kinds.
2. Desires of many Kinds.
3. Delight of many Kinds.

1: 35–37
1. Threshold of the Day.
2. Threshold of God.
3. Threshold of Discovery.

1: 40–42
1. Confident approach.
2. Compassionate attitude.
3. Courageous act.
4. Clean again.

2: 2–12
1. Jesus preaches to the crowd.
2. Jesus proclaims forgiveness.
3. Jesus perplexes his enemies.
4. Jesus proves his claim.
5. Jesus provokes surprise and praise.

2: 14
1. Jesus came.
2. Jesus saw.
3. Jesus conquered.

2: 15–17
1. Something new in religion.
2. Nothing new in religion.
3. Not Narrowness but Newness of life.

2: 18–20

1. A New Worry for the Sc. and Ph.
2. A New Way of life to the Sc. and Ph.
3. A Necessary Warning.

2: 21–22

1. Not Repairs but Renewal.
2. Not Refill but Renunciation.
3. Not Resistance but Readiness.

2: 24, 27, 28

1. Churlish condemnation.
2. Christ's counsel.
3. Christ's claim.

3: 1–6

1. Christ's Custom.
2. Christ's Call.
3. Christ's Challenge.
4. Christ's Compassion.
5. Cure Completed.

3: 7–12

1. Christ's Cures draw the Crowds.
2. Christ's Concern for the Crowds.
3. Christ's Concern for the Continuation of His Ministry.

3: 13

1. The Place of the Call—
2. The Pattern of the Call—
3. The Promptness of the Response—

3: 14–15

1. Empowered to serve the Lord.
2. Elected to know the Lord.
3. Employed to broadcast the Word and bring healing to men.

3: 19b

1. A Group with a Master.
2. A Group with a Message.
3. A Group that was Marked.

3: 20–22

1. Miracles draw the multitudes together.
2. Misunderstanding draws the relatives together.
3. Madness draws his enemies together.

3: 23–27

1. Peace demands a Central Loyalty on the Horizon.
2. Peace demands a Central Loyalty on the hearth at home.
3. Peace demands a Central Loyalty in the heart.

3: 28–30

1. A great Evangel.
2. A great Exception.
3. A great Envy.

3: 31–35

1. A common Love of God.
2. A common Loyalty to the Lord.
3. A common Life to share.
4. A common Looking forward.

4: 2–9

1. Good Seed needs Soil ready to receive it.
2. Gospel of Jesus needs a Soul ready to receive it.
3. Gospel of Jesus needs a Soul ready to proclaim it.

4: 25

1. Understanding leads to greater understanding in our Experience of Life,
2. in our Knowledge of the World,
3. in our Mastery of living.

4: 26–29

1. Though unexplained, the Kingdom of God will come.
2. Though unseen, it will come.
3. Though we are unbelieving to the end, it will yet come in fullness because Jesus has come already.

4: 30–32

1. Watch the Single Grain.
2. Wonder at the Greatness.
3. [Welcome the Grace of the Gospel.

4: 35–41

When
1. Critical Experiences overtake us and
2. Consequences overwhelm us and
3. Concern opens up our Prayers,
4. Christ rides the storm with us.

5: 1–20

1. The Conflict of Light and Darkness.
2. The Challenge of Light to Darkness.
3. The Change to Light from Darkness.
4. The charge of Christ to the redeemed Demoniac.

5: 21–24, 35–43

1. Sorrow breaks down Barriers.
2. Sympathy brings Blessing.
3. Scorn hinders Healing.
4. Seeing is Believing.

6: 1–3

1. Were they too near to see Him as he was?
2. Were they too blind to see who He really was?
3. Were they too proud to see greatness in one of their own?

6: 4–6

1. Because He was Unrecognised He was Unhonoured.
2. Because of their Unbelief He was Unable to heal.
3. Though Unappreciated He remained Undaunted.

6: 7–13

1. The Master calls.
2. The Mission begins.
3. The Method outlined.
4. The Message proclaimed.

6: 14–20

1. Coming of John had challenged him.
2. Conscience was aroused at last.
3. Cowardice had corrupted him.
4. Conduct had condemned him.

6: 35–41

1. After campaigning for the Faith—the Companionship of Jesus.
2. When clouds foregather—the Compassion of Jesus.
3. When companions hesitate—behold the Commands of Jesus.
4. When crowds are waiting—behold the Communion of Jesus.

6: 42–44

1. Mercy always Satisfies.
2. Mercy always Sufficient.
3. Mercy always Surprises.

6: 45–51

1. The Consideration of Jesus.
2. The Contemplation of Jesus.
3. The Concern of Jesus.
4. The Control of Jesus.

6: 53–56

1. A hunted Lord.
2. A healing Lord.
3. A holy Lord.

7: 1–23

1. For them Religion consisted of Ritual alone.
2. For Him Religion was Righteousness.
3. For them outward practices were more important than inner purity.
4. For Him outward practices were the expression of inner purity.

7: 24

1. Jesus could not be hidden from Society.
2. Jesus could not be hidden from Sufferers.
3. Jesus could not be hidden from Sinners.

7: 31–37

1. His Concern for the handicapped.
2. His Call for help.
3. His Command to him who was healed.
4. The Consequence of the Cure.

8: 11–12

SIGNS THEY DID NOT SEE.

1. Faith of my Followers—not a Firework Display.
2. Facts of Common Day—not a Fairy Land of Fancy.
3. Fact of Me—not of Miracles alone.

8: 14–21

1. Unprepared for the Crossing.
2. Unaware of threatening Corruption.
3. Understanding not who Christ is.

8: 22–26

1. The care of Jesus for this man.
2. The character of the Cure.
3. The Completeness of the Cure.

8: 27–30

1. The Decision He made.
2. The Difference they noted.
3. The Declaration they made.
4. The Discipline imposed upon them.

8: 31

1. The Cost of Redemption.
2. The Cause of Rejection.
3. The Crowning Resurrection.

8: 34–35

1. The Terms of Discipleship.
2. The Training for Discipleship.
3. The Truth of Discipleship.
4. The Triumph of Discipleship.

8: 36–38

1. Christ's Challenge to our Sense of Values.
2. Christ's Certainty of the Sanity of Virtue.
3. Christ's Concern for those who Shun Him, on the Day of Visitation.

9: 1

1. The Encouragement of Jesus.
2. The Endurance of the Church.
3. The Expansion of the Church.

9: 2–8

1. A Mountain-Top Experience.
2. A Mystery Explained.
3. A Mission Established.
4. A Man Excelling.

9: 14, 19, 24, 28–29

1. Jesus—the Centre of Hope
2. Jesus—the Centre of Healing.
3. Jesus—the Centre of Happiness.
4. Jesus—the Secret of Helpfulness.

9: 33–37

1. Ashamed of their Conversation.
2. Ambition should be converted.
3. Ambassadors are sometimes Common folk.

9: 38–41

1. The Pride of Privilege.
2. The Privileges of Persons.
3. The Persons who Please the Lord.

9: 50a

1. Preserves from Deterioration.
2. Preserves from Dullness.
3. Preserves from Disease.

10: 13–16

1. Ignorance of True Greatness.
2. Invitation to True Greatness.
3. Interpretation of True Greatness.

10: 17–22

1. Wanting the Gift sublime.
2. Wanting one thing more.
3. Wanting his Goods too much.

10: 23–27

1. A startling Statement.
2. A Searching Simplicity.
3. A sad Shout.
4. A Sublime Secret.

10: 28–31

1. A great Confidence expressed.
2. A great Confidence shaken.
3. A great Confidence restored.
4. A great Conclusion drawn.

10: 32–34

1. The Journey onwards.
2. The Jesus before them.
3. The Joy denied them.
4. The Judgement awaiting Him.
5. The Justification promised them.

10: 35–45

1 An Unworthy Request.
2. An Unexpected Reply.
3. An Urgent Reproof.
4. An Uncompromising Redeemer.

10: 46–52

1. The Cry from the Dust.
2. The Compassion to Deliver.
3. The Courage that was rewarded.

11: 1–10

1. The Fulfilling of Prophecy.
2. The Fact of Preparation.
3. The Faith of Pilgrims.
4. The Fullness of Praise.

11: 11

1. The Deliberation of Jesus.
2. The Dedication of Jesus.
3. The Decision of Jesus.

11: 15–17

1. He disapproved of their Dishonesty.
2. He was disappointed with the Desecration of the Temple.
3. He was distressed at the Divisions men make.

11: 22–26

1. Is our God big enough?
2. Is our Faith eager enough?
3. Is our readiness to forgive real enough?

11: 27–33

1. Divine Authority is questioned.
2. Direct Answer is denied them.
3. Divine Activity, not human authority, is what matters.

12: 1–11

1. God's Provision for his servants.
2. God's Plan for his servants.
3. God's Progress with his servants.
4. God's Prayer for his Son.
5. God's Punishment of Sin.
4. God's Praise is sung.

12: 13–17

1. An Offence intended.
2. An Observation made.
3. An Obligation explained.
4. An Obedience clarified.

12: 18–27

1. The Resurrection is doubted.
2. Their Reasoning is challenged.
3. Revelation has been given.
4. Resurrection is confirmed.

12: 28–34

1. A Man's Admiration leads to Enquiry.
2. The Lord's Answer is given eagerly.
3. An Alliance corrects an Error.
4. The Lord's Approval reveals His Esteem.

12: 38–40

1. Pride that draws attention to itself.
2. Prominence that flatters this Pride.
3. Prayers that are Hypocrisy.
4. Punishment that is prepared.

12: 41–44

1. Those with much gave much.
2. Those with little gave everything.
3. He who had nothing gave Himself.

13: 2–13

1. Disorder is prophesied.
2. Dismay is evident.
3. Deception is possible.
4. Distress there will be.
5. Declaration of Good News must continue.
6. Deliverance there will be.

13: 26, 32, 33

1. The Promise of His coming.
2. The Privilege of the Knowledge of His coming.
3. The Preparation this calls for.

14: 1, 10

1. The Setting—a crowded city.
2. The Scheming of a Callous Company.
3. The Servant who lost character.

14: 3

1. A home that was avoided.
2. A man who was lonely.
3. A Saviour who was lonely, too.
4. A Woman who loved greatly.
5. A Deed that is remembered.

14: 12–21

1. The Lord's last meeting place was unknown but not unprepared for.
2. Some of His disciples were unknown but not unprepared.
3. The Lord's Accusation was searching but they were not unprepared for it.
4. The Lord's Courage was unswerving but they were not unprepared for that.

14: 22–25

1. A Symbol of Sacrifice.
2. A Symbol of Service.
3. A Symbol of Certainty.

14: 27–28

1. Loyalty shines through.
2. Love's certainty.
3. Leadership returns.

14: 29–30

1. The Pride of Peter.
2. The Protest of Peter.
3. The Prediction concerning Peter.

14: 32–42

1. Jesus did not want to die.
2. Jesus did not doubt God's Power even then.
3. Jesus did not shrink from the fulfilling of the Will of God.
4. Jesus did not shrink from facing his enemies.

14: 43–45

1. Judas could wait no longer.
2. Judas came with a crowd.
3. Judas came with a Kiss that Cursed him for ever.

14: 46–50

1. Unquiet conscience of the crowd.
2. Untroubled heart of the Lord.
3. Uncontrolled fear of the disciples.

14: 54

1. Was Peter curious?
2. Was Peter conscience-stricken?
3. Was Peter a coward?

14: 55–64

1. Dishonesty of Witnesses.
2. Despair of His accusers.
3. Decision they made.
4. Dignity of Jesus.

14: 67–72

1. A fine Tribute.
2. A fiery Trial.
3. The final Truth.

15: 3

1. Was it the Silence of Condemnation?
2. Was it the Silence of Contempt?
3. Was it the Silence of Conflict?
4. Was it the Silence of broken Communications?
5. Was it the Silence of Communion?

15: 8–11, 13

1. They demanded the Maintenance of Tradition (*v. 8*).
2. They demanded Mercy for a Murderer (*v. 11*).
3. They demanded Murder for the Merciful One (*v. 13*).

15: 15

1. Afraid to be unpopular.
2. Abdicated from seat of responsibility.
3. Assented to cruelty.
4. Authorised the crucifixion of Jesus.

15: 21

1. Unexpected summons.
2. Unwilling obedience.
3. Unusual Burden.
4. Unsuspected privilege.

15: 29–32

1. A Challenge to His Power.
2. A Challenge to His Privileged Sonship.
3. A Challenge to His Patience.

15: 33, 35, 36

1. When there should have been LIGHT there was DARKNESS.
2. When there should have been Understanding, there was Misunderstanding.
3. Where there should have been TRIBUTE, there was one who wanted to Test a Theory.
4. Where before there had been Uncertainty—now there was Certainty.

15: 39–46

1. A Great Tribute from a Centurion.
2. A Greater Tribute from Several Women.
3. A Greater Tribute still from a Leader of the Sanhedrin.

16: 3, 4, 5b, 6, 8

Difficulties in the way of Faith:—
1. Doubt common to us all.
2. Darkness prevalent everywhere.
3. Dismay at what is happening, then
4. Discovery and Decision.

16: 12

1. To those whose ages are different.
2. To those whose backgrounds are different.
3. To those whose understanding is different.

16: 14, 15

1. Jesus entered their fellowship.
2. Jesus expected their Faith.
3. Jesus established their Mission.

16: 19, 20

1. The understanding we must have.
2. The Undertaking upon which we embark.
3. The Undergirding we can expect.

Luke

1: 1-4
1. The Claim he wants to establish.
2. The Certainty he wants to share.
3. The Christ he wants to honour.

1: 8-11
1. The Work of the Lord.
2. The Witnesses of the Work of the Lord.
3. The Wonder of the Work of the Lord.

1: 10-14
1. The Place of Prayer.
2. The Place of Proclamation.
3. The Place of Promise.
4. The Place of Pardon.

1: 17
1. The Lord's Forerunner.
2. The Lord's Family Concern.
3. The Lord's Faithful.

1: 30-33
1. Jesus—Divinely Sent.
2. Jesus—Divinely a Saviour.
3. Jesus—Divinely Sufficient.

1: 35-38
1. The Fact to be accepted.
2. The Faith that is required.
3. The Father who overrules.
4. The Faith that responds.

1: 48-50
1. The Lord's Condescension.
2. The Lord's Consideration.
3. The Lord's Compassion.

1: 51-55
1. False Virtues vanish before the Lord.
2. False Barriers break down before the Lord.
3. False Values vanish before the Lord.

1: 56-66
1. The Gift received.
2. The Gratitude expressed.
3. The Goal before Him.
4. The Grace upon Him.

1: 67-75
1. Divine Performance—Faith Vindicated.
2. Divine Prophecy—Faith Challenged.
3. Divine Purpose—Faith Obedient.

1: 76-79
1. The Pilot of Salvation.
2. The Pioneer of Salvation.
3. The Pattern of Salvation.
4. The Preparation for Salvation.

2: 1-7
1. The Census: Political requirement.
2. The Christ: Prophecy fulfilled.
3. The Challenge: Personal.

2: 7
1. The Lord Jesus Christ—Unrecognised.
2. The Lord Jesus Christ—Unwanted.
3. The Lord Jesus Christ—Unhonoured.

2: 8–11

1. The Plight of the World.
2. The Light of the World.
3. The Life of the World.

2: 12–14

1. The Loving-kindness of God.
2. The Lowliness of God.
3. The Language of Heaven.

2: 15–20

1. The Vision of the Shepherds.
2. The Vow of the Shepherds.
3. The Visitation to the Shepherds.

2: 21–24

1. The Pattern of His Home.
2. The Priority in His Home.
3. The Poverty of His Home.

2: 25–32

1. The Man who waited.
2. The Man who welcomed.
3. The Man who won through.

2: 34–35

1. Judgement before Christ.
2. Justification in Christ.
3. Jealousy because of Christ.
4. Joylessness because of Christ.

2: 36–38

1. She was Old but still Obedient.
2. She had known sorrow but was still Sweet.
3. She was Thankful and still Thinking of others.

2: 41–52

1. A Blurred Understanding.
2. A Bold Utterance.
3. A Brave Undertaking.

3: 2

1. God gives the Word.
2. God finds the Worker.
3. God comes to the Wilderness.

3: 3–6

1. The Prophecy comes to life.
2. The Prophet challenges life.
3. The Promise of life.

3: 7–9

1. The Truth he proclaims is not challenged.
2. The Traditions of which they were so proud were challenged.
3. The Turning-point has arrived.

3: 10–17

1. Conviction is being born in them.
2. Compassion is commended to them.
3. Conscientiousness is encouraged.
4. Christ is commended to them.

3: 19–20

1. The Iniquity of Herod.
2. The Injustices of Herod.
3. The Intention of Herod.

3: 21–22

1. Identified with the sin of the people.
2. Inspired to serve the people.
3. Insight into His service for the people.

3: 23

1. What about the Silent Years?
2. What about the Sacrificial Years?
3. What about the Satisfying Years?

3: 23–38

1. The Humiliation of the Son of God.
2. The honour of the Son of God.
3. The hour of the Son of God.

4: 1–2

1. The Plenitude of the Power of God.
2. The Pathway of the Power of God.
3. The Persecution of the Power of God.

4: 2–13

1. Tempted to forget His Manhood.
2. Tempted along the line of His Mission in the world.
3. Tempted along the line of His Message to the world.

4: 2–13

1. The Lord's Fasting.
2. The Lord's Fight.
3. The Lord's Fullness.

4: 14–15

1. His Return.
2. His Reputation.
3. His Resolution.

4: 16–21

1. The Saviour's Enterprise.
2. The Saviour's Example.
3. The Saviour's Encouragement.

4: 22–29

1. At first: Admiration.
2. Then: Animosity.
3. Later: Advocacy.
4. At last: Anger.

4: 30–32

1. His Movements were unhindered.
2. His Habits were untiring.
3. His Teaching was untraditional.

4: 33–37

1. The Saviour dealt with people as they were.
2. The Saviour dealt with people's beliefs as they were then held.
3. The Saviour dealt with people because their need was obvious.

4: 38–39

1. Love seeking.
2. Love Succeeding.
3. Love Serving.

4: 40–44

1. His Healing Ministry.
2. His Holy Ministry.
3. His Helpful Ministry.
4. His Hopeful Ministry.

5: 1–7

1. The Authority He exercised.
2. The Opportunity they accepted.
3. The Obedience they gave.
4. The Overflow they received.

5: 8–11

1. A Full Boat— the Miracle.
2. A Full Heart—the Man.
3. A Full-time job—the Mission.

5: 12–13

1. The Homage rendered.
2. The Hope expressed.
3. The Hour extended.
4. The Healing that followed.

5: 14–15

1. The Charge given.
2. The Conditions imposed.
3. The Clamour arising.

5: 16–17

1. He went to seek the Father's Hospitality.
2. He returned to meet the Pharisees' Hatred.
3. He remained to know the Father's Help.

5: 18–26

1. The Faith that worked.
2. The Forgiveness that had not been tried.
3. The Failure of their understanding.
4. The Favour of God known.
5. The Fear of God experienced.

5: 27–28

1. He renounced one Reputation and found a better one.
2. He renounced his material Resources and found others.
3. He renounced one Ruler and found Another.

5: 29–31

1. He shows his Joy.
2. He shares his Joy.
3. He scandalises the Kill-Joys.
4. He serves his Lord through his Joy.

5: 33–35

1. Christian Gladness and religious gloom.
2. Christian Fellowship and religious fears.
3. Christian Fortitude and religious faiths.

5: 36–39

1. Are we too fond of the Past?
2. Are we too frightened of what is New?
3. Are we forgetting the greatness of our God?

6: 1–5

1. Law to them greater than human need.
2. Love alone can meet human need.
3. Love knows no law but human need.

6: 6–11

1. The Lord's Courage.
2. The Lord's Command of the Situation.
3. The Lord's Concern for the Man.
4. The Lord's Consciousness of Healing Power.
5. The Consequences.

6: 13

1. He chose them to share His Companionship.
2. He chose them to share His Compassion.
3. He chose them to share His Commission.

6: 17–19

1. They heard Him.
2. They were healed by Him.
3. They fixed their hopes upon Him.

6: 20–26

1. Unexpected Words.
2. Unexpected Rewards.
3. Unexpected Warnings.

6: 27–34

1. Do we listen carefully?
2. Do we love carefully?
3. Do we live carefully?

6: 35

1. Wish them well.
2. Treat them well.
3. Support them well.
4. All will be well.

6: 36–38

1. The Ultimate Standard.
2. The Universal Principle.
3. The Unexpected Provision.

6: 39–40

1. Leadership demands Light.
2. Leadership demands Love.
3. Leadership gives Light.

6: 41–42

1. The Blindness of Self-Righteousness.
2. The Burden of Self-Knowledge.
3. The Blessing of Self-Criticism.

6: 45

1. The Heart makes Character.
2. The Heart dictates our Conduct.
3. The Heart directs our Conversation.

6: 46–49

1. Not Praise alone but Performance also.
2. Not for immediate Profit but for long-term peace of mind.
3. Not without Preparation but according to Plan.

7: 1–6

1. Social Barriers down.
2. Religious Barriers down.
3. Political Barriers down.
4. All Barriers down.

7: 6–10
1. The Centurion's Self-Abasement.
2. The Centurion's Sense of Authority.
3. The Saviour's Approval.
4. The Servant's affliction cured.

7: 11–16
1. The Heart that was breaking.
2. The Heart that blessed.
3. The Heart that beat again.
4. The Hearts that burned.

7: 19–23
1. From the Wilderness to the Window.
2. From Understanding to Uncertainty.
3. From Evidence to Enlightenment.

7: 28
1. The Tribute to a great Age.
2. The Threshold of a new Age.
3. The Truth for a new Age.

7: 31–35
1. They were unresponsive.
2. They were inconsistent.
3. They were without insight.

7: 36–48
1. An Invitation accepted.
2. An Incident arouses comment.
3. An Insight unexpected.
4. An Interpretation given.

7: 44–46
1. No honour unto the Lord.
2. No humility before the Lord.
3. No honesty with the Lord.

7: 37, 44–48
1. The Gifts of a Sinner.
2. The Grace of the Saviour.
3. The Gospel of the Second Chance.

8: 1–3
1. The Word of God is not bound.
2. The Witness to God is not bound.
3. The Will of God is not bound.

8: 4–8
1. In the Lord's work, hard work is to be expected.
2. In the Lord's work, hardship is to be expected.
3. In the Lord's time, harvest is sure.

8: 11
1. It must be preached.
2. It must be preserved.
3. It must prosper.

8: 16–17
1. Let us not be ashamed of our Faith.
2. Let us not be ashamed to share our Faith.
3. Let us not be ashamed to let our Faith shine.

8: 18
1. A Responsibility we must accept.
2. A Reward we receive.
3. A Retribution we may expect.

8: 19–21
1. The Discipline He had known.
2. The Decision He had made.
3. The Destiny He had chosen.

8: 22
1. The Request—His Order.
2. The Response—their Obedience.
3. The Reward—their Opportunity.

8: 23–25
1. The Lord's Communion.
2. The Lord's Confidence.
3. The Lord's Control.
4. The Lord's Concern.

8: 22–25
1. A rough Crossing.
2. A royal Companion.
3. A real Compassion.
4. A royal Concern.
5. A ready Confession.

8: 26–36

1. Light reveals the darkness.
2. Light rebukes the darkness.
3. Light redeems the darkness.

8: 38–39

1. A Privilege denied.
2. A Purpose declared.
3. A Providence acknowledged.

8: 41–42, 49–56

1. What a man will do for someone he loves.
2. What the Saviour will do for anyone in need.
3. What the Saviour did in spite of laughter and scorn.
4. What the Situation revealed to all concerned.

8: 43–48

1. She was beyond human cure.
2. She was byond human care.
3. She was beyond human caution.
4. She was not beyond the Saviour's compassion.

9: 1–2

1. They shared in the fellowship of a common Lord.
2. They shared a common Authority.
3. They shared a common Purpose.

9: 6

1. They were equipped to serve.
2. They were equipped to speak.
3. They were equipped to save.

9: 7–9

1. The Challenge a man must face.
2. The Conscience that would not be denied.
3. The Curiosity that would be satisfied.

9: 10–17

1. His Concern for the Apostles.
2. His Compassion for his followers.
3. His Command of the situation.
4. His Communion with the Father.
5. His Confidence in the Father.

9: 18–22

1. What is the Public Testimony to Me?
2. What is your Personal Testimony to Me?
3. This is Personal Testimony about Myself.

9: 23

1. Discipleship calls for Discipline.
2. Discipline calls for Self-Denial.
3. Denial calls for Diligence.

9: 24–25

1. The seeming Contradiction.
2. The sure Compensation.
3. The solemn Consideration.

9: 26

1. The Record.
2. The Reckoning.
3. The Return.

9: 28

1. Peter—the Giant.
2. James—the Good.
3. John—the Gentle.

9: 29–36

1. The Communion of the Master.
2. The Confirmation of His Ministry.
3. The Communication to His Men.
4. The Conviction of His Men.

9: 33

1. The Tryst.
2. The Temptation.
3. The Truth.

9: 37–42

1. His Communion.
2. His Contact with human need.
3. His Compassion.
4. His Cure.

9: 43–45

1. The Wonder.
2. The Warning.
3. The Waiting.

9: 46–48
1. Childishness.
2. Childlikeness.
3. Christlikeness.

9: 49–50
1. A Pardonable Jealousy.
2. Plain Justice.
3. A Precious Judgement.

9: 51–56
1. The Glory.
2. The Gesture.
3. The Grief.
4. The Gospel.

9: 57–62
1. Count the Cost.
2. Come without delay.
3. Come without reserve.

10: 2
1. Men are waiting for the Gospel.
2. Men are wanted to proclaim the Gospel.
3. Men are wanted with Gospel power.

10: 3–9
1. They will be without Defence.
2. They must travel without Delay.
3. They must travel without Distraction.
4. They must be without Desire of a personal nature.
5. They must preach Deliverance.

10: 10–16
1. The great Responsibility.
2. The great Revelation.
3. The great Retribution.
4. The great Rebellion.

10: 17–20
1. His Enterprise, not theirs.
2. His Excellence, not theirs.
3. His Enabling, not theirs.

10: 21–22
1. The Disclosure of God's Power to the simple-hearted.
2. The Disclosure of God's Plan to His Son.
3. The Disclosure of God's Person through His Son.
4. The Disclosure of God's Person to those Christ chooses.

10: 25–29
1. He asked the right question.
2. He asked the right Person.
3. He gave the right reply.
4. He was shown the right way of life.

10: 30–37
1. Compassion for the unwise who are in need.
2. Compassion for the unknown who are in need.
3. Compassion for those unable to cope with their own need.

10: 38–42
1. Martha was somewhat overcome.
2. The Lord was certainly overshadowed.
3. Mary was overflowing.

11: 1
1. They had noticed the Difference.
2. They knew the Difficulties.
3. They now know the Director.

11: 2
1. The Supremacy of God, the Father.
2. The Sacredness of the Father's name.
3. The Certainty of the Father's rule.
4. The Scope of the Father's rule.

11: 3–4
1. The Lord will supply our material needs.
2. The Lord will provide for our Spiritual needs.
3. The Lord will instruct our Moral obligations.

11: 5–13
1. Endurance in our Prayers.
2. Expectancy in our Prayers.
3. Endowment in our Prayers.

11: 14–19
1. The Service He had rendered.
2. The Slander He received.
3. The Sign He was asked to obtain.
4. The Simplicity of His reply.

11: 23
1. Christ calls for Decision.
2. Christ calls for Dedication.
3. Christ calls for Diligence.

11: 24–26
1. Spiritual Life—a constant Warfare.
2. Spiritual Life—demands constant Watchfulness.
3. Spiritual Life—demands a constant Walk with God.

11: 27–28
1. Love's Outpouring.
2. Love's Obedience.
3. Love's Outlet.

11: 29–32
1. Unlike people of N. they were unresponsive.
2. Unlike people of N. they were unrepentant.
3. Unlike people of N. they were unashamed.
4. Unlike people of N. they were unbelieving.

11: 33–36
1. The Gospel is for all to live by.
2. The Gospel is for all to see by.
3. The Gospel is for all to love by.

11: 37–42
1. They were more concerned about Legalism than Love.
2. They were more concerned about Externals than about Inner Excellence.
3. They were more concerned about Trifles than about the Truth of God.

11: 43–44
1. Are we free from Pride of Place?
2. Are we free from Pride of Position?
3. Are we unaware of our Pride?

11: 45–52
1. They impose Burdens and inspire no Blessing.
2. They thought more of Remembrance than of Righteousness.
3. They were Blind to God and wanted others to be Blind also.

12: 1–7
1. They must beware of False Godliness.
2. They must brave the Fear of Consequences.
3. They must believe in the Fathers providing Care.

12: 8–9
1. No Age Limit.
2. No Class Limit.
3. No Colour Limit.
4. No Country Limit.

12: 10
1. They were blaspheming the Righteousness of God.
2. They became Blind to the Fact of God.
3. They were beyond Repentance and therefore beyond Forgiveness.

12: 13–15, 21
1. The Word that was revealing.
2. The Watchfulness that is required.
3. The Wealth that is rewarding.

12: 16–21
1. His very Prosperity was from God.
2. His very Prosperity made him Godless.
3. His very Prosperity turned to Poverty.

12: 22–31

1. A Word to the Believer.
2. A Way for the Believer.
3. A Witness to the Believer.
4. A Work for the Believer.

12: 32–34

1. The Resources at our Disposal.
2. The Resources that do not fail.
3. The Resources that reveal our Faith.

12: 35–40

1. Happy are they who await their Lord.
2. Happy are they upon whom the Lord waits.
3. Happy are they who keep on waiting.

12: 42–48

1. Happy is he who has done what he ought to have done.
2. Unhappy is he who delays doing what he ought to do.
3. Unhappy is he who denies responsibility for doing anything at all.
4. Happiest of all: he who does more than duty demanded.

12: 49

1. Symbol of Heat.
2. Symbol of Humiliation.
3. Symbol of Holiness.

12: 50

1. The Crisis.
2. The Cross.
3. The Cost.

12: 51–53

1. The Presumption.
2. The Prediction.
3. The Penalty.

12: 54–59

1. The Kingdom has come but they know it not.
2. The King has come but they know Him not.
3. The Call has come but they heed it not.

13: 1–5

1. The Lord corrects popular opinions.
2. The Lord condemns popular obstinacy.
3. The Lord calls for the people's obedience.

13: 6–9

1. Despite a Place of Privilege, it offered no Praise. The First Chance.
2. Despite much Patience, it deserves to Perish. The Second Chance.
3. Despite more Patience, it did Perish. The Last Chance.

13: 10–17

1. The Woman was helpless.
2. The Lord gave healing.
3. The Ruler was hopeless.
4. The People were happy.

13: 18–19

1. The Source of the Kingdom.
2. The Size of the Kingdom.
3. The Shelter provided by the Kingdom.

13: 20–21

1. It comes from without.
2. It works from within.
3. It works.

13: 22

1. No time to be lost.
2. No opportunity to be lost.
3. No Vision to be lost.

13: 23–24

1. The Anxiety—Fear.
2. The Answer—Fight.
3. The Award—Final.

13: 25–27

1. The Experience.
2. The Excuse.
3. The Explanation.

13: 28–30

1. Their Expectations will be disappointed.
2. Their Exclusiveness will disappear.
3. Their Estimate of greatness will suffer reverse.

13: 31–33

1. The Gathering Storm.
2. The Gallant Stand.
3. The Great Steadfastness.

13: 34–35

1. The Despair He must have felt.
2. The Disappointment He must have known.
3. The Destruction He predicted.

14: 1–6

1. He accepts hospitality.
2. He bestows healing.
3. He silences hatred.

14: 7–11

1. The Welcome into the Kingdom.
2. The Warning from the King.
3. The Welfare of the subjects of the King.

14: 12–14

1. Do we give to get?
2. Do we give for glory?
3. Do we give for the glory of God?

14: 15–24

1. The Feast to which they were invited.
2. The Folly of their refusal.
3. The Feeble-Folk who accepted.
4. The Fellowship that always has room.
5. The Feast that will be denied.

14: 26–27

1. The Love that calls.
2. The Loyalty demanded.
3. The Life dedication.

14: 33

1. The Call to us all.
2. The Cost to us all.
3. The Consequence to us all.

14: 34–35

1. Salt differs from that into which it is put.
2. Salt preserves that into which it is put.
3. Salt flavours that into which it is put.

15: 1–7

1. The Pursuit of the Lord.
2. The Perseverance of the Lord.
3. The Pride of the Lord.
4. The Purpose of the Lord.

15: 8–10

1. Precious but lost.
2. Pursued until found.
3. Pleased when found.

15: 11–24

1. The Understanding Father.
2. The Unprofitable Son.
3. The Unwanted Son.
4. The Unworthy Son.
5. The Unexpected Father.
6. The Unreserved Welcome of the Father.

15: 25–32

1. The Joy of the Household.
2. The Jealousy of the Elder Son.
3. The Justification of the Father.

16: 1–9

1. The Enterprise of the Man of the World.
2. The Example to the Man of Faith.
3. The Encouragement to the Man of Faith.

16: 10–13

1. The Question concerning Stewardship.
2. The Qualifications for Stewardship.
3. The Quality of the Steward.

16: 13
1. The Demand.
2. The Decision.
3. The Declaration.

16: 14
1. They Derided Him.
2. Many delay concerning Him.
3. All must decide sooner or later.

16: 15
1. Prosperity no sign of goodness.
2. Prosperity can separate from God.
3. Prosperity can separate from one's fellows.

16: 16
1. Life needs Law.
2. Love needs Law.
3. Family Life needs Law.

16: 19
1. He lived without a Conscience.
2. He lived without Compassion.
3. He lived on to find no Compromise.

17: 1-2
1. Prepare for Temptations that will come.
2. Pray that Temptations do not come through us.
3. Prepare for a Tortured Conscience if they do.

17: 3-4
1. Let us live responsibly.
2. Let us befriend those who offend.
3. Let us forgive without reserve.

17: 5-6
1. What we all want to declare.
2. What we all need to hear.
3. What we all can always share.

17: 7-10
1. The Saviour commands our Service.
2. Our Service is but our Duty.
3. Our Duty is but part payment of our Debt.

17: 11-14
1. Their Need brings them together in Poverty.
2. Their Need brings them to the right Person.
3. Their Need brings them new Power.

17: 15-19
1. He was thankful for his cure.
2. He was thoughtful because of his cure.
3. He was thorough about his thanks.
4. He was thoroughly healed, body and soul.

17: 20-25
1. Faith alone will know.
2. Faith alone will be prepared.
3. Faith alone will understand.

17: 26-37
1. The Lord Jesus Christ will come again.
2. The Lord Jesus Christ will come suddenly.
3. The Lord Jesus Christ will come to justify the faithful.
4. The Lord Jesus Christ will come when He is ready to come.

18: 1-8
1. The Necessity of Prayer.
2. The Natural attitude towards Prayer.
3. The New attitude towards Prayer.
4. The Need for Patience in Prayer.
5. The Need for Preparation in Prayer.

18: 9-14
1. An Expression of Pride.
2. An Entreaty for Pardon.
3. An Example of true Prayer.

18: 15-17
1. The Saviour's Winsomeness.
2. The Saviour's Welcome.
3. The Saviour's Warning.

18: 18–24
1. He was unhappy.
2. He was uncommitted.
3. He was unready.

18: 25–27
1. There are some things money cannot buy—Life.
2. There are some things men cannot do—Life Abundant.
3. There are some things only God can do—Life Eternal.

18: 28–30
1. The Claim he made or The Protest.
2. The Conditions to be fulfilled, The Purpose.
3. The Consequences that follow, The Promise.

18: 31–34
1. His Determination to go on to Jerusalem.
2. His Destiny to be met in Jerusalem.
3. His Deliverance up to death.
4. His Deliverance unto life.
5. The Disciples' Darkened Minds.

18: 35–43
1. The Blind man lived in a dark world.
2. He longed to be delivered from it.
3. The Lord met him.
4. The Lord delivered him.
5. The Light of discipleship.

19: 1–9
1. He lived in Comfort.
2. He did not lack Courage.
3. He was welcomed by Christ.
4. He was wonderfully converted.

19: 10
1. The Saviour is here.
2. The Saviour is here seeking us.
3. The Saviour is here seeking to save us.
4. The Saviour saves to bring us home again.

19: 12–27
1. The Certainty of His Return.
2. The Confidence He showed.
3. The Conduct He condemned.
4. The Conduct He approved.

19: 28
1. Uphill all the way because of Unbelief.
2. Uphill all the way because of Unreadiness.
3. Uphill all the way because of Unrighteousness.

19: 29–36
1. The Lord's Preparation.
2. The Lord's Plan.
3. The Lord's Purpose.

19: 36–40
1. The Courage shown.
2. The Challenge implied.
3. The Kingdom declared.
4. The Criticism offered.
5. The Conviction expressed.

19: 41–44
1. The Homecoming.
2. The Heartbreak.
3. The Hour.

19: 45–48
1. Indignation in action.
2. Injustice reveals itself.
3. Independence at work.

20: 1–8
1. The Opposition hears the Word.
2. The Opposition hardens against the Word.
3. The Opposition is humiliated by the Word.

20: 9–16
1. The Plan of God.
2. The Prophets of God.
3. The Patience of God.
4. The Passion of His Son.
5. The Punishment inflicted.

20: 17–18

1. The Lord knew He would be rejected.
2. The Lord knew He would rise again.
3. The Lord knew judgement would be revealed through Him.

20: 19–26

1. They were cowardly.
2. They were crafty.
3. They were confused.

20: 27–40

1. The Mockery of the Faith of Others.
2. The Method Jesus employed to answer them.
3. The Miracle Jesus confirmed.
4. The Mastery they recognised.

20: 45–47

1. They boast of their Pride of Appearance.
2. Pride of Position.
3. Pride of Place and yet
4. They abuse their Privileges and
5. They act the part.

21: 1–4

1. The Lord knew their Circumstances.
2. The Lord knew their Contributions.
3. The Lord knew the Cost to them.

21: 5–15

1. The Lord of Life saw life whole.
2. The Lord of Life saw life as under God's control.
3. The Lord of Life saw life as a struggle within the soul.

21: 16–19

1. The Faithful will know Pain.
2. The Faithful will know Persecution.
3. The Faithful will know His Protection.
4. The Faithful will exercise Patience.

21: 25–28

1. The Lord's Revelation.
2. The Lord's Return.
3. The Lord's Redemption.

21: 29–36

1. The Second Coming.
2. The Sacred Commission.
3. The Steadfast Character.
4. The Servant's Call.

21: 37–38

1. The Responsibility He Carried.
2. The Rest He craved.
3. The Refreshment He gave.

22: 1–6

1. The Dark Plot.
2. The Darkened Mind.
3. The Darker Preparations.

22: 7–14

1. The Gracious Preparation.
2. The Gracious Provision.
3. The Gracious Privilege.

22: 15–20

1. A Feast realised.
2. A Faith recorded.
3. A Fellowship established.
4. A Forgiveness offered.

22: 19

1. How easily we forget.
2. How enduring is the Lord's forgiveness.
3. How easily we forget to forgive.

22: 21–23

1. Is He betrayed by our hypocrisy?
2. Is He betrayed by our neglect?
3. Is He betrayed by our indifference?
4. Is He betrayed by our ignorance?

22: 24–30

1. A Holy Memory.
2. A Harrowing Moment.
3. A Humble Master.
4. A Heavenly Ministry.

22: 31–33

1. Satan leaves no-one alone.
2. The Saviour lets no-one fight alone.
3. The Saviour lets no-one fall alone.

22: 35–38

1. Want—they never knew with Him.
2. Willingness—they must show without Him.
3. To Wait—they must be ready.
4. Warfare—they must expect.

22: 39–42

1. A Familiar Place.
2. A Friend's Prayer.
3. A Filial Prayer.
4. The Final Prayer:

22: 43–46

1. The Stranger.
2. The Struggle.
3. The Sadness.
4. The Secret.

22: 47–53

1. Cowardice in Company.
2. Control of Christ.
3. Companions of Christ.
4. Challenge of Christ.

22: 55–62

1. The Conduct of a loving heart.
2. The Confusion of a loving heart.
3. The Collapse of a loving heart.

22: 61–62

1. Conscience strikes him.
2. Conscience stabs him.
3. Conscience shatters him.

22: 61–62

1. The Look that accused him.
2. The Look that reminded him.
3. The Look that broke down his defences.

22: 63–64

1. The Mockery to which He was subjected.
2. The Hostility they showed Him.
3. The Blindness that prevented them from seeing Him properly.

22: 66–71

1. The Question they put to Him.
2. The Conviction He expressed.
3. The Conclusion they came to.

23: 1–7

1. They feared the Lord.
2. They found the Lord Disturbing.
3. They forgot the Lord's character.

23: 8–11

1. Words in Vain.
2. Worthless in Value.
3. Warped in Vision.

23: 13–25

1. He tells them his Conviction.
2. He is tormented in his conscience.
3. He tramples upon his conscience.

23: 26

1. The Humiliation of Simon.
2. The Honour of Simon.
3. The Heritage of Simon.

23: 27–31

1. The Lord predicts their Infirmities.
2. The Lord prays for their Instruction.
3. The Lord protests His Innocence.

23: 33

1. He was born to save Sinners.
2. He lived amongst Sinners.
3. He died between Sinners.

23: 34a

1. Loving Obedience to the Father.
2. Love outpoured in Forgiveness.
3. Love obscuring the Offence.

23: 34b–38

1. The attitude of Irreverence.
2. The attitude of Idleness.
3. The attitude of Iniquity.
4. The attitude of Irresponsibility.
5. The Inscription.

23: 38

1. The Language of the Common people.
2. The Language of those in Control.
3. The Language of the Covenant people.

23: 39–43

1. The Desperate Cry.
2. The Deliberate Confession.
3. The Decisive Companionship.

23: 44–46

1. The World of God in mourning.
2. The Way to God was opening.
3. The Warfare of God was over.

23: 47–49

1. The Tribute of an Unbeliever.
2. The Tribute of the Undiscerning.
3. The Tribute of the Undefeated.

23: 50–53

1. The Man who did not consent to the Saviour's death.
2. The Man who did not come out on the Lord's side.
3. The Man who showed his Loyalty, too late.

24: 1–12

1. Seeking the Lord but looking in the wrong place.
2. Seeking the Lord but lacking the right faith.
3. Seeking the Lord but lost in bewilderment.

24: 2

1. Rolled away—the Stone of Doubt.
2. Rolled away—the Stone of Darkness.
3. Rolled away—the Stone of Death.

24: 13–29

1. The Lengthening Shadows.
2. The Listening Stranger.
3. The Language of Sadness.
4. The Literature of Certainty.
5. The Light of the Saviour.

24: 28–29

1. The Courtesy of the Lord.
2. The Constraint of the couple.
3. The Companionship shared.

24: 32–33

1. The Feeling they shared.
2. The Fellowship they shared.
3. The Faith they shared.

24: 34

1. The Conviction.
2. The Communication.
3. The Consideration.

24: 36–40

1. The simplicity of it.
2. The Salutation.
3. The Scare.
4. Their Salvation.

24: 41–43

1. Their hearts were full.
2. His hunger was real.
3. His humility, also, was real.

24: 44–49

1. The History.
2. The Heritage.
3. The Honour.
4. The Harvest to come.
5. The Holy Equipment.

24: 50–53

1. From Upper Room to Open-Air.
2. From Fellowship to Faith.
3. From Gloom to Gladness.

John

1: 1–6
1. The Will of God declared.
2. The Work of God described.
3. The Witness to God demonstrated.

1: 6–7
1. A Man with a Message.
2. A Man with a Master.
3. A Man with a Ministry.

1: 5
1. The Contrast.
2. The Conflict.
3. The Conquest.

1: 9–12
1. The Test.
2. The Tragedy.
3. The Triumph.

1: 13
1. Conversion: not of human origin.
2. Conversion: not by human effort.
3. Conversion: but by heavenly Grace.

1: 14
1. The Limitation.
2. The Lowliness.
3. The Love.
4. The Loveliness.

1: 15–16
1. The Privilege.
2. The Preparation.
3. The Pre-eminence.
4. The Precious Gifts of Grace.

1: 18
1. The Declaration.
2. The Divine Son.
3. The Divine Disclosure.

1: 19–27
1. A Man of Integrity.
2. A Man who Interprets.
3. A Man of Insight.

1: 29–33
1. The Utterance of Faith.
2. The Uttermost in Faith.
3. The Understanding of Faith.

1: 32–34
1. A Divine Investiture.
2. A Disclosure of Ignorance.
3. A Direct Instruction.
4. A Definite Inspiration.

1: 35–39
1. The Vision of a Warrior.
2. The Value of Witness.
3. The Venture and the Welcome.

1: 39
1. The Obedience they gave.
2. The Opening of their eyes.
3. The Opportunity presented them.
4. The Outcome.

1: 40–41
1. Andrew: his conversion.
2.   his concern.
3.   his contentment.

194

1: 41b–42
1. The Discovery made.
2. The Duty done.
3. The Distinction conferred.

1: 45–46
1. The Discovery.
2. The Diligence.
3. The Doubter.
4. The Declaration.

1: 43–46
1. The Encounter that transforms.
2. The Experience that must be shared.
3. The Excuse that was made.
4. The Enlightenment through Example and Experiment.

1: 47–51
1. The Approach.
2. The Assessment.
3. The Affliction.
4. The Amazement.
5. The Answer.
6. The Appointment.

2: 1–11
1. Her concern for everyone.
2. Her confidence in Jesus.
3. Their co-operation with each other.
4. His Command.
5. Their Contentment.
6. His Challenge.

2: 13–17
1. Instead of Worship—Worldliness.
2. Instead of Offering—Offence.
3. Instead of Devotion—Dishonesty.

2: 18–22
1. What are His credentials?
2. What a glorious conviction.
3. What a glad consequence.

2: 23–25
1. The Success of His Power over men.
2. The Secret of His Power over men.
3. The Symbolism of His Power over men.
4. The Searching of His Power.

3: 1–8
1. Wealthy but Wondering.
2. Courteous but Cautious.
3. Master of religion but misunderstanding.
4. Slave of formalism, not servant of Freedom.

3: 4–8
1. That is impossible.
2. This is imperative.
3. This is not Imagination.
4. This you cannot imprison.

3: 8
1. We cannot see it.
2. We cannot silence it.
3. We cannot secure it.
4. We cannot standardise them.

3: 9–11
1. A man unconvinced.
2. A man uninformed.
3. A man unbelieving.

3: 14–15
1. Lifted to inspire Salvation from Death.
2. Lifted to suffer for sin.
3. Lifted to inspire to holiness.
4. Lifted to inspire to heavenly living.

3: 16
1. A Holy Venture.
2. A Holy Vehicle.
3. A Holy Victory.

3: 16
1. The Love that stoops.
2. The Love that serves.
3. The Love that saves.

3: 17
1. A mighty Action.
2. A mighty Affliction.
3. A mighty Affection.
4. A mighty Atonement.

3: 18–21

1. The Encouragement of Belief.
2. The Emptiness of Unbelief.
3. The Enmity of Unbelief.
4. The Error of Unbelief.
5. The Enlargement of Belief.

3: 26–30

1. A Great Herald.
2. A Great-hearted friend.
3. A great Humility.
4. A great Honour.

3: 34

1. Authorized.
2. Authentic.
3. Abounding.

3: 36

1. If we believe, we belong.
2. If we believe not, we do not belong.
3. If we believe not, we pass judgement upon ourselves.

4: 7–9

1. Humanity of Jesus asserts itself.
2. Hunger of disciples breaks down prejudices.
3. Honour of Jesus establishes a principle.

4: 10–15

1. The Courtesy of Jesus.
2. The Concern of the woman.
3. The consternation of the woman.
4. The challenge of Jesus.
5. The conclusion of the woman.

4: 15–18

1. Her past life.
2. Her present life.
3. Her promised life.

4: 19–26, 28–29

1. Conversation continues.
2. Confusion increases.
3. Conviction invited.
4. Confession made.

4: 27–30

1. A group silenced.
2. A woman satisfied.
3. A community seeking.

4: 31–35

1. Misunderstanding of the disciples.
2. Mission of the Master.
3. Manifest opportunity before them.

4: 39–42

1. The Value of Personal Evidence.
2. The Value of Personal Encouragement.
3. The Value of Personal Encounter.

4: 44

1. Was it because of familiarity?
2. Was it because people seldom know what is good for them?
3. Was it because of the Fear of what they might lose if they accepted Him?

4: 46–53

1. The Interest shown.
2. The Integrity that was put to the test.
3. The Importunity revealed.
4. The Instruction given.
5. The Inspiration known.
6. The Incredible that happened.
7. The Indwelling experienced.

5: 1–9

1. Books of the Law.
2. Broken-hearted masses.
3. Bondage in their wanderings.
4. Born-again experience.

5: 1–9

1. The Plight of Man.
2. The Perseverance of the man.
3. The Power of man's Saviour.
4. The Penalty incurred.

5: 10–16

1. A dying Authority.
2. The Living Authority.
3. The new Authentic Voice.
4. The old Authoritarianism.

5: 17–18
1. The Criterion—Mercy knows no rest.
2. The Criticism—Misunderstanding knows no rest.
3. The Claim—Majesty and Meekness.

5: 19–20
1. Here we have Identity of Will.
2. Here we have Identity of Work.
3. Here we have Identity of Witness.

5: 21–23
1. An Ancient Creed recognised.
2. A New Claim recorded.
3. A New Criterion received.

5: 24
1. The Personal Word.
2. The Personal Relationship.
3. The Personal Freedom.

5: 25
1. The Promise made.
2. The Power released.
3. The Personality restored.

5: 26–29
1. Have we recognised the Authority of Christ?
2. Have we lived as Advocates of Christ?
3. Have we lived as Adversaries of Christ?

5: 33–38
1. John's Testimony that burnt itself out.
2. Jesus' Tribute to John.
3. Jesus, the Truth of God and Life still burns.

5: 39–41
1. The Mistake they made.
2. The Motives that were confused.
3. The Method they ignored.
4. The Man they passed by.

6: 5–14
1. His Concern for the hungry.
2. His Challenge to Philip.
3. His Choice of a lad's Offering.
4. His Command to the disciples.
5. The Consequences of the Miracle.

6: 5–14
1. He saw the need.
2. He sought help.
3. He sanctified an offering.
4. He served the others.
5. He saved what was left.

6: 15
1. The Clamour.
2. The Crisis.
3. The Calm.

6: 18–21
1. Without Christ: Alarm.
2. Waiting for Christ: Action.
3. With Christ: Arrival.

6: 22–29
1. The Lord is missing.
2. The Lord is misunderstood.
3. The Lord Explains meaning of Miracle.
4. The Lord explains meaning of His Ministry.

6: 30–35
1. Their Curiosity.
2. Their Claim.
3. His Correction.
4. His Claim.

6: 35
1. Always necessary—cannot live without it.
2. Always nourishing—cannot flourish without it.
3. Always new—can never tire of it.

6: 40
1. The Intention of God.
2. The Invitation of God.
3. The Indwelling of God.
4. The Inheritance of God.

6: 41–45
1. The Resentment they feel.
2. The Resistance they offer.
3. The Reward they refuse.

6: 50
1. Essential Life in Christ.
2. Experience of that life in Christ.
3. Eternal Life in Christ.

6: 60–64
1. A Claim rejected.
2. A Consideration resisted.
3. A Contrast recorded.

6: 60, 64, 66
1. They resist His claim.
2. They refuse to trust Him.
3. They reject Him altogether.

6: 67–71
1. The Dismay.
2. Their Decision.
3. The Deserter.

7: 2–8
1. A subtle temptation.
2. A strange tribute.
3. A suitable time.
4. A sacred testimony.

7: 12–13, 31
1. Discussion about Him.
2. Division because of Him.
3. Discretion regarding Him.
4. Decision for Him.

7: 25–31
1. The Confusion in their midst.
2. The Conceit in their minds.
3. The Conviction of the Master.
4. The Condemnation of the Master.
5. The Conclusion of the multitude.

7: 32–38
1. Unrest among the Leaders.
2. Ultimatum of the Lord.
3. Unbelief of the Leaders.
4. Unexpectedness of the Lord.

7: 40–52
1. Unprofitable Discussion.
2. Unseemly Disfavour.
3. Unexpected Defenders.
4. Unrepentant Disgust.

8: 3–9
1. The men who knew no shame.
2. The woman who had no name.
3. The Lord who was put to shame.

8: 9
1. How easily we pass judgement.
2. How easily we excuse ourselves.
3. How easily we think we avoid judgement.

8: 1–11
1. The Interruption.
2. The Interview.
3. The Iniquity.
4. The Instruction.

8: 12
1. The Source of Light.
2. The Scope of Light.
3. The Service of Light.

8: 14, 18–19
1. His Sense of fellowship with God.
2. His Sense of Freedom in God.
3. His Sense of Failure for God.

8: 21–25
1. Unfit for heaven.
2. Unable to hear.
3. Unwilling to have Him.
4. Unwise to refuse Him.

8: 28–30
1. The Offering of His Life.
2. The Opening of their eyes.
3. The Obedience unto death.
4. The Obedience unto Life.

8: 31–32
1. Look at Him.
2. Learn of Him.
3. Live in Him.
4. Liberty in Him.

8: 33–41
1. Their Pride in a name of Privilege.
2. Their Pride in the story of the Past.
3. Their Pride in Presumption, not Performance.

8: 42–44
1. The Accusation.
2. The Anointing.
3. The Adversary.

8: 45–47
1. Truth they know not.
2. Truth they care not for.
3. Truth that condemns them.

8: 55–58
1. He understands the mind of God.
2. He undertakes the Will of God.
3. He is unique in Himself.

8: 59
1. Beaten in Argument.
2. Beaten in Action.
3. Beaten in Authority.

9: 1–3
1. The Compassion of Jesus.
2. The Confusion of the Disciples.
3. The Conclusion of Jesus.

9: 1–5
1. Blind without Christ.
2. Blessed with Christ.
3. Begin with Christ, now.

9: 6–7
1. He had regard for the man's need.
2. He respected the practices of that day.
3. He restored the man's vision.

9: 13–16
1. The Pharisees: Malice at work.
2. The Man: Matter of fact.
3. The Miracle: Menace to their faith.

9: 11, 17, 38
1. Man: Witness.
2. Prophet: Wonder.
3. Son of God: Worship.

9: 25
1. The Query.
2. The Confidence.
3. The Confession.

9: 35–38
1. The Penalty.
2. The Pursuit.
3. The Preparation.
4. The Privilege.
5. The Praise.

9: 39–41
1. The new Standard.
2. The new Status.
3. The new Sickness.

10: 1–4
1. Christ issues a warning.
2. Christ offers a welcome.
3. Christ knows the way.
4. Christ knows the wayfarers.

10: 9
1. An Encounter with a Friend.
2. An Entry into the Fellowship.
3. The Enjoyment of Freedom.

10: 10b, 11, 14
1. The Proclamation.
2. The Prophecy.
3. The Pride of Possession.

10: 10b
1. The Divine Operation.
2. The Divine Offering.
3. The Divine Overflow.

10: 16
1. A World won for Christ.
2. A World Church one in Christ.
3. A World with one Christ.

10: 17–18
1. His Vision of the Cross.
2. His Voluntary acceptance of it.
3. His Vow concerning the Cross.

10: 19–21
1. The Hearing they gave Him.
2. The Hatred some showed.
3. The Hesitation of others.

10: 28
1. Now: Life Invisible.
2. Later: Life Indestructible.
3. Afterward: Life Inaccessible.

10: 30
1. One—Spiritually.
2. One—in seeking man.
3. One—in saving man.

10: 37–38
1. The Justice of His Claim.
2. Their Judgement upon His Compassion.
3. The Justification of His Consecration.

10: 39–42
1. Rest.
2. Recollection.
3. Reputation.
4. Refreshment.

11: 1–5, 20–46
1. The Request of two loving hearts.
2. The Response of His loving heart.
3. The Resurrection of a loving heart.
4. The Revelation through His loving heart.

11: 9–10
1. Rejoice in the time you have.
2. Redeem the time you have.
3. Remember the time you have.

11: 21–28
1. Love Bleeding.
2. Love Begging.
3. Love Brightening.
4. Love Beckoning.

11: 35
1. The Affliction of His friends.
2. The Affection for His friends.
3. The Anguish of His heart.
4. The Awakening because of this.

11: 40–44
1. A Pledge that had been given.
2. A Pledge about to be redeemed.
3. A Person who was restored.

11: 47–54
1. Bewilderment evident.
2. Blindness prevails.
3. Battle begins.

11: 54–57
1. A murderous plot.
2. A merciful provision.
3. A murmuring populace.
4. A miserable price.

12: 3–7
1. Mary: overcome.
2. Mary's Gift: Overflow.
3. The Lord's Acceptance: overshadowing of the cross.
4. The Spikenard's perfume: overrunning the house.

12: 9–11
1. The Object of their curiosity.
2. The Origin of their curiosity.
3. The Outcome of their curiosity.

12: 12–15, 19
1. People welcome their Lord.
2. Prophecy comes to life.
3. Peace comes to the living.
4. Panic comes to the Leaders.

12: 23–26
1. Glory by Death, not by Domination.
2. Glory by Service, not by Selfishness.
3. Glory by Poverty, not by Possessions.

12: 27–28
1. The Anguish.
2. The Achievement.
3. The Appeal.
4. The Approval.

12: 32–33
1. The Crisis.
2. The Cross.
3. The Constraint.

12: 42–43
1. Disciples in secret.
2. Discipline too strong for them.
3. Double-minded in service.

12: 44–47
1. In Christ, God challenges us.
2. In Christ, God judges us.
3. In Christ, God comforts us.
4. In Christ, God comes to us.

13: 2–5, 11
1. The Honour of God in His hands.
2. The Humility of God in His service.
3. The Humiliation of God in His knowledge.

13: 13–17
1. The Honour He acknowledges.
2. The Humility He approves.
3. The Happiness they will attain.

13: 20
1. The Master who sends.
2. The Messenger who is sent.
3. The Mercy he serves.

13: 21–33
1. All were unworthy.
2. All were uninformed.
3. All were unready.

13: 31–32
1. The Cross: Revelation of God's Love.
2. The Cross: Revelation of God's Love in Christ.
3. The Cross: Revelation of God's Love of Christ.

13: 34
1. He loves without reserve, always.
2. He loves without response, sometimes.
3. He loves without restriction.
4. He loves without Reward.

13: 36–38
1. The Loneliness that was threatening.
2. The Love that was preparing.
3. The Loyalty that was protesting.
4. The Lord who was prophesying.

14: 1
1. The Fear that is common to us all.
2. The Father who controls all that happens to us.
3. The Faith that comforts us all.

14: 2–3
1. Room for all.
2. Ready for all.
3. Returning to us all.

14: 4–6
1. Declaration.
2. Doubt.
3. Disclosure.

14: 8–12
1. The Mystery he wanted to understand.
2. The Master he did not understand.
3. The Ministry he did not understand.
4. The Miracle he would understand.

14: 13–14
1. The Promise.
2. The Pattern.
3. The Performance.
4. The Praise.

14: 15–17
1. The Example.
2. The Equipment.
3. The Evidence.
4. The Endowment.

H

14: 18–20
1. The Disciples are reassured.
2. The Declaration of Resurrection.
3. From Despair to Revelation.

14: 21
1. The Pattern of Obedience.
2. The Proof of Obedience.
3. The Privilege of Obedience.

14: 27a
1. The Peace that is positive.
2. The Peace that is personal.
3. The Peace that is permanent.

14: 27b–29
1. The Call to Courage.
2. The Call to Confidence.
3. The Call to Contentment.
4. The Call to Calmness.

15: 1–2, 5
1. The Source of our Energy in Witness.
2. The Source of our Encouragement in Witness.
3. The Source of our Enterprise in Witness.

15: 3–4
1. The Cleansing Power of Christ.
2. The Continuing Power in Christ.
3. The Communicating Power through Christ.

15: 6–8
1. Out of touch with Christ: we perish.
2. In touch with Christ: we prosper.
3. The Touch of Christ upon us: the Praise of God.

15: 11
1. The Purpose of His Preaching.
2. The Pattern of the Preacher.
3. The Privilege He has prepared.

15: 16
1. Called of Christ.
2. Courier for Christ.
3. Confident in Christ.

15: 18–20
1. Standard for Loyalty.
2. Suffering for Loyalty.
3. Such is Loyalty.

15: 21–25
1. Ignorance of God—their condemnation.
2. Incarnation deepens their condemnation.
3. Iniquity demands condemnation.

15: 26–27
1. Mercy of God in control.
2. My Ministry will be confirmed.
3. My Messengers will be equipped.

16: 1–4
1. Disciples must expect Persecution.
2. Disciples must expect to be deprived of Privileges.
3. Disciples are warned these things will happen because enemies are dead to God.

16: 4b–7
1. The Lord's Insight.
2. Their Indifference.
3. Their Infirmity.
4. His Intention.
5. His Interpretation.

16: 8–11
1. The Holy Spirit—exposing Sin.
2. The Holy Spirit — exalting righteousness.
3. The Holy Spirit — exacting judgement.

16: 12–15
1. Consideration shown—Truth withheld.
2. Confidence shared — Truth promised.
3. Comunication revealed — Truth interpreted.
4. Comprehension — Truth to the Utmost.

16: 16–21

1. The Mystery before them.
2. The Misunderstanding of them all.
3. The Meaning He explains to them.

16: 22–23

1. Now—Regret.
2. Later—Return.
3. Always—Retained.
4. At that day—Reconciled.

16: 23b–24

1. Act on My Authority.
2. Accept the Opportunity.
3. Anticipate the Overflow.

16: 26–27

1. Divine Access.
2. Divine Action.
3. Divine Acceptance.

16: 30–31

1. Their Declaration.
2. Their Decision.
3. His Doubt.

16: 32

1. Warning of Desertion.
2. Warning of Desolation.
3. Word of Devotion.

16: 33

1. Word of Compassion.
2. Word of Contrast.
3. Word of Courage.

17: 1–2

1. The Confidence of Jesus.
2. The Cross of Jesus.
3. The Contrast of Jesus.

17: 3

1. The Gift of God.
2. The Glory of God.
3. The Grace of God.

17: 4–6

1. Jesus has unveiled the Power of God.
2. Jesus has undertaken to the uttermost the Purpose of God.
3. Jesus has unveiled the Personality of God.
4. Jesus utters an unforgettable Prayer.

17: 11–15

1. The Basis of Unity: Spiritual.
2. The Bond of Unity: The Saviour's Joy.
3. The Burden of Unity: saving Grace of God.

17: 20–23

1. Unity in Christ—Basis of Evangelism.
2. Undergirding of Christ—Buttress of Evangelism.
3. Understanding of Christ—Boldness of Evangelism.

17: 24–26

1. The Vision of Another world.
2. The Valour in this world.
3. The Vanity of this world.
4. The Vow unto this world.

18: 1–2

1. The Garden: a Place of Blessing.
2. The Garden: a Place of Beauty.
3. The Garden: a Place of Betrayal.

18: 3–6

1. Under cover of night.
2. Equipped with might.
3. Overwhelmed by the Right.

18: 7–9

1. The Courage of Jesus.
2. The Calm of Jesus.
3. The Consideration of Jesus.
4. The Consecration of Jesus.

18: 18b

1. He was disgusted with himself.
2. He had disgraced the fellowship.
3. He had denied his Lord.

18: 22–24
1. An Act of Cowardice—Jesus was bound.
2. An Act of stricken Conscience—Jesus was right.
3. An Act of Condemnation—They were wrong.

18: 28–39
1. They wanted to by-pass Responsibility.
2. They prejudiced their prisoner.
3. The Pride of Pilate.
4. The Patience of Jesus.
5. The Personal Opinion of Pilate.

18: 39–40
1. The Rejection.
2. The Reminder.
3. The Result—Resurrection.

19: 1–9
1. The cruelty of the soldiers.
2. The Cowardice of Pilate.
3. The Conduct of the Crowd.
4. The Calm of Jesus.

19: 12–16
1. Curiosity at work.
2. Contempt at work.
3. Conscience at work.
4. Compromise at work.
5. Collapse at last.

19: 22
1. The Conflict in his soul.
2. The contrast in his behaviour.
3. The Conclusion he had come to too late.

19: 23–24
1. The Indecency of the Soldiers.
2. The Indifference of the soldiers.
3. The Ignorance of the soldiers.

19: 25–27
1. The Loyalty of Love.
2. The Lingering Light.
3. The Loving-kindness of the Lord.

19: 31–37
1. They thought of Tradition, not of Truth.
2. He was tortured but triumphant.
3. He was torn but was still testifying.

19: 38–42
1. Late comers to Christ.
2. Labourers secretly for Christ.
3. Last Service for Christ.

20: 1–8
1. Love impatient.
2. Love impressed.
3. Love impetuous.
4. Love's Insight.

20: 11–16
1. A Loving heart in tears.
2. A Loving heart transfixed.
3. A Loving heart turns round.
4. A Loving heart triumphant.

20: 11, 14, 16
1. Love looking down.
2. Love looking round.
3. Love looking up.

20: 16–18
1. The Greeting she heard.
2. The Grip of her hold on the Lord.
3. The Glory she shared.

20: 16–18
1. The Voice she heard.
2. The Violence of her hold.
3. The Vision she shared.

20: 19–21
1. A Place of Memory.
2. A Place of Meeting.
3. A Place of Mission.

20: 21–23
1. The Greatness of the Call.
2. The Greatness of the Gift.
3. The Greatness of the Gospel.

20: 24–25

1. Where had he been?
2. What he now heard.
3. Why he would not believe.

20: 26–29

1. Thomas still uncertain.
2. Thomas understood by the Lord.
3. Thomas went to the utmost for his Lord.
4. Thomas uncondemned for his doubts.

20: 30–31

1. The Light of Revelation
2. The Love revealed.
3. The Life received.

21: 1–7

1. Jesus is risen.
2. Jesus is real.
3. Jesus is recognised.

21: 9–11

1. The Welcome of Jesus.
2. The Word of Jesus.
3. The World for Jesus.

21: 15–19

1. Love on Trial.
2. Love's Tribute.
3. Love's Triumph.

21: 24

1. A Man of Witness.
2. A Man who became a Writer.
3. A Man of his Word.

The Acts of the Apostles

1: 1–5
1. The Continuation of the Ministry.
2. The Command for the Ministry.
3. The Credentials of the Ministry.
4. The Character of the Ministry.

1: 6–8
1. Not Place but Power.
2. Not Pride but Price.
3. Not Promise but Performance.

1: 9–11
1. The Blessing of His Word.
2. The Benediction of their Experience.
3. Behold—His Return.

1: 12–13
1. The Place of Privilege.
2. The Place of Prayer.
3. The Place of Power.

1: 14
1. A Tribute to Boldness.
2. A Tradition that was Broken.
3. A Triumph over Barriers.

1: 15–26
1. The Authority of Scripture.
2. The Anxiety of the Fellowship.
3. The Authority of an Apostle.

1: 26
1. They asked for Guidance.
2. They acknowledged the Lord's Choice.
3. They acted accordingly.

2: 1
REVIVAL
1. Continuance in Prayer.
2. Convictions in Partnership.
3. Confession of Powerlessness.

2: 2
1. Unexpected.
2. Unseen.
3. Uncontrollable.

2: 3–4
1. No explanation of it.
2. No exemption from it.
3. No experience like it.

2: 6, 11–13
1. The Holy Spirit in charge.
2. The Holy Spirit interpreting.
3. The Holy Spirit inspiring.
4. The Holy Spirit instantly misunderstood.

2: 16–21
1. Prophecy comes to fulfilment.
2. Preaching comes with fire.
3. Prayers offered in faith.

2: 22–24
1. Jesus—a man approved of God.
2. Jesus—a man attested by Miracles, Signs.
3. Jesus—a man appointed to die.
4. Jesus—a man anointed to life.

2: 32
1. This Jesus—Fulfilment of Prophecy.
2. This Jesus—First fruits of them that slept.
3. This Jesus—Fact of Personal Experience.

2: 33

1. Jesus—Ascended to Power.
2. Jesus—Authorised with Power.
3. Jesus—Appears with Power.
4. Jesus—Abides in Power.

2: 37–41

1. They were convicted.
2. They were challenged.
3. They were converted.

2: 42

1. The Basis of Unity—
2. The Blessing of Unity—
3. The Beginning of Unity—
4. The Building of Unity—

2: 43–47

1. The Mark of Revival.
2. The Miracle of Revival.
3. The Manifestation of Revival.
4. The Meaning of Revival.

3: 1–8

1. A man who was afflicted.
2. Two men who were accosted.
3. Two men under Authority.

3: 9

1. The Evidence.
2. The Enlightenment.
3. The Experience.

3: 12–13

1. Beyond us to Him.
2. Beyond Present to the Past.
3. Beyond Death to Life.

3: 14–15

1. The Accusation made.
2. The Accomplished fact.
3. The Amazing Truth.
4. The Apostolic Testimony.

3: 16

1. The Authority of the Lord.
2. The Assurance of the Apostles.
3. The Awakening of the Man.

3: 19

1. The Call to Repent.
2. The Challenge of Conversion.
3. The Consequence of Conversion.

3: 18, 22

1. Advent of Christ is prophesied.
2. Affliction of Christ is prophesied.
3. Authority of Christ is prophesied.

4: 1–4

1. Terrified of losing temporal power.
2. Terrified on hearing the Truth.
3. Terrified of breaking with Tradition.
4. Triumph of Testimony to Truth.

4: 8–10

1. A man transfigured.
2. A man transformed.
3. A man translated.
4. A man triumphant.

4: 13

1. The Boldness of their Behaviour.
2. The Boldness of their Belief.
3. The Boldness of their Belonging.

4: 22

1. It was assumed he was beyond help.
2. It was assumed he was beyond hope.
3. It was assumed he was beyond healing.

4: 29–30

1. The Menace awaiting them.
2. The Men awaiting.
3. The Miracles they await.
4. The Ministry upon which they wait.

4: 31

1. The Prayer for Revival.
2. The Place of Revival.
3. The Proof of Revival.
4. The Purpose of Revival.

4: 32–35
1. They shared a Common Purpose.
2. They shared a Common Life.
3. They shared a Common Blessing.
4. They shared a Common Concern for Others.

5: 1–4
1. The Demands of Fellowship.
2. The Disappointment within the Fellowship.
3. The Disgrace to the Fellowship.

5: 12–16
1. The Authority of the Apostles.
2. The Awe in which they were held.
3. The Awakening among the people.

5: 17–25
1. Human Opposition on the alert.
2. Divine Opponent also on the alert.
3. Divine Opportunity presented to them.
4. Divine Overruling prepares the way.

5: 29–32
1. The Principle of their Obedience.
2. The Proclamation of their Offence.
3. The Purpose of their Obedience.
4. The Power within their Obedience.

5: 34–40
1. A Providence unexpected.
2. A Persecution delayed.
3. A Principle well stated.

5: 41–42
1. The Joy in which they shared.
2. The Suffering in which they shared.
3. The Message in which they shared.

6: 1–6
1. Animosity creeps in.
2. Action is called for.
3. Appointments are made.

6: 7
1. The Spread of Apostolic Teaching.
2. The Strategy of Attack.
3. The Surprising Additions.
4. The Success of Stephen's Witness.

6: 9–15
1. Contention begins.
2. Conscience is stirred.
3. Cowardice prevails.
4. Calmness challenges them.

7: 1–53
1. The Faith of Adventure which Stephen commends.
2. The Faith in Action which he describes.
3. The Faith that angered God.
4. The Faith that angered his opponents.

7: 54–60
1. Condemned by their folly.
2. Stephen Confirmed in his faith.
3. Cowardly in their fears.
4. Stephen Content to forgive.

7: 60c–8: 1
1. Consenting to Stephen's death.
2. Conducting persecution of Church.
3. Contributing to Expansion of Church.

8: 4–8
1. Persecuted but still preaching.
2. Pioneering amongst century-old aliens.
3. Persuading the people with power.
4. Praise gladdens the hearts of the people.

8: 13, 18, 19, 24
1. Baptised but not born again.
2. Wondering but still worldly.
3. Interested but not instructed.
4. Penitent but Prayerless.

8: 26-39

1. The Obedience of a Christian believer.
2. The Opportunity of a Christian believer.
3. The Overflow of a Christian believer.
4. The Overcoming of a Christian believer.

9: 1-6

1. Satanic Enthusiasm against Christ.
2. Sudden Encounter with Christ.
3. Strange Enquiry by Christ.
4. Sacred Engagement with Christ.

9: 8

1. Overpowered—Pride brought low.
2. Overshadowed — Purpose now broken.
3. Overtaken—Leader is now led.

9: 15-18

1. The Holy Spirit Guiding.
2. The Holy Spirit Forgiving.
3. The Holy Spirit Healing.
4. The Holy Spirit Anointing.

9: 19b, 20-22

1. He confers with fellow Christians.
2. He confesses to what Christ has done for him.
3. He continues despite opposition.
4. He is condemned to death.

9: 26-39

1. The Suspicion he aroused.
2. The Sincerity that convinced.
3. The Sin he faced up to.

9: 34-35

1. The Power displayed.
2. The Person employed.
3. The Purpose revealed.

9: 38-41

1. The Confidence shown.
2. The Consternation evident.
3. The Communion sought.
4. The Cure that followed.

10: 1-2

1. The First Gentile convert.
2. Faithful Churchman.
3. Feared God.
4. Family shared his faith.
5. Flourished in Kindliness.

10: 3-6, 13-15, 34

1. God calls.
2. God confirms.
3. God co-ordinates.
4. God challenges.
5. God's children.

10: 36-43

1. Peace with God through Christ.
2. Power from God in Christ.
3. Price before God paid by Christ.
4. Pardon from God in Christ.

10: 44-48

1. God at work in Conviction.
2. God at work creating Community.
3. God at work building His Church.

11: 16-18

1. God's Promise is now realised.
2. God's Power to all is now shared.
3. God's Praise is now given.
4. God's Pardon for all is now recognised.

11: 20-21

1. The Servants of God at Antioch—Anonymous.
2. The Salvation of God—Assurance.
3. The Support of God—Anointing.

11: 22-26

1. The Movement spreads.
2. The Murmurs begin.
3. The Man who came.
4. The Man who was called.

11: 26c

1. Known by the Faith that was scorned.
2. Known by the Lord whom they served.
3. Known by the Courage they showed.

11: 27–30
1. A Test of their Faith.
2. A Testimonial to their Faith.
3. A Triumph of Faith.

12: 4, 5b, 7–11
1. The Importance of Peter.
2. The Importunity of their Prayers.
3. The Impotence of their Keepers.
4. The Insight given to Peter.

12: 12
1. A holy place of Refreshment.
2. A holy place of Reunion.
3. A holy place of Remembrance.

12: 13–16
1. Too surprised to open the door.
2. Too sceptical to believe the news.
3. Too sensible not to believe Peter.

13: 2–3
1. The Edict of the Holy Spirit.
2. The Equipment by the Holy Spirit.
3. The Enterprise of the Holy Spirit.

13: 4–11
1. The Holy Spirit directs the Advance.
2. The Holy Spirit disturbs the Adversary.
3. The Holy Spirit demolishes the Adversary.

13: 16–32
1. The Reminder of God's Providence in the past.
2. The Record of God's Purposes in the past.
3. The Realization of God's Promises in the past.
4. The Resurrection—God's Power in the present.

13: 23, 29, 31
1. Old Testament prophecies fulfilled in birth of Christ.
2. Old Testament prophecies fulfilled in death of Christ.
3. Old Testament prophecies fulfilled in resurrection of Christ.

13: 38–41
1. The Source of Forgiveness.
2. The Secret of Forgiveness.
3. The Satisfaction of Forgiveness.
4. The Surprise of Forgiveness.

13: 43–47
1. Opportunity beckons.
2. Opposition begins.
3. Obligation becomes clear.
4. Outreach becomes obvious.

13: 48
1. Praise is forthcoming.
2. Privilege asserts itself.
3. Persecution follows.
4. Protection is afforded.
5. Precious is the Word that remains.

14: 2–6
1. The Word of the Lord displeases many.
2. The Word of the Lord divides the people.
3. The Word of the Lord directs the Apostles.

14: 8–18
1. The Healing by the Holy Spirit.
2. The Humiliation of the Apostles.
3. The Honour of God's name.

14: 19–20
1. The Subtlety they practiced.
2. The Suffering they inflicted.
3. The Sermon they must have remembered.

14: 22
1. Establishing them in the Faith.
2. Encouraging them in their Faith.
3. Expounding the suffering ere the Kingdom comes.

14: 26–27
1. The Grace of God equips for Service.
2. The Grace of God experienced in Service.
3. The Grace of God emancipates.

15: 1–3
1. Rebuked and on trial for the Gospel.
2. Representing the triumph of the Gospel.
3. Redeeming the time by the Gospel.

15: 8–11
1. The Evidence of Divine Approval.
2. The Endeavours that failed.
3. The Evangel of Divine Grace.

15: 13–19
1. The Visitation of the Gentiles.
2. The Verdict of the Apostles.
3. The Vindication of the Gospel.

16: 1–5
1. The Lord's Provision.
2. The Apostle's Prudence.
3. The Lord's Praise in the growing Church.

16: 6–10
1. The Check to their plans.
2. The Challenge to alter their plans.
3. The Choice to obey.

16: 13–15
1. The Ground that is prepared.
2. The Gospel is preached.
3. The Grace that is practical.

16: 16–23
1. They encounter Opposition that is Valuable.
2. They exorcise the Evil from her.
3. They engage with Vested Interests.
4. They endure much Violence.

16: 25
1. In bonds but not in bondage.
2. In darkness but undaunted.
3. In prison but prayerful.
4. In pain but full of praise.

16: 28–34
1. The Cry that saved.
2. The Cry to be saved.
3. The Christ who saves.
4. The Christ who serves.

17: 2–4
1. The Foundation of his convictions.
2. The Faith he confessed.
3. The Faith that convinced.

17: 6b
1. A Tribute to the Power of the Gospel.
2. A Tribute to the Poverty of Pagan Religion.
3. A Tribute to the Providence of God.

17: 11–12
1. A Bible-reading Community.
2. A Bible-believing Community.
3. A Bible-blessed Community.

17: 13
1. The Power of the Gospel.
2. The Panic of the Jews.
3. The Persecution of the Gentiles.
4. The Preservation of the Gospel.

17: 15–23
1. The Disciples who are unknown.
2. The Journey into the unknown.
3. The Jesus who is unknown.
4. The God who is unknown.

17: 32–34
1. Some were unbelieving.
2. Some were undecided.
3. Some understood.

18: 5–11
1. Hearing the Word but hardening their hearts.
2. Holding forth the Word but humbled in heart.
3. Hearing a Word and honouring the Lord.

18: 24–26
1. Eloquent but not Enlightened.
2. Bold but not Born-again.
3. Knowledgeable but knowing not the Holy Spirit.

19: 2–5

1. They were believing Christians but knew not the Blessing.
2. They were struggling Christians who knew not Strength.
3. They were dedicated Christians but not delivered Christians.

19: 9–10

1. Ephesus—A Centre of Idolatry.
2. School—A Centre of Instruction.
3. Asia—A Centre of Inspiration.

19: 11–12

1. The Source of Healing.
2. The Medium of Healing.
3. The Miracle of Healing.

19: 18–20

1. They cut adrift from the Past.
2. They counted the cost.
3. They contributed to the victory of Grace.

19: 24, 35, 30

1. Saving the Silver—Demetrius.
2. Saving his skin—Town Clerk.
3. Saving his soul—Paul.

20: 18–32

1. He has preached a full Gospel.
2. He is prepared to face the future with God.
3. He pleads for faithful stewardship in the Gospel.
4. He proceeds to warn them of false Teachers.
5. He prays that their Faith fail not.

20: 28

1. Rise to your Responsibilities.
2. Refresh those who hunger and thirst.
3. Remember the debt you owe.

21: 11–14

1. The Warnings of the people.
2. The Warrior of the Gospel.
3. The Will of God.

21: 19

1. A Gospel Ministry.
2. A Guided Ministry.
3. A Glorious Ministry.

21: 30–22: 22

1. The Cowardice of the Mob.
2. The Courage of the Man of God.
2. The Claims of the Man of God.
4. The Charity of the Man of God.
5. The Confession of the Man of God.
6. The Consequences to the Man of God.

21: 37; 22: 2; 22: 21

1. The Perseverance of Paul.
2. The Power of Paul's Personality.
3. The Pattern of Paul's Ministry.

22: 3, 6, 15

1. Born in Tarsus.
2. Brought up in Jerusalem.
3. Born-again in Damascus.
4. Brought the Gospel to men everywhere.

22: 28

1. The Freedom he had bought.
2. The Freedom we cannot buy.
3. The Freedom that has been bought for us.

23: 1–3

1. Misrepresenting God.
2. Misinterpreting God's Law.
3. Mishandling God's Servant.

23: 6b, 7b, 9

1. Declaration of a basic truth.
2. Division by a basic belief.
3. Dread of consequences.

23: 10–11

1. The Lord's Compassion for Paul.
2. The Lord's Comfort for Paul.
3. The Lord's Command to Paul.

23: 12–23
1. A cruel Plot.
2. A kind Providence.
3. A careful Provision.

23: 27
1. Cruelty of Jews.
2. Courtesy of Roman Soldiers.
3. Calm of Paul.

24: 14–16
1. His manly confession.
2. His magnificent creed.
3. His meekness of conduct.

24: 25
1. A right attitude towards God.
2. A right attitude towards ourselves.
3. A right attitude towards the Future.

24: 27
1. Bound but not Beaten.
2. Bribed but not Broken.
3. Banished but still Believing.

25: 10–12
1. Faith protesting.
2. Faith professing.
3. Faith prophesying.

26: 12–20
1. The Fact of his experience.
2. The Force of his experience.
3. The Fulness of his experience.
4. The Finality of his experience.
5. The Fruitfulness of his experience.

26: 24, 25–29
1. The Fervour of his words.
2. The Fire in his bones.
3. The Flame in his heart.

27: 20–25
1. Gloom everywhere.
2. Gladness returns.
3. God intervenes.

27: 29
1. The Anchor of Common Sense.
2. The Anchor of Christian Conviction.
3. The Anchor of Christian Patience.
4. The Anchor of Christian Courage.

27: 35–36
1. He offers Encouragement.
2. He sets an Example.
3. He inspires Endurance.

28: 3–6
1. Not ashamed to lend a hand.
2. Not afraid of what was in his hand.
3. Not alarmed by what he overheard.

28: 8
1. Compassion—in person.
2. Communion—in prayer.
3. Cure—through prayer.

28: 14–15
1. The Lord has prepared a Welcome.
2. The Lord has prepared a Way.
3. The Lord has prepared Witnesses on the Way.

28: 23–31
1. Awaiting Judgement and preaching Jesus.
2. Under Authority but speaking with Authority of the Scriptures.
3. Ambition realised but for ever an Ambassador.

Romans

1: 1-5
1. Jesus Christ—rooted in history.
2. Jesus Christ—risen with power.
3. Jesus Christ—recognised as divine.
4. Jesus Christ—raised to reign over us.

1: 7
1. A Glorious Truth.
2. A Glorious Tribute.
3. A Glorious Transmission.

1: 8
1. To whom his thanksgiving is addressed.
2. By whom his thanksgiving is addressed.
3. For whom his thanksgiving is addressed.

1: 9-12
1. He prays in the presence of One he has never seen.
2. He prays for men and women he has never seen.
3. He prays for an experience both may share.

1: 14-15
1. The scope of his Mission.
2. The source of his Mission.
3. The secret of his Mission.

1: 16, 17
1. Pride in his Message.
2. Purpose of his Message.
3. Power through his Message.
4. Pattern revealed through the Message.

1: 18-21
1. The Wrath of God against Sin.
2. The Wrath of God because of Sin.
3. The Wrath of God challenging Sin.

1: 22-24
1. The folly of human wisdom.
2. The folly of human wickedness.
3. The finale of human waywardness.

1: 25
1. An ancient heresy with us still.
2. An ancient hypocrisy with us still.
3. An ancient homage with us still.

2: 2-4
1. Judgement is not our privilege.
2. Judgement is God's prerogative.
3. Judgement bypasses no one.
4. Judgement can lead to Repentance.

2: 6-11
1. Divine Reward to those who do good.
2. Divine Retribution to those who do evil.
3. Divine Respect for what we are.

2: 13-16
1. The Justice of Divine Judgement.
2. The Jewish Idea of Judgement.
3. The Gentile approach to Judgement.
4. The Jesus who judges all.

2: 17-29
1. A proud heritage.
2. A possible hypocrisy.
3. A proclaimed hatred.
4. A pattern of holiness.

3: 1–4

1. The Truth that was deposited with them.
2. The Truth they sometimes disobeyed.
3. The Truth they could not deny.
4. The Truth that will not die.

3: 19–20

1. Sin made Law necessary.
2. Sin makes keeping of the Law impossible.
3. Sin, therefore, is self-condemned.

3: 21–26

1. Not in us but in Him.
2. Not by us but by Him.
3. Not unto us but unto Him.

3: 28–31

1. A bold declaration.
2. A blessed deliverance.
3. A blessing in disguise.

4: 1–3

1. An analogy from the past.
2. An argument from the past.
3. An answer from the past.

4: 14–17

1. By Faith alone we get right with God.
2. By Faith alone we know the favour of God.
3. By Faith alone we get to know God.

4: 23–25

1. The Incredible did happen.
2. The Incredible can happen again.
3. The Incredible must happen again. if God be GOD.

5: 1

1. The Venture of Faith.
2. The Victory of Faith.
3. The Vehicle of Faith.

5: 2–5

1. Christ—Mediator of God's Grace.
2. Christ—Mediator of God's Goodness.
3. Christ—Mediator of God's Glory.

5: 6

1. In our helplessness—Christ—Supreme.
2. In our helplessness—Christ—Sinless.
3. In our helplessness—Christ—Saviour.

5: 8

1. The Hospitality of the love of God.
2. The Helplessness of those He would entertain.
3. The Heritage into which we enter.

5: 11

1. The Source of Christian Joy.
2. The Substance of Christian Joy.
3. The Solemnity of Christian Joy.

5: 16–17

1. Man fashioned for Immortality.
2. Man forfeited that Immortality.
3. Man, forgiven, wins Immortality.

5: 18–19

1. Disobedience of Adam—Sin enters.
2. Disobedience of Adam—Sin involves everyone.
3. Obedience of Christ—Salvation made known.
4. Obedience of Christ—Salvation offered everyone.

6: 8–9

1. Christ died upon the Cross.
2. Christ died for us upon the Cross.
3. Christ delivered from power of death.
4. Christ delivers us also from the power of death.

6: 10

1. Christ died: Sin's power exhausted itself.
2. Christ rose: God's power expressing itself.
3. Christ evermore: God's Evangel to Man.

6: 12–14

1. Demands of Salvation—Right Living.
2. Dedication of Self—Right Outlook.
3. Dominion of Sin—Routed for ever.

6: 22

1. Freed from Bondage of Slavery.
2. Free to serve the Saviour.
3. Forward unto Sanctification.
4. Finally—Forever with the Lord.

6: 23

1. Sin pays—Dividends.
2. Sin pays—Death.
3. Salvation is Free.
4. Salvation is For Ever.

7: 5, 7, 11

1. Sin is deadly.
2. Sin is defiling.
3. Sin is deceitful.

7: 13

1. Experience tells us SIN can be attractive.
2. Experience tells us SIN has its advocates.
3. Experience tells us SIN is abhorrent.

7: 19–25

1. The Complexity of the Struggle.
2. The Confusion within his Soul.
3. The Cry from his Soul.
4. The Conviction of his Soul.

8: 1

1. The Outburst.
2. The Overcomers.
3. The Overflow.

8: 6–9

1. If we are worldly—let us look out.
2. If we are unworldly—let us look up.
3. If we are worldly—we frustrate God's Purposes.
4. If we are unworldly—we help to fulfil God's Purposes.

8: 10–11

1. When Christ dwells within—Death to natural man.
2. When Christ dwells within—Divine Life to every man.
3. When Christ dwells within—Divine Power operates in every man.

8: 14–15

1. Conversion implies following the Father's Guidance.
2. Conversion implies freedom from Fear's Power.
3. Conversion implies fullness of Sonship.

8: 16–18

1. God confirms our conviction of Sonship.
2. God confers an inheritance with this Sonship.
3. God calls us to share His Suffering and His glory.
4. God contrasts present Trial and Future Triumph.

8: 22–25

1. The World awaits its redemption.
2. We, too, await our full redemption.
3. We will keep on waiting—Hopefully.

8: 26

1. An Inspiration acknowledged.
2. An Infirmity confessed.
3. An Intercession shared.

8: 28–29

1. No uncertainty.
2. Nothing excluded.
3. Not everyone included.
4. Nothing unprepared.

8: 31–32
1. Our Security is of God.
2. Our Salvation is of God.
3. Our Satisfaction is of God.

8: 34
1. Christ for us died.
2. Christ for us rose.
3. Christ in us reigns.
4. Christ for us remembers.

8: 35–39
1. A Statement of Christian Confidence.
2. The Source of Christian Confidence.
3. The Steadfastness of Christian Confidence.

9: 14–26
1. Is God unjust?
2. Has God favourites?
3. Does God get His own Way?

9: 30–33
1. Problem.
   How do we get right with God?
2. Proposed Solution.
   By our own Achievements.
3. Prepared Solution.
   By faith in Christ's Atonement alone.

10: 1–4
1. They were Enthusiastic but not Enlightened.
2. They were Enterprising but had not 'Entered into'.
3. They were Experts but not Expectant.

10: 8, 9
1. Salvation is Unfettered.
2. Salvation is Faith in Fact of Christ.
3. Salvation is Faith in Death of Christ.
4. Salvation is Faith in Resurrection of Christ.

10: 11–13
1. Christian Faith is satisfying.
2. Christian Faith simplifies.
3. Christian Faith is searching.

10: 14–15
1. Prayer implies a Person addressed.
2. Person addressed implies a Proclamation.
3. Proclamation implies a Preacher.
4. Preacher implies a Providence.

11: 4, 5
1. God picks His own Trusted Servants.
2. God preserves His own Truth.
3. God prevails with those who Testify to Him.

11: 11, 12
1. Failure overruled.
2. Faith overflowing.
3. Future overcoming.

11: 13–15
1. Holds down his job seriously.
2. Holds out hope for conversion of fellow-Jews.
3. Holds up before them a possible Miracle.

11: 22
1. A Fact to ponder.
2. A Fact to proclaim.
3. A Faith to persevere in.

11: 28–29
1. Unbelieving but not useless.
2. Unbelieving but not unloved.
3. Unbelieving but not unwanted.

11: 33
1. The Majesty of God.
2. The Mastery of God's Knowledge.
3. The Mystery of God's Ways.

12: 1
In response to God's Mercies, then, let us offer
1. The Worship of our hearts.
2. The Work of our hands.
3. The Witness of our heads.

12: 3–5

1. Does Faith instruct our thought about ourselves?
2. Does Faith inspire our fellowship with others?
3. Does Faith issue in service for others?

12: 9–19

1. Christian's attitude towards fellow-Christians.
2. Christian's attitude towards himself.
3. Christian's attitude towards the World.
4. Christian's attitude towards God.

12: 19–21

1. Be not offended easily.
2. Be on the offensive early with Good.
3. Be an Overcomer, on the side of good.

13: 1–10

1. We are called to be good Citizens.
2. We are called to be good Christians.
3. We are called to be considerate.

13: 11–14

1. Daylight is failing for us.
2. Dawn is breaking for Him.
3. Darkness must have its day.
4. Daybreak will have its way.

14: 1–12

1. Our attitude towards Others—Is it of Conviction or Convention?
2. Our attitude towards our God—Is it of Conviction or Convention?
3. Our attitude towards Ourselves—Is it of Conviction or Convention?
4. God's attitude towards Us.

14: 13–18

1. We have a Lord to serve.
2. We have a Love to preserve.
3. We have a Liberty to respect.
4. We have Lives to save.

14: 23b

1. We commit sin if we violate our own Conscience.
2. We commit sin if we violate another's Conscience.
3. We commit sin if we make a virtue of Compromise.

15: 3, 4

1. The Source of Interpretation: Christ.
2. The Source of Instruction: God's dealings with Jews in the Past.
3. The Source of Inspiration: God's promises for the Present.

15: 8

1. Christ came to confirm the Trustworthiness of God.
2. Christ came to confirm the Promises of God.
3. Christ came to encourage the People of God.

15: 5, 13

1. The God of Patience.
2. The God of Consolation.
3. The God of Hope.

15: 15, 16

1. A Great Claim.
2. A Great Commission.
3. A Great climax.

15: 19–20

1. The Source of his preaching.
2. The Scale of his preaching.
3. The Scope of his preaching.

15: 25–27

1. Conviction and Concern.
2. Gospel and Generosity.
3. Principles and Practice.

16: 1–2

A Quiet Revolution?
1. Phebe—A Sister.
2.   —A Servant.
3.   —A Succourer.

16: 3–5

1. Priscilla and Aquila—Helpful.
2. Priscilla and Aquila—Heroic.
3. Priscilla and Aquila—Honoured.
4. Priscilla and Aquila—Hospitable.

16: 5b–15

1. Apostolic Remembrance.
2. Apostolic Record.
3. Apostolic Romance?

16: 17–20

1. The Supremacy of Christian Teaching.
2. The Subtlety of unChristian Teachers.
3. The Sincerity of Christian Fellowship.
4. The Safeguards of Christian Fellowship.

16: 22

1. Tertius—One who was Intelligent.
2. Tertius—One who was Interested.
3. Tertius—One who was Industrious.

16: 25, 26

1. Gospel is with Power.
2. Gospel is that which was Promised.
3. Gospel is that which was Prepared.
4. Gospel is for all People.
5. Gospel fulfils the Purposes of God.

I Corinthians

1: 4–5
The Grace of God.
1. Source of Blessing in Life.
2. Source of Boldness in Speech.
3. Source of Balance in Understanding.

1: 7b, 8, 9
1. The Coming of the Lord.
2. The Confirmation by the Lord.
3. The Challenge from the Lord.
4. The Comfort in the Lord.

1: 10–17
1. An Urgent Direction.
2. An Unworthy Division.
3. An Unfaithful Distinction.
4. An Unchangeable Decision.

1: 18
1. A Strange Declaration.
2. A Startling Division.
3. A Strong Doctrine.

1: 25–28
1. Paradox is here.
2. Parable is here.
3. Prophecy is here.
4. Performance is here.

1: 30
1. Christ—the Wisdom of God.
2. Christ—the Way to God.
3. Christ—the Word of God.
4. Christ—the Word of Life.

2: 1–5
Apostolic Preaching.
1. Great Simplicities of the Gospels (*v. 1, 2*).
2. Great searching of Heart (*v. 3*).
3. Great Signs of Grace (*v. 4, 5*).

2: 9
1. Promises of God to those who love him.
2. Provision of God for those who love him.
3. Preparation of God for those who love him.

2: 12–14
1. The Claim he makes (*v. 12a*).
2. The Commission he receives (*v. 12b, 13*).
3. The Conclusion he comes to (*v. 14*).

3: 1, 2
1. The Confession he makes.
2. The Condition he deplores.
3. The Contrast he describes.

3: 9
1. A bold statement to make.
2. A bold start to announce.
3. A bold structure to build.

3: 10–15
1. The Fact of the Church (*v. 10*).
2. The Foundation of the Church (*v. 11*).
3. The Faith of the Church.

3: 16–17

1. A lofty ideal (*v. 16a*).
2. A loving Inspiration (*v. 16b*).
3. A living Image (*v. 17*).

4: 5

1. Mercy not Judgement is required of us.
2. Mysteries will be made plain.
3. Motives will be made clear.
4. Merit will be rewarded.

4: 7b

1. The DEBT we acknowledge.
2. The DOUBT we expect.
3. The DEED we accept.

4: 9

1. Last in estimation of the world.
2. Least in esteem of the world.
3. Lifted up as example to the world.

4: 20

1. This Kingdom is Different.
2. This Kingdom is not a matter of Discussion.
3. This Kingdom is a matter of Deeds.

5: 6

1. Unsuspected Dangers.
2. Unexpected Developments.
3. Unresting Diligence.

5: 8

1. The Sacrifice made (*v. 7b*).
2. The Service promised (*v. 8a*).
3. The Standard accepted (*v. 8b*).

6: 2a

1. The Fear of Judgement.
2. The Fact of Judgement.
3. The Foundation of Judgement.

6: 11a

1. Life as it was.
2. Lives as they were.
3. Lives as they now are.

8: 13

1. The Conviction which is expressed.
2. The Concern which is evident.
3. The Courtesy which is exemplified.

9: 16

1. No cause for personal pride.
2. No claim to personal power.
3. No Christ to proclaim would break his heart.

9: 24, 25, 27b

1. Have a Destination in Life.
2. Hold to your Disciplines in Life.
3. Honour your Declarations in Life.

10: 7–10

Temptations—Ancient and Modern.
1. Idolatry (*v. 7*).
2. Impurity (*v. 8*).
3. Ingratitude (*v. 9, 10*).

10: 13

Temptations are:
1. Universal.
2. Understood.
3. Undergirded.

10: 21

1. Commemoration demands Consistency.
2. Fellowship demands Faithfulness.

10: 32

1. Do nothing to offend people whose Faith is different from our own.
2. Do nothing to offend people who appear to have no faith at all.
3. Do nothing to offend people whose Faith is the same as our own.

11: 24–25

1. The Simplicity of the Utterance of Jesus.
2. The Solemnity of Unity in Jesus.
3. The Splendour of the Uttermost of Jesus.

11: 26–29
1. The Testimony (v. 26).
2. The Transgression (v. 27).
3. The Test (v. 28).
4. The Truth of the Matter. (v. 29).

12: 3
1. The Word of Instruction.
2. The Word of Insight.
3. The Word of Inspiration.

12: 4–7
1. Many Gifts but the same Giver.
2. Many Methods but the same Master.
3. Many Results but the same Redeemer.

14: 3
Preaching should be:
1. Morally Uplifting.
2. Manifestly Understanding.
3. Mightily Upholding.

15: 3–4
Foundations of the Gospel Message:
1. Revelation (v. 3).
2. Redemption (v. 3b).
3. Resurrection (v. 4).

15: 9–10
1. The Modesty of his Claim.
2. The Miracle of his Change.
3. The Mission he accomplished.

15: 13, 14, 15
1. If there is no Resurrection—Christ did not rise.
2. If Christ did not rise—there is no Christian Gospel.
3. If there is no Christian Gospel—we mock the honour of God.

15: 26
Is Death the End?
1. Yes: of ALL Sorrow.
2. Yes: of ALL Suffering.
3. Yes: of ALL Searching.

15: 33
1. The Caution.
2. The Conversation.
3. The Conduct.

15: 35–44
1. The Argument (v. 35).
2. The Analogy (v. 36–39).
3. The Answer (v. 42–45).

15: 55–57
1. Faith attacking (v. 55).
2. Faith analysing (v. 56).
3. Faith's assurance (v. 57).

15: 58
1. The Call.
2. The Character.
3. The Consecration.
4. The Conviction.

16: 1, 2
1. The Ministry to which they were invited.
2. The Method they were recommended.
3. The Means they were to share.

16: 8, 9
1. An Obligation to respect (v. 8).
2. An Opportunity to use (v. 9a).
3. Obstacles to overcome (v. 9b).

16: 13
1. Takes no chances.
2. Treasure your Convictions.
3. Tremble not because of Contempt.

16: 19
A. and P.
1. Well to do.
2. Well-disposed.
3. Well-loved (Romans 16: 3).

II Corinthians

1: 1–2
1. His Authority.
2. His Objective.
3. His Offering.

1: 3–4
1. Thank God for His comfort to know.
2. Thank God for His Compassion to experience.
3. Thank God for His Comfort to share.

1: 5–7
1. The Lord is involved in our suffering.
2. The Lord inspires our endurance of it.
3. The Lord instructs us in our suffering.

1: 8–11
1. Extremity of our Despair.
2. Enlightenment in our Despair.
3. Encouragement in our Despair.

1: 12–14
1. Conscience is clear.
2. Conduct is correct.
3. Correspondence is consistent.

1: 19–22
1. Jesus, our concern when preaching.
2. Jesus, our confirmation of the promises of God.
3. Jesus, who communicates conviction concerning life eternal.

2: 1–11
1. Not Domination but Discipline.
2. Not Hurt but Healing.
3. Not Vindictiveness but Victory.

2: 12–14
1. The Lord provides the Objective.
2. The Lord provides the Opportunity.
3. The Lord provides the Obedience.

2: 15–16
1. Christians: are we unsurpassed in character?
2. Christians: are we unavoidable in contact?
3. Christians: are we universal in our concern?

2: 16–17
1. The Standard before us.
2. The Status we claim.
3. The Sincerity demanded of us.

3: 1–3
1. Christians should be as a letter: Readable.
2. Christian should be as a letter: Reflecting Mind of the writer.
3. Christians should be as a letter: Recognisable as from the writer.
4. Christians should be as a letter: Real not Unreal.

3: 4–6
1. Not our strength but the Saviour's.
2. Not our ministry but the Master's.
3. Not of Law but of Love.

223

3: 7–11
1. The Revelation that was revered.
2. The Revelation of Righteousness.
3. The Revelation of Reconciliation.

3: 12–16
1. The Triumph of Freedom.
2. The Tradition they feared.
3. The Truth they found.

3: 17–18
1. Resurrection Glory.
2. Reflected Glory.
3. Reconciled Glory.

4: 1–2
1. His Call to Service.
2. His Equipment for Service.
3. His Credentials for Service.
4. His Confession in Service.

4: 3–5
1. Some will not hear the Gospel.
2. Satan will not have the Gospel.
3. Salvation in Christ, not in us, is the Gospel.

4: 6
1. The Source of Inspiration.
2. The Source of Instruction
3. The Source of Insight.

4: 7–10
1. The need for Humility.
2. The fact of Humiliation.
3. The Debt of Honour.

4: 14
1. A great Conviction.
2. A great Confession.
3. A great Confidence.

4: 16–18
1. The Encouragement of Hope.
2. The Endurance of Hope.
3. The Enterprise of Hope.
4. The Enlightenment of Hope.

5: 1–5
1. The Christian's Home.
2. The Christian's Heritage.
3. The Christian Hope.

5: 6–10
1. The Desire.
2. The Demand.
3. The Discipline.

5: 11–14a
1. The Open Vision: his understanding.
2. The Open Book: his Integrity.
3. The Overcoming Love: his Insight.

5: 14b–15
1. The Cross for all.
2. The Condemnation of all.
3. The Claim upon all.

5: 16–7
1. A New Valuation.
2. A New Vision.
3. A New Venture.

5: 18–19
1. The Source of our Reconciliation.
2. The Saviour who reconciles.
3. The Scope of this Reconciliation.
4. The Servants of this Reconciliation.

5: 20
1. The Man with a Master.
2. The Man with a Mission.
3. The Man well-marked by others.

5: 21
1. The Cost of Reconciliation.
2. The Character of the Reconciler.
3. The Consequence of Reconciliation.

6: 1–2
1. God works with us.
2. God works through us.
3. God works for a Decision.
4. God warns of Damnation.

6: 3–10

1. The Panorama of Troubles.
2. The Panoply of Truth.
3. The Paradox of Tributes.
4. The Parable of Triumph.

6: 11–13

1. He speaks without Fear.
2. He speaks as though on Fire.
3. He speaks in Freedom.

6: 14–18

1. We must take sides as Christians.
2. We must make a stand as Christians.
3. We must serve by being separate as Christians.

7: 1

1. The Promises we may claim.
2. The Preparation for that claim.
3. The Perfection to which we must aim.

7: 2–4

1. His conscience is clear.
2. His companionship is theirs.
3. His criticism is not for them..
4. His confidence is because of them.

7: 7–16

1. Understanding returns to them.
2. Under-study rewards the trust placed in him.
3. Unreserved welcome refreshes his heart.

7: 10

1. God can use sorrow to save.
2. World uses sorrow to separate.
3. Godly sorrow will want to make Restitution.

8: 1–5

1. They were generous in their Affliction.
2. They were generous in their affection.
3. They were generous in their allegiance.

8: 9

1. The Revelation they know.
2. The Resolution they should know.
3. The Revolution they would know.

8: 16–24

1. Initiative.
2. Integrity.
3. Industry.
4. Insight.

9: 2, 6

1. Enthusiasm inspires Enthusiasm.
2. Meanness inspires meanness.
3. Liberality inspires liberality.

9: 7

1. Generosity—Dictated by the Heart.
   (a) not drawn from us.
   (b) not a matter of Duty.
   (c) but because we delight to give.

9: 8–15

1. We can thank God for His Bounty toward us.
2. We can thoughtfully bless those in need.
3. They will thank God for our goodness to them.
4. They will thank God for the Gospel that prompted this goodness.

9: 15

1. The Gift beyond Praise.
2. The Gift beyond our Prayers.
3. The Gift beyond Price.

10: 3–8

1. The Supremacy of Spiritual Truth.
2. The Safe-guarding of this Truth.
3. The Sincerity of his Spiritual Testimony.

10: 12–17

1. A False Comparison.
2. A Foolish Comparison.
3. A Fair Comparison.
4. A Final Comparison.

10: 15–16

1. The Offer of Christ in the Gospel.
2. The Obligation to declare the Gospel.
3. The Opportunity to share the Gospel Overland and Overseas.

11: 3

1. The Simplicity of Faith.
2. The Simplicity of Fact.
3. The Simplicity of Fellowship.

11: 7–15

1. He knew what he was doing.
2. He knew Whom he served.
3. He knew who the adversary was.

11: 21–31

1. His Resentment for the Honour of Christ.
2. His Record, in the service of Christ.
3. His Resources, in the service of Christ.

12: 7–10

1. Purpose of his infirmity.
2. Prayer in his infirmity.
3. Power through his infirmity.
4. Praise in his infirmity.

12: 20–21

1. Disappointment.
2. Discussion.
3. Disunity.
4. Disgrace.

13: 11

1. Follow on to know the Lord.
2. Find Joy in His Fellowship.
3. Find Unity in His Fellowship.
4. Find Peace in His Fellowship.

13: 14

1. The Gift.
2. The Giver.
3. The Glory.

13: 14

1. Love's Expression.
2. Love's Existence.
3. Love's Enterprise.

Galatians

1: 4

1. Sacrifice of Jesus was willingly made.
2. Sacrifice of Jesus was deliberately made.
3. Salvation in Jesus was divinely planned.

1: 6–9

1. Even then there were Substitutes for the Gospel.
2. Even then there was Strife among the Godly.
3. Even then there were true Servants of God.

1: 11–12

1. Gospel is not a human Invention (made).
2. Gospel is not a human Inheritance (received).
3. Gospel is a Divine Inspiration (GIVEN).

1: 16–17, 24

1. The experience through which he passed (v. 16)
2. The examination of what that meant (v. 17b).
3. The exchange that involved (v. 17c).
4. The excellence of the consequences (v. 24).

2: 9, 10

Right hand of fellowship.

1. Symbol of Acceptance into Fellowship.
2. Symbol of Authority within the Fellowship.
3. Symbol of Action by the Fellowship.

2: 14

1. Behaviour is the test of Conviction.
2. Brotherhood is the test of Character.
3. Blessing is the test of Compassion.

2: 16 end to 20

1. Inability of Law to effect Salvation (v. 16d).
2. Inadequacy of Law to express Salvation (v. 19).
3. Inspiration of Love expressed in Sacrifice of Christ (v. 20).

2: 21

1. Refuses to reject the Love of God.
2. Regulations alone cannot make a man good.
3. Reconciliation demands a crucified Saviour.

3: 6

1. The Fact of Faith. 'believed'.
2. The Finality of Faith. 'accounted'.
3. The Flower of Faith. 'for righteousness'.

3: 8–9

1. Promised to Abraham.
2. Prevailed with Abraham.
3. Partners with Abraham.

3: 11b

1. Fact of Experience deserving our consideration.
2. Found on Experiment to be true.
3. Fountain of Evangelical Witness.

227

3: 13

1. Christ has saved us from Hopelessness.
2. Christ has been sacrificed for our Helplessness.
3. Christ has the secret of our Healing and Holiness.

3: 26

1. The Certainty. 'ye are'.
2. The Claim. 'all'.
3. The Conditions. 'by faith'.

3: 28

1. Statehood no longer important.
2. Station is life no longer important.
3. Sex-distinctions no longer important.

4: 8, 10, 19

1. Ritual is no substitute for Religion (v. 8).
2. Remembrance is no substitute for Religion (v. 10).
3. Religion has no real Substitute for true Religion is *Christ* in us (v. 19).

5: 1

1. Liberty from Bondage to False Fears.
2. Liberty from Bondage to False Gods.
3. Liberty from Bondage to False Salvation.

5: 6

1. Nothing we can do can merit Salvation.
2. Nothing we do not do can merit Salvation.
3. Nothing more than Faith—active in Loving Kindness—makes Salvation real.

5: 9

1. Despise not small things.
2. Despise not silent things.
3. Despise not secret things.

5: 13–15

1. The Announcement—Liberty (v. 13a).
2. The Admonition—Licence (v. 13b).
3. The Absolute—Love (v. 14).
4. The Alternative—Loss (v. 15).

5: 16–24

1. The ADVICE (v. 16).
2. The ANALYSIS (v. 17–23).
3. The ACHIEVEMENT (v. 24).

6: 2

1. Carrying a burden is the lot of everyone.
2. Carrying another's lightens our own.
3. Caring for others honours the Lord, lifts up CHRIST.

6: 7

1. A Proclamation made.
2. A Principle stated.
3. A Promise affirmed.

6: 9

1. A Conviction declared.
2. A Condition made.
3. A Consequence stated.

6: 14–15

1. A Wholesome Fear. 'God forbid'.
2. A Holy Fact. 'in the cross'.
3. A Whole Faith. 'new creation'.

Ephesians

1: 1–2
1. His Credentials.
2. His Claim.
3. His Courtesy.

1: 7
1. The Source of our Redemption.
2. The Sign of our Redemption.
3. The Satisfaction of our Redemption.

1: 9–12
1. Revelation of Divine Purpose.
2. Repair of broken Paradise.
3. Recovery of True Praise.

1: 13–14
1. Christ the Object of our Trust.
2. Christ, the Origin of Saving Truth.
3. Christ, ordained to Triumph.

1: 20–23
1. Raised to Life.
2. Raised to Leadership.
3. Raised to Liberty.
4. Raised to Long-suffering.

2: 4, 5, 6
1. Condemnation.
2. Conversion.
3. Conquest.
4. Conduct.

2: 8–9
1. Grace—unexpected Generosity of God.
2. Salvation—undeserved Gift of God.
3. Faith—unchangeable Goodness of God.

2: 10
1. We are Objects of Divine Craftsmanship—Creator.
2. We are Objects of Divine Compassion—Creatures.
3. Objective is Directed Service—Controlled living.

2: 12, 13
1. Condition.
2. Contrast.
3. Cost.

2: 19–22
1. Transformation.
2. Transaction.
3. Transfiguration.

3: 3, 4, 6
1. The Apostle's Claim.
2. The Apostle's Concern.
3. The Apostle's Challenge.

3: 8
1. Beyond our knowledge.
2. Beyond our calculation.
3. Beyond our finding.
4. By Faith alone.

3: 18
1. Breadth—world embracing.
2. Length—Evermore.
3. Depth—Enduring.
4. Height—Ennobling.

3: 19
1. The Paradox of the Love of Christ.
   (a) Knowledge never means all knowledge.
   (b) Knowledge of Love does not always mean all knowledge of all Love.
   (c) Knowledge of Love of Christ is knowledge of Eternal Love in Time's Expression of it.
2. The Pre-eminence of the Love of Christ.

3: 20–21
1. Declaration of Faith.
2. Development of Thought.
3. Direction of Praise.

4: 1–3
1. Consistency in Life.
2. Courtesy and Courage.
3. Consideration for others.
4. Committed to Christian Unity.

4: 7
1. God's Resources are Abundant.
2. God's Resources are Available to all.
3. God's Resources are according to need.

4: 10
1. Christ came down—Incarnation.
2. Christ went up—Ascension.
3. Christ everywhere—Pentecost.

4: 11
1. Persons with different tasks.
2. Plan of Campaign:—
   (a) Enrichment of Believers.
   (b) Adornment of Ministry.
   (c) Enlightenment of Church.
3. Purpose over all—The Day of the Lord—the consummation of all things in Christ.

4: 14–16
1. Firmly rooted in the Faith.
2. Stoutly resist Falsehood.
3. Strongly growing in Christian Confidence.
4. Showing Unity of Effort in Power of Love.

4: 22–24
1. An Act of Will.
2. An Acknowledgement of Sin.
3. An Awakening to new Hope.
4. An arising to New Life.

4: 32
1. For Bitterness—Kindness.
2. For Self-Assertion—Gentleness.
3. For Malice—Generosity.

5: 1–2
1. The Command.
2. The Comparison.
3. The Cost.

5: 5–6
1. The Wrath of God cometh because of Grosser Sins,
2. Grubby-mindedness.
3. Greed.

5: 32
1. A Great Mystery.
2. A Great Mediator.
3. A Great Manifestation.

6: 1–4
1. Expected of Children
   (a) Obedience.
   (b) Honour.
2. Expected of Parents
   (a) To be worthy of Obedience.
   (b) Set an example of Honour by honouring the Lord.

6: 11–18
1. Prepare for Battle.
2. Put on Battle Dress.
3. Pray with Boldness.

6: 20
1. Bonds of Affliction.
2. Bonds of Affection.
3. Bonds of Authority.
4. Bonds of Assurance.

6: 21–22
1. By Correspondence with them.
2. By Companions sent to him.
3. By Comfort bestowed upon them.

Philippians

1: 1, 2

The Restraint of Greatness.
1. Call themselves SERVANTS.
2. Call others Saints.
3. Call upon them Salutations.

1: 3–6
1. A Constant Source of Thanksgiving to him.
2. A Continuing sense of fellowship with them.
3. Confidence in their loyalty to the end.

1: 7

Both when
1. Denied his freedom and when
2. Defending his freedom in Christ or
3. Demonstrating his freedom in Christ, all were sharing a common Gift—the Grace divine.

1: 9

Prayer of Paul:
1. That their Love may grow.
2. That their love may grow in knowledge.
3. That their love may grow in understanding.

Purpose he has in mind:
1. That they may have a high sense of values.
2. That they may be harmless in behaviour.
3. That they may be holy in character. The Power: Christ Jesus.

1: 12–20
1. The fact of Imprisonment.
2. The fact of Interpretation.
3. The fact of Insight.

1: 21
1. His witness is personal.
2. His witness is to a Person.
3. His witness is profitable.

1: 23, 24
1. A Choice must be made.
2. Consideration must be shown.
3. Christ must be honoured.

1: 27, 28
1. Is their faith in Christ unshakeable?
2. Is their witness to Christ united?
3. Is their courage for Christ unshaken?

2: 5–9
1. Christ: Divine by nature.
2. Christ: Discarded this for a time to to share our mortal life.
3. Christ: Delivered up to Death.
4. Christ: Declared to be Saviour of all men.

2: 12–13
1. Salvation must be worked out in life.
2. Salvation cannot be earned.
3. Salvation cannot be denied though it can be rejected.

2: 25

Magnanimity of a Warrior:
1. Brother—in Christ—That was the Tie.
2. Companion—for Christ—that was the task.
3. Fellow-soldier—of Christ—therein —their triumph.

3: 2

1. The Caution.
2. The Claim.
3. The Conviction.

3: 7, 8, 9, 11b

1. New Values.
2. New Ventures.
3. New Victory.
4. New Vision.

3: 13–14

The Allegiance of a warrior.
1. Conversion still a mystery to him.
2. Concentrates on what he can do.
3. Consecrates himself to the call of God.

3: 19

1. Without consideration for spiritual things.
2. Without conscience.
3. Without concern for their soul's future.

4: 6, 7

1. The Lord is always available.
2. The Lord is always accessible.
3. The Lord is always on the alert.

4: 11–13

1. The Possession of a contented mind.
2. The Possession of a courageous heart.
3. The Possession of a Christian faith.

4: 19

1. Source of his supply.
2. Certainty of his supply.
3. Scope of his supply.
4. Substance of his supply.

4: 22

1. Christian companions in prison.
2. Christian consideration from prison.
3. Christian converts in prison.

Colossians

1: 15, 20–22
1. Revealer of the character of God.
2. Reconciler of rebellion of the world.
3. Redeemer of Sin of Men.

1: 7–8
1. A Fellow Prisoner.
2. A faithful Servant.
3. A fruitful ministry.

1: 9–10
1. That they may be filled with Wisdom.
2. That they may be faithful in their witness.
3. That they may be fruitful in their Work.

1: 11–14
1. That they may be fortified for any emergency.
2. That they may be fervent in thanksgiving.
3. That their forgiveness be realised afresh.

1: 23b
1. Continue in Faith's Fundamentals.
2. Constant in Hope.
3. Cherish the Gospel.

1: 24
1. Makes no complaint about his suffering.
2. Means to complete his suffering.
3. Ministers to Christ's suffering for his church.

1: 25–27
1. Called to serve a divine Commission.
2. Called to preach a divine Word.
3. Considered worthy of a divine secret.
4. Comforted by a divine Saviour.

1: 28–29
1. Subject of his preaching—Christ.
2. Object of his preaching—Commitment.
3. Objective of his preaching—Perfection.
4. Origin of his preaching—Experience.

2: 6, 7
1. Gospel they have received.
2. Grace that is promised.
3. Growth they will make.
4. Godliness that will result.

2: 8–16
1. Warning Lights.
    1. Humanism.
    2. Ritualism.
    3. Regulations.
2. Wonderful Life in
    1. Christ—all sufficient.
    2. Christ—all men's Saviour.
    3. Christ—always strong Son of God.

3: 1–4
1. Seek those interests that release power.
2. Set your heart on things permanent.
3. Share in the Lord's gracious promises.

I

3: 15

1. The Peace that is permanent.
2. The Peace that prevails.
3. The Peace that is the Pathway to fellowship with others.
4. The Peace of which the secret is Praise.

4: 6

Apostolic advice on approach to 'outsiders'.

1. Speech should be patient.
2. Speech should be palatable.
3. Speech should be perceptive.

3: 17

1. Be thorough.
2. Be thoughtful.
3. Be thankful.

4: 15b

1. Known by risks he took.
2. Known by the Royalty he served.
3. Known by the respect he won.

I and II Thessalonians

1: 2–5
1. The Wisdom of Paul's Approach to Thessalonians.
2. The Worth of their Achievements.
3. The Wonder of his Appointment.

1: 9–10
1. A religion that creates comment.
2. A religion that produces conversions.
3. A religion that promises compassion in our condemnation.

2: 7–8
1. The Excellence of the consideration shown.
2. The Example of the Constraint revealed.
3. The Experience of the Communion shared.

2: 10–12
1. The Example.
2. Then the Exhortation.
3. Later the Emulation.
4. Finally the Encouragement.

2: 18
1. Was it due to lack of Opportunity?
2. Was it due to want of Obedience?
3. Was it due to fear of Opposition?
4. Was it just an oversight?

3: 12–13
1. The Source of our Service.
2. The Scope of our Service.
3. The Standard of our Service.
4. The Stewardship of our Service.

4: 3–8
1. The Purpose of God.
2. The Prohibitions of God.
3. The Pattern of God.
4. The Power of God.

4: 11–12
1. A helpful Reminder is offered.
2. A fearless reputation to aim at.
3. A full recompense is promised.

4: 13–14
1. The Banishment of Doubt.
2. The Bondage of Darkness.
3. The Bearer of Deliverance.

4: 16–18
1. To fulfil prophecy.
2. To fulfil Promises.
3. To fortify personal Faith.

5: 1–6
1. He will come unexpectedly.
2. Some will be unprepared.
3. Some will be unbelieving.
4. Let us not be unready.

5: 9–10
1. The Destiny from which we escape.
2. The Deliverance into which we are brought.
3. The Dignity upon us bestowed.

5: 16–17
1. Happy in the Lord
2. Hopeful in the Lord   } always.
3. Honouring the Lord

1: 3-4

1. Their Faith grew strongly—Inward.
2. Their Love abounded—Outward.
3. Their hope endures—Upward.

1: 11-12

1. The Prayer of the Apostle.
2. The Purpose of the Prayer.
3. The Power to realize the purpose.

2: 1-4

1. The Urgency of the Appeal.
2. The Unrest of the Alarmist.
3. The Ungodliness of the anti-Christ.

2: 7

1. An Evil to be acknowledged.
2. A Challenge to be accepted.
3. A Truth to be announced.

2: 13-17

1. Chosen to Salvation.
2. Called to Sanctification.
3. Comforted to Serve.

3: 1, 2

1. The Request he makes.
2. The Revival he prays for.
3. The Relief he seeks.
4. The Regret he expresses.

3: 6-14

1. Worldliness condemned.
2. Waywardness condemned.
3. Work commended.
4. Well-doing commended.

I and II Timothy

1: 2b
1. Jesus, the Author of our Salvation.
2. Christ, the Authority for our Salvation.
3. Lord, the Authority for our Service.

1: 3–7
1. The Truth of the Gospel has its disciples.
2. The Truth of the Gospel has its disciplines.
3. The Truth of the Gospel has its discoveries.

1: 8–11
1. Lawlessness is native to Man.
2. Law is needful to Man.
3. Love is necessary to complete Man.

1: 12–14
1. The Gratitude of the Sinner.
2. The Grace of the Saviour.
3. The Greatness of the Service.

1: 15
1. Fact of Sin is to be assumed.
2. Fact of Salvation without Christ must be denied.
3. Fact of Salvation in Christ must be affirmed.

1: 16–17
1. The Enterprise of Paul's Conversion.
2. The Energy shown forth in his conversion.
3. The Example of his conversion.
4. The Excellence of his conversion.

2: 1, 2, 8
1. Priority in practice.
2. Prayer for all men.
3. Prayer by all men.

2: 5, 6
1. There is one Almighty Father.
2. There is but one Advocate.
3. There is but one Atonement.

3: 1–7
1. Piety must be practical.
2. Prominence calls for prudence.
3. Power needs patience.
4. Popularity but not pride.

3: 15
1. The Church is a divine Possession.
2. The Church serves a divine purpose.
3. The Church stands for a divine principle.

3: 16
1. Divine appearing.
2. Divine approval.
3. Divine announcement.
4. Christ accepted in the world.
5. Christ accepted in heaven.

4: 1–3
1. Failures in spiritual living.
2. Failures in sincerity of life.
3. Failures in simplicity of believing.

4: 6
1. The Conditions imposed.
2. The Commendation promised.
3. The Character outlined.

237

4: 9–10
1. The Supremacy of the Spiritual.
2. The Suffering it involves.
3. The Struggle it calls for.
4. The Saviour who inspires.

6: 3–5
1. Not Novelty but Newness of life.
2. Not Gain but Godliness.
3. Not Friction but Fellowship.

6: 6–11
1. The Wealth that awaits us.
2. The Wealth that avoids us.
3. The Wealth that answers our needs.
4. The Wealth that afflicts us.
5. The Wealth that amazes us.

6: 12
1. The Warfare in which we fight.
2. The Weapons with which we fight.
3. The World for which we fight.

6: 17–19
1. Wealth can create contempt for others.
2. Wealth can encourage faith in fleeting things.
3. Wealth can contribute towards welfare of others.
4. Wealth can be converted.

II

1: 6, 7
1. Recall our first Dedication.
2. Renew our Resources of Strength.
3. Renew our Resources of Sympathy.
4. Renew our Resources of Self-denial.

1: 8
1. Let us advertise our Faith.
2. Let us accept hardship for the Faith.
3. Let us be armed with Faith's Inspiration.

1: 10
1. Risen after Death and tribulation.
2. Robbed Death of its Terror.
3. Revealed Life in all its triumph.

1: 12
1. The Christ for whom he suffers.
2. The Christ of his convictions.
3. The Christ of his Confession.

1: 16–17
1. A Man of Encouragement.
2. A Man of Enlightenment.
3. A Man of Enterprise.

2: 3
1. The Hardness of Separation.
2. The Hardness of Strife.
3. The Hardness of Standing still.

2: 9b
The Word of God is not bound by
1. Our inherited views.
2. Our Ignorance.
3. Our Intelligence.

2: 11–13
1. A glorious conviction.
2. A glorious compensation.
3. A gentle caution.
4. A glorious consummation.

2: 15
1. Go all out to be worthy before God.
2. Go all out to be workmanlike before the world.
3. Go all out to witness faithfully to all men.

2: 19
1. Resurrection beyond denial.
2. Recognition beyond doubt.
3. Righteousness beyond dispute.

3: 5
1. Outwardly religious but inwardly rebellious.
2. A Veneer—not vital.
3. Respectable but not real.

3: 12
1. A Prediction that has come true.
2. A Perseverance that has won through.
3. A Presence that shines through.

3: 15

1. The Word of God.
2. The Work it has accomplished.
3. The Way it opens up.
4. The Wonder it reveals.

3: 16–17

1. The Source of the Word.
2. The Soul of the Word.
3. The Sufficiency of the Word.

4: 6

1. His Departure implies Duty done.
2. His Departure implies Destination.
3. His Departure implies Discovery.

4: 11

1. A Man of no mean intelligence.
2. A man of no mean Industry.
3. A man of no mean inspiration.

Titus

1: 1, 2
1. The Source of Faith.
2. The Strength of Faith.
3. The Secret of Faith.

2: 11
1. Salvation is of God.
2. Salvation is for all.
3. Salvation should issue in Godly living.
4. Salvation is a foretaste of glory.

3: 4–7
1. Loving-kindness of God—
   an Offering to us.
   in operation for us.
   overflowing for us.
   obtaining for us.

Philemon

1
1. Prisoner for a Principle.
2. Prisoner for a Person.
3. Prisoner for a Purpose.

1–7
1. He was well-to-do.
2. He was well-disposed towards others.
3. He was a witness in his own home.

10–15
1. He had run away.
2. He had received Christ.
3. He must make restitution.

Hebrews

1: 1–2
1. The Morning of Truth—God.
2. The Message of Truth—Revelation.
3. The Messengers of Truth—Prophets.
4. The Majesty of Truth—Christ the Lord.

2: 1, 2, 3a
1. Therefore: Be Diligent.
2. For: Be Discerning.
3. If: Be Decided.

2: 3b, 4
Salvation.
1. Words of our Lord—Christian Gospel.
2. Witness of Disciples—Corroboration.
3. Works of God—Confirmation.

2: 8–9
1. Sovereignty of Man—Responsibility.
2. Limitations of Man—Restraint.
3. Salvation of Man—Reconciliation.

2: 16, 18
1. Christ came to endure Suffering.
2. Christ could have avoided Suffering.
3. Christ came, also, to use Suffering.
4. Christ claims to redeem the Suffering.

3: 8–13
1. Warning from History.
2. Word concerning the Heart.
3. Witness with Humility.

3; 17–4: 10
1. Restlessness issues from Unbelief.
2. Rest issues from Righteousness.
3. Restfulness issues from Faith,

4: 13
1. None can hide from God.
2. No hypocrisy can stand up to God.
3. No escape from God's Concern.

4: 14
1. Personal Possession. 'we have'.
2. Perfect Priesthood. 'Son of God'.
3. Personal Profession. 'hold fast our profession'.

4: 15, 16
1. The Claim (*v. 15a*).
2. The Comparison (*v. 15b*).
3. The Confidence (*v. 16*).

5: 7, 8, 9
1. The Humanity of our Lord (*v. 7*).
2. The Humility of our Lord. 'Though a Son'.
3. The Holiness of our Lord. 'being made perfect'.
4. The Honour of our Lord. 'became author'.

5: 11, 12–14
1. The Observation (*v. 11*).
2. The Neglected Obligation (*v. 12a*).
3. The regrettable Offence (*v. 12b*).
4. The present Opportunity (*v. 14*).

6: 3–6, 9

1. A Terrible Sentence.
2. A Tragic Possibility.
3. A Triumphant Hope.

6: 10–12

God is not unfair—He rewards those who

1. Are untiring in Work for others.
2. Are unwavering in Witness to others.
3. Are unwearying in Watchfulness.

6: 13, 17–20

1. Promised to a Man of Faith (*v. 13*).
2. Confirmed to Men of Faith (*v. 17*).
3. Enriches the Meaning of Faith (*v. 19–20*).

7: 25

1. End of a Discussion. 'Wherefore'.
2. Entry of a Deliverer. 'he is able'.
3. Encouragement to Decision. 'seeing'.

7: 26–28

1. The Character of a Saviour (*v. 26*).
2. The Quality of the Sacrifice (*v. 27*).
3. The Consecration to Service (*v. 28*).

8: 1, 2

1. Christ—The Majesty of God.
2. Christ—The Minister of God.
3. Christ—The Mediator of God.

9: 2–3

1. Revelation to man. 'Candlestick'.
2. Response by man. 'Table, loaves'.
3. Remembrance by man. 'Incense'.

9: 27–28

1. The Certainty of Departure.
2. The Certainty of Destiny.
3. The Certainty of Deliverance.
4. The Certainty of Daybreak.

10: 17

1. The Comprehensiveness of Forgiveness.
2. The Compassion of Forgiveness.
3. The Completeness of Forgiveness.

10: 23–25

1. Let us Witness to Others.
2. Let us Work for Others.
3. Let us Worship with Others.
4. Let us Wait and Watch with Others.

10: 29

An analysis of Sin.

1. To scorn the Saviour.
2. To belittle the Sacrifice.
3. To insult His Spirit.

10: 35–37

1. The Value of Faith—an investment in the Goodness of God.
2. The Victory of Faith—an investiture of Glory.
3. The Vision of Faith—an invitation to share the final glory.

11: 6

1. The Faith that pleases God.
2. The Fact of God.
3. The Favour of God.

11: 1

1. Explanation: Faith is Confidence on which we base our hope as Christians.
2. Exposition: What is this Hope?
   (*a*) That God is trustworthy.
   (*b*) That this is God's world.
3. Expectation: Reward (*v. 16b*).

11: 7

1. Noah trusted God implicitly.
2. Noah treated God's Word reverently.
3. Noah triumphed over ridicule.
4. Noah testified in an unbelieving world.
5. Noah teaches Value of absolute Trust.

11: 8–10
1. There is a time for Adventure.
2. There is a time for Obedience.
3. There is a time for Courage.

11: 12
'As good as dead.'
1. As Abraham—so CHRIST on CROSS.
2. As Land of Promise—so CHURCH today.
3. As City with foundation—so KINGDOM of GOD.

11: 24–27
Moses forsook Egypt. i.e.
1. (a) Security
   (b) Status   } (v. 27).
   (c) Shelter
2. Moses faithful to his friends (v. 24–25).
3. Moses fearless in leadership (v. 27).
4. Moses farseeing in Faith (v. 27)

11: 32, 39, 40
1. The End of the Story. (v. 32).
2. The Examples of Glory (v. 39).
3. The Encouragement to greater glory (v. 40).

12: 1–2
1. A Great Company (seeing).
2. A great Confession (let us).
3. A great Challenge (let us run).
4. A great Companion (looking unto Jesus).

12: 3a
1. Hostility towards His Teaching.
2. Hostility towards His Triumphs.
3. Hostility towards His Titles.

12: 6–8
1. Discipline—a token of Divine Favour.
2. Discipline—a test of Discipleship.
3. Discipline—a triumph of Dedication.

12: 12, 13
1. The need for Encouragement (v. 12a).
2. The need for Enthusiasm (v. 12b).
3. The need for Enterprise (v. 13).

12: 14–16
1. *Demands of a Christian Life.*
   (a) Let right relationships be your aim.
   (b) Let right living be your objective.
2. *Darkness that threatens our Life.*
   (a) Falling behind in Goodness.
   (b) Forgetfulness of God.
   (c) Failure in Moral Standards.

12: 28–29
1. Permanence of our fellowship with God.
2. Privilege of our service for God.
3. Proclamation of nature of God.

13: 1–6
Principles to remember:
1. HOSPITALITY.
2. SYMPATHY.
3. Domestic Happiness.
4. Don't be envious of others' possessions.
5. Put your faith to Work.

13: 8
1. Earthly saviours pass on: He passes by.
2. Earthly saviours stay for a while: He stays.
3. Earthly saviours serve their generation: He serves all generations.

13: 12
1. Driven out of town—No Room there!
2. Died out of town—No Mercy there!
3. Decorated with a Crown—No Victory there for me!

13: 13–16

Called to

1. Share His Rejection by the World (*v. 13*).
2. Shun the Rewards of this World (*v. 14*).
3. Show the Redeemer to the World (*v. 15*).
4. Share our Religion with the World (*v. 16*).

13: 17

1. An Order of Obedience.
2. A Recognition of Responsibility.
3. A Plea for Partnership.

13: 20–21

1. A God of Peace.
2. A God of Power.
3. A God, the Pattern of Leadership.
4. A God who works through Persons.
5. A God to Proclaim.

James

1: 2–8

1. When faith is challenged, welcome opportunity to prove that it works.
2. When faith lacks understanding, welcome opportunity to trust God fully.
3. When faith is uncertain of God, He withholds His gifts and graces.

1: 9–11

1. The Poor have cause to rejoice: God has revealed the riches of His Grace to them.
2. The Rich, also, have cause to rejoice: God has revealed their poverty to them.
3. Both Rich and Poor alike are debtors.

1: 12–15

1. Temptation from without, when endured, brings its reward.
2. Temptation from within, when encouraged, brings its reckoning.
3. Temptation's human origin should be recognized.

1: 17–18

1. All good has its source in God.
2. God is unchangeably good.
3. Godliness is the reflection in us of the Goodness of God.

1: 19–20

1. Hasten to listen.
2. Hesitate to speak.
3. Hold on to your temper.
4. Heat of the moment never serves the good purpose of God.

1: 21

1. Be separate from Evil.
2. Be strong in the Lord.
3. Be sure of your Redemption.

1: 23–25

1. The Parable.
2. The Paradox.
3. The Privilege.

1: 26–27

1. The Challenge: Is our worship real?
2. The Control: Is our tongue converted?
3. The Consequence: is that surprising?
4. The Character of our religion: Outward or Inward? Service and Separation.

2: 1–13

1. The Exhortation to the Faithful.
2. The Example of Faithlessness.
3. The Enterprise of Faith.
4. The Exclusive Claim of Faith.

2: 14–23

1. An important question.
2. An imperfect creed.
3. An imperfect conviction.
4. An important consequence.

3: 1–3

1. Mistakes are common to us all.
2. Mastery is the concern of us all.
3. Much can be controlled by little.

JAMES

3: 7–10
1. The Impossibility.
2. The Inconsistency.
3. The Indiscretion.

3: 13–18
1. Wisdom implies waiting upon God.
2. Worldliness is the denial of God.
3. Wholesome living makes for Peace.

4: 1–7a
1. Animosity reveals inner tension.
2. Answers to prayer reveal absolute trust.
3. Allegiance to the world's ways makes us enemies of God.
4. Allegiance to God makes us the friends of God.

4: 7b–10
1. Stand up to the Devil: he's a coward.
2. Stand fast by the Lord: He's your Companion.
3. Stand up to yourself: Humility is the crying need.

4: 13–17
1. Tomorrow—unknown.
2. Life—uncertain.
3. Good undone—unworthy.

5: 1–6
1. Condemnation of Graft.
2. Corruption of Greed.
3. Consequence of Godlessness.

5: 7–8
1. The Patience that prevails.
2. The Parable that explains.
3. The Promise that inspires.

5: 10–11
1. Examples of Endurance from the Past.
2. Encouragement from the Present.
3. Enlightenment from the Lord.

5: 12
1. Let us not protest too much.
2. Let us not profess too much.
3. Let us not presume too much.

5: 13–15
1. Let us take our temptations to the Lord.
2. Let us take our triumphs to the Lord.
3. Let us take our tribulations to the Lord.
4. Let us take our transgressions to the Lord.

5: 16b
1. The Power available.
2. The Prayer that prevails.
3. The Person who prays.

5: 19–20
1. The Fact of Conversion.
2. The Freedom conversion brings.
3. The Forgiveness to which Conversion witnesses.

I Peter

1: 1
1. The Man of three Denials.
2. The Man of three Questions.
3. The Man of three Answers.
   His three-fold Ministry:
1. To those who deny Christ.
2. To those who question Christ's Claims.
3. To those who are fully committed.

1: 2
1. Chosen of God.
2. Cherished by God.
3. Cleansed by God.

1: 3–5
1. To God be the praise.
2. From God a new Promise.
3. In God a new Power.
4. From God a new Privilege.
5. In God a new Perspective.

1: 7–9
1. Beyond sight but not beyond the soul.
2. Beyond sight but not beyond Surrender.
3. Beyond sight but not beyond Salvation.

1: 15–17
1. A Challenging Standard.
2. A Challenge to Steadfastness.
3. A Call to Stewardship.

1: 17–20
1. Back up our Prayers with Performance.
2. Bought with a Price—the Precious Blood.
3. Before time, for all people—Preparation.

1: 23–25
1. The Word of Grace.
2. The Workmanship of Grace.
3. The Witness to Grace.

2: 1–3
1. Real Conversion changes our attitude towards others.
2. Real Conversion changes our attitude towards ourselves.
3. Causes Gratitude towards God to abound.

2: 4
1. A Solid Stone.
2. A Serviceable Stone.
3. A Satisfying Stone.
4. A Select Stone.

2: 7–8
1. Precious to those who believe.
2. Perverse to those who believe not.
3. Paradoxical, also, to those who believe not.

2: 9
1. Divided from the world.
2. Dedicated to the Word.
3. Divinely ordained.
4. Different from the world.
5. Delivered from the world.

2: 11–12
1. No permanent home here.
2. No policy of slackness for us.
3. No pride must mar our behaviour.
4. No perseverance goes unrewarded.

2: 13–16

1. Respect all lawful authority.
2. Respect the law of the land.
3. Respect the liberty so dearly won.

2: 20–24

1. Christians called to patient endurance.
2. Christ the pattern of endurance.
3. Christ, the power to redeem our suffering.

2: 25

1. A natural thing to do.
2. A supernatural thing to happen.
3. A superlative truth to know.

3: 8, 9

1. Let Unity prevail.
2. Let understanding prevail.
3. Let uprightness prevail.

3: 15, 16

1. Get right with God.
2. Get ready for man.
3. Get right within ourselves.

3: 18

1. The Sacrifice that is final.
2. The Sacrifice that is full.
3. The Sacrifice that won our forgiveness.

4: 1–2

1. Christ was ordained to suffer.
2. Christ would obey His Father's will.
3. Christ would offer Himself for men.

4: 3–5

1. The Past from which we have been called.
2. The Price we must pay.
3. The Punishment we may expect.
4. The Presence before whom all will give account.

4: 7–8

1. The Consummation awaiting us.
2. The Control demanded of us.
3. The Confidence expressed in us.
4. The Consideration expected of us.

4: 10–11

1. Share our Gifts to God's Praise.
2. Share our Gospel as from God.
3. Share our Goods as unto God.

4: 12–13

1. Suffering, for Christians, is not an alien affliction.
2. Suffering, for Christians, is an Alliance with Christ in His Suffering.
3. Suffering, for Christians, is an assurance of Final Acceptance.

4: 17–19

1. The Proclamation of Judgement.
2. The Place of Judgement.
3. The Peril of Judgement.
4. The Petition to the Judge.

5: 1

1. A Servant of the Church.
2. A Spectator of the Sufferings of the Church.
3. A Sharer in the future glory of the Church.

5: 4–5

1. The Promise of His coming.
2. The Preparation for His coming.
3. The Pride that protests.
4. The Prize that is promised.

5: 8, 9

1. Keep the Lights burning.
2. Keep the Enemy at bay.
3. Keep your weapons in order.
4. Keep a sense of perspective.

5: 10

1. Our Help in ages past.
2. Our Hope for years to come.
3. Our Healing now, and ever.

II Peter

1: 3, 4
1. The Source of Spiritual Life.
2. The Secret of Spiritual Life.
3. The Satisfaction of Spiritual Life.
4. The Splendour of Spiritual Life.

1: 10–11
1. Let our Conduct confirm our claim to be Christian.
2. Let our conduct confirm our character as Christians.
3. Let our conduct consolidate our acceptance as Christians.

1: 16–20
1. The Claim to be true.
2. The Confirmation of the Truth.
3. The Consummation of the Truth.

1: 20–21
1. Scriptural prophecy not derived from human interpretation of life.
2. Scriptural prophecy not derived from human intelligence at all.
3. Scriptural prophecy derived from divine Inspiration.

2: 1–10
1. The Faith always under fire.
2. The Fellowship always under fire.
3. The Freedom worth fighting for.

2: 17
1. Full of Promise but Empty in Performance.
2. Full of shadow but showerless.
3. Full of Fury but no real fight in them.

2: 20–21
1. What, by the Grace of God, a man can achieve.
2. What, by neglect of Christ, a man may accomplish.
3. What, by that neglect, a man may come to.

3: 3–10
1. The Promise of His Coming.
2. The Patience that calls for.
3. The Purpose that implies.
4. The Power that will be revealed.

3: 11–13
1. The Call to Christian Believers.
2. The Conviction of Christian Believers.
3. The Confidence of Christian Believers.
4. The Character of Christian Beliefs.

I John

1: 1–3
1. CHRIST a fact of history.
2. CHRIST a fact of experience.
3. CHRIST a fact of Eternity.

1: 5–7
1. Divine Light that ends the bondage of our fears.
2. Divine Light that exposes the backsliding of our faith.
3. Divine Light that expresses the Bond of our fellowship.
4. Divine Light that enters the soul when cleansed of Sin.

1: 5
1. It shatters the darkness.
2. It shows the way.
3. It shares its glory.

1: 8–10
1. How honest are we?
2. How happy are we?
3. How humble are we?

2: 1–2
1. The Infirmity we all share.
2. The Intercession we all share.
3. The Indebtedness we all share.

2: 6
1. The Claim we make.
2. The conscience we need.
3. The Christ we follow.

2: 10
1. Loving kindness makes for fellowship.
2. Loving kindness has no fears.
3. Loving kindness has no falls.

2: 15b, 16, 17
1. A salutary reminder.
2. A sobering realization.
3. A sure reward.

2: 18b
1. Anti-christs deny foundations of religion.
2. Anti-christs deny facts of Christian religion.
3. Anti-christs deny faith of Christians.

3: 1
1. Love beyond our desiring.
2. Love beyond our deserving.
3. Love beyond our doubting.

3: 2
1. A present happiness.
2. A precious hope.
3. A promised heaven.

3: 8b
1. Assumes tragic fact of Sin.
2. Announces failure of Sin.
3. Advertises triumph over Sin.

3: 10
1. The Contrast implied.
2. The character described.
3. The consequence drawn.

3: 14
1. The strong assurance.
2. The saving experience.
3. The simple explanation.

3: 16
1. The Love that concerns us.
2. The Love that was crucified for us.
3. The Love that claims us.

3: 20
1. The conscience that condemns us.
2. The compassion that comforts us.
3. The consideration that cleanses us.

3: 23–24
1. The Belief that redeems.
2. The Behaviour that is representative.
3. The Blessing that awaits us.

4: 5
1. The Mark of the world is upon them.
2. The Message of the world is upon their lips.
3. The Man of the world waits upon them.

4: 10–11
1. Love described.
2. Love demonstrated.
3. Love descending.
4. Love demanding.

4: 12
1. God is not known to our sight.
2. God is known through our service.
3. God is known to sustain our service.

4: 15
1. No barriers here.
2. No competition here.
3. No restrictions here.

4: 18
1. The Miracle of Love's Power.
2. The Ministry of Love's Power.
3. The Mercy of Love's Power.

4: 19
1. The Proclamation.
2. The Priority.
3. The Passion.

5: 6
1. The Son of God has come.
2. The Son of God has come to serve.
3. The Son of God has come to be sacrificed for us.

5: 11–12
1. Real life is the Gift of God.
2. Real life is given in God's Son.
3. Real life is not found anywhere else.

5: 14–15
1. Are we confident in our prayers?
2. Are we conforming to His plan?
3. Are we convinced of His Providence?

5: 16b–17
1. Some sins are beyond repentance.
2. Some sins are beyond prayer.
3. All sins are acts of rebellion.
4. Some sins are acquitted through prayer.

5: 19
1. The Certainty of the Christian.
2. The Claim of the Christian.
3. The Comprehension of the Christian.

II John

III John

1–8, 11
1. He was well-loved.
2. He was a good witness.
3. He was a good worker.
4. He must be watchful.

5–8
1. Hospitable to the Gospel.
2. Helping forward the Gospel.
3. Honouring the Lord.

Jude

1–2

1. Called to service of the Lord.
2. Kept in service of the Lord.
3. Competent in service of the Lord.

3–4

1. He appeals for strong advocacy of the Gospel.
2. He appeals to them to be on the alert.
3. He warns against anti-God activities.
4. He warns of anti-Christ in their midst.

5–9

1. A Warning from the Past.
2. The Wickedness of the Present.
3. A Word concerning the future.

12–13

1. Promise but no performance.
2. Promise but powerless.
3. Flowering but fruitless.
4. Full of Fury but soon forgotten.
5. Homeless and helpless.

17–19

1. Mockers.
2. Mischief-makers.
3. Merciless.

20–21

1. Faith for a foundation.
2. Prayer for faithfulness.
3. Hope for forgiveness.

24–25

1. Lift up your heads.
2. Lift up your eyes.
3. Lift up your hearts.

Revelation

1:1
1. From Whom the Revelation has come.
2. Through Whom the Revelation has come.
3. For whom the Revelation has come.
4. By whom the Revelation has been made.

1:4
1. Word of Divine Comfort to Whole Church.
2. Word of Divine Power to Whole Church.
3. Word of Divine Remembrance to Whole Church.

1:5a
1. Jesus Christ: Mediator of Life.
2. Jesus Christ: Emancipator from Death.
3. Jesus Christ: Imperial in Life.

1:5b6
1. The Love that condescends.
2. The Love that cleanses.
3. The Love that creates Fellowship.

1:7
1. Nothing can stop His Coming.
2. No one can avoid His coming.
3. No one can escape from His coming.

1:8
1. The One Author of Life.
2. The One Authentic Explanation of Life.
3. The One Authority in Life.

1:9
1. The Exile.
2. The Example.
3. The Evangelist.

1:12–16
1. His Word to all the Churches.
2. His Witness in all the Churches.
3. His Warning to all the Churches.

1:17–8
1. Overcome by the Vision.
2. Overshadowed by the Victor.
3. Overwhelmed by the Victory.

2:1
1. The Church by Divine Appointment
2. The Church: a Divine Possession.
3. In the Church: a Divine Presence.

2:2–5
1. He recognizes their zeal.
2. He recognizes their zealous regard for Goodness.
3. He recognizes their zealous regard for Truth.
4. He rebukes them for their lack of Love.
5. He recalls them to Fundamentals.

2:8–10
1. Always present to comfort.
2. Always prevailing to convince of triumph.
3. Always praying that we be faithful.
4. Always perfecting our Witness.

256

2: 12–3

1. The Power of Christ risen.
2. The Praise He gives.
3. The Place in which they must endure.
4. The Patience they have exercised.

2: 14–6

1. Are they consenting to Evil?
2. Are they concerned about weaker brethren?
3. Are they converted truly to the Lord?

2: 18

1. The Son of God risen.
2. The Son of God recording.
3. The Son of God ready for action.

2: 19–23

1. Encouragement is given.
2. Entreaty is made.
3. Enmity is recognised.
4. Estrangement and Exclusion.

2: 26–28

1. The Supremacy of their Experience.
2. The Steadfastness of their Obedience.
3. The Certainty of their Endurance.
4. The Sureness of their Encounter.

3: 1–6

1. The Condemnation.
2. The Concern.
3. The Challenge.
4. The Consideration.
5. The Comfort.

3: 7

1. A Faith to inspire.
2. A Foundation upon which to build.
3. A Fellowship to be sure of.

3: 8–10

1. They have been saved to Serve.
2. They are small; but steadfast in Christ's Love.
3. They are unimportant, may be, but unconquerable.
4. They have kept the Faith: that will be honoured by the Lord.

3: 12–13

1. The Gift of Consecration.
2. The Gift of Courage.
3. The Gift of Confession in Christ's Service.

3: 14–16

1. Inspired Authority.
2. Insipid Allegiance.
3. Inevitable Affliction.

3: 17–19

1. They were Prosperous but did not know they were Poor.
2. They were Independent but did not know they were Ignorant.
3. They were Arrogant but not Abandoned.

3: 20

1. The Patience of Christ.
2. The Person Christ seeks.
3. The Purpose of Christ.

4: 1–2

1. Anticipation.
2. Access.
3. Authority.

4: 3–6a

1. Symbolic of Salvation.
2. Symbolic of Storm.
3. Symbolic of Scale of Salvation.
4. Symbolic of Serenity.

4: 6b–7

1. Our God is a Lord of Power.
2. Our God is a Lord of Patience.
3. Our God deals with us Personally.
4. God is Praiseworthy and will prevail.

4: 8

1. Our God is not incapable.
2. Our God is not indifferent.
3. Our God is not unworthy.

4: 9–11
1. The Testimony of Nature.
2. The Testimony of the Church.
3. The Tribute of Faith.

5: 1
1. There is a Divine Purpose for the world.
2. There is a Bountiful Purpose for the world.
3. There is an unalterable Purpose for the world.

5: 2–5
1. The Question—can God be known?
2. The Confession—man unaided cannot discover God.
3. The Consolation—God makes Himself known.

5: 6
1. Christ—satisfies the hopes of the past.
2. Christ—sacrificed but strong to save.
3. Christ—silent but shining upon the world for ever.

5: 7–11
1. He acts with authority.
2. He accepts their praise.
3. He has accomplished salvation.
4. He authorises personal approach to God, most High.

5: 12 (1)
1. Christ—the Power of God—to save.
2. Christ—the Power of God—to sustain.
3. Christ—the Power of God—to sanctify.

5: 12 (2)
1. Christ—the riches of God—to redeem the promises.
2. Christ—the riches of God—to redeem our poverty.
3. Christ—the riches of God—to redeem our pain.

5: 12 (3)
1. Christ—the Wisdom of God—to lighten our darkness.
2. Christ—the Wisdom of God—to liberate our fears.
3. Christ—the Wisdom of God—to lead us unto life.

5: 12 (4)
1. Christ—the Strength of God—to overthrow evil.
2. Christ—the Strength of God—to overcome temptation.
3. Christ—the Strength of God—to overshadow our weakness.

5: 12 (5)
1. Christ—the Honour of God—worthy of Worship.
2. Christ—the Honour of God—worthy of Witness.
3. Christ—the Honour of God—to withstand the World.

5: 12 (6)
1. Christ—the Glory of God—seen in His Birth.
2. Christ—the Glory of God—seen in His Life.
3. Christ—the Glory of God—seen in His Death.
4. Christ—the Glory of God—seen in His Resurrection.

5: 12 (7)
1. Christ—the Blessing of God—in the Gospel He brings.
2. Christ—the Blessing of God—in the Grace He reveals.
3. Christ—the Blessing of God—in the Goodness He shares.

6: 1–17
1. A Vision of a Famine of Happiness.
2. A Vision of a Famine of Peace.
3. A Vision of a Famine of Food.
4. A Vision of a Famine of Health.
5. A Vision of a Famine of Hope.
6. A Vision of a Famine of Confidence.

7: 1–10

1. The Coming Provocation.
2. The Comforting Provision.
3. The Companions in Praise.

7: 13–17

1. The Vision continued.
2. The Virtue conferred.
3. The Victory confirmed.
4. The Vow of Consolation.

8: 1, 3–5

1. Where Prayers are expected.
2. Prayers that rise from the Earth.
3. Prayers that return to the Earth.

8: 6

1. The Call to Attention.
2. The Call to Arms.
3. The Call to Action.

8: 7–12

1. Man must expect Judgement.
2. Mercy is greater than Judgement.
3. Mercy calls for Justice also.

8: 13

1. The Lord's Ways are sometimes unexpected.
2. The Lord's Ways are sometimes unseen.
3. The Lord's Ways are sometimes unfettered.

9: 1–6

1. The Mischief caused by Sin.
2. The Misery caused by Sin.
3. The Mercy despite our Sin.

9: 20–21

1. They had been delivered but denied the Deliverer.
2. They had been blessed but were still Blind.
3. They had been warned but were still wicked.

10: 1–2

1. The Mystery of God.
2. The Majesty of Christ.
3. The Manuscript of Revelation.
4. The Measure of Grace.

10: 9–11

1. The Message of God has been revealed for Life.
2. The Message of God must be realized in Life.
3. The Message of God must be repeatedly proclaimed.

11: 1–2

1. The Preservation of the Faithful.
2. The Persecution of the Faithful.
3. The Perseverance of the Faithful.

11: 7–13

1. The Stern struggle between Evil and Good.
2. The Seeming Success of Evil over Good.
3. The Celebration of Evil over Good.
4. The Surprise of Evil by Good.

11: 15–19

1. Prophecy ultimately realized.
2. Praise rendered by the whole Church.
3. Preservation of the Faithful promised.
4. Panorama of God's Glory unveiled.

12: 1–6

1. The Vision of Advent.
2. The Vicious Adversary.
3. The Victory announced.

12: 7–11

1. The Conflict waged.
2. The Conquest won.
3. The Confidence restored.

12: 13–17

1. Beaten but not broken.
2. Persecuted but not powerless.
3. Punished but preserved.

13: 1–18

1. Persecution symbolised by Roman Power.
2. Paganism symbolised by Roman Practices.
3. Purpose of God symbolised by Patience of His People.

14: 1

1. The Mark of Divine Possession.
2. The Mark of Patriotism in the Kingdom.
3. The Mark of Protection from the Evil One.
4. The Mark of Purchase by the Possessor.
5. The Mark of Providence within the Kingdom.

14: 2

1. The Voice of God—Deep—Meaningful.
2. The Voice of God—Decisive—Masterful.
3. The Voice of God—Delightful—Melodious.

14: 3–5

1. Out of Tribulation a new Tribute of Praise.
2. Out of Fellowship a New Faith.
3. Out of Sacrifice a new Certainty.

14: 6

1. The Good News for all Time.
2. The Good News for all Men.
3. The Good News for all circumstances.

14: 7

1. The Call to Worship.
2. The Challenge to Worship.
3. The Creator whom we worship.

14: 8

1. The Contrast.
2. The Collapse.
3. The Cause.

14: 9–12

1. The great need for Christian Witness.
2. The great Wickedness.
3. The great Work to be done.

14: 13

1. The Happy Warrior.
2. The Heart of the Warrior.
3. The Heritage of the Warrior.

14: 14–20

1. The Christ of Glory.
2. The Christ of Judgement,
3. The Contrasting Judgements.
4. The Completeness of the Judgement.

15: 2–4

1. At the last, Faith is justified.
2. At the last, Hopes are realized.
3. At the last, Love is triumphant.

15:5–8

1. Man is reminded of the Eternal Law of God.
2. Man is rebuked by the Eternal Law of God.
3. Man cannot run away from the Law of God.
4. Man cannot restrain the Law of God.

16: 1–21

1. Punished but still unrepentant.
2. Provided for but still unbelieving.
3. Pleaded with but still unmoved.

16: 13–15

1. The Temptation to surrender Faith.
2. The Temptation to succumb to Falsehood.
3. The Triumph awaiting the Faithful.

17: 14

1. The Adversaries of the Lord.
2. The Achievement of the Lord.
3. The Allies of the Lord.

18: 1–3
1. The Light from which he came.
2. The Light that shone.
3. The Light that shattered the darkness.

18: 4–5
1. The Iniquity around them.
2. The Invitation they receive.
3. The Integrity they must safeguard.

18: 6–16
1. Indulgence creates Injustices.
2. Pride kills Pity.
3. Prosperity can create Poverty.
4. Luxury can kill love.

18: 17–20
1. From Plenty to Poverty.
2. From Prosperity to Self-Pity.
3. From Possessions to Persons.

18: 20
1. Judgement belongs to God.
2. Justice we may expect from God.
3. Joy we receive from God.

18: 21–24
1. Powerful but Pagan.
2. Prosperous but Proud.
3. Civilised but now Silent.

19: 1–2
1. The Salvation of God calls for Thanksgiving.
2. The Glory of God calls for our Testimony.
3. The Honour of God calls for our Thoughtfulness.
4. The Power of God calls for our Trust.

19: 5
1. God is worthy of Praise.
2. God is worthy of the Witness of the Prophets.
3. God is worthy of the Witness of all Peoples.

19: 6
1. An Exclamation of Faith.
2. An Encouragement to the Faithful.
3. An Enlightenment of the Faithful.

19: 7–8
1. The Tribute of Praise.
2. The Trysting Place.
3. The Triumph of the Pilgrims.

19: 9
1. A Love to be cherished.
2. A Love to be shared.
3. A Love that glows.
4. A Love that never fails.

19: 10
1. The Mysterious Revelation.
2. The Mistaken Response.
3. The Master Responsibility.

19: 11
1. The Risen Christ—in Command.
2. The Risen Christ—our Confidence.
3. The Risen Christ—our real Communion.
4. The Risen Christ—our Conscience.

19: 12
1. His Judgement is for all.
2. His Rule is over all.
3. His Nature is beyond all.

19: 13
1. Christ risen—The Word of Power.
2. Christ risen—the Word of Pardon.
3. Christ risen—the Word of Promise.
4. Christ risen—the Word of Peace.

19: 14–16
1. The Unseen Resources.
2. The Unexpected Retribution.
3. The Unchallenged Royalty.

20: 1-3
1. Conquest of Evil is the divine Prerogative.
2. Conquest of Evil calls for Disciples' Partnership.
3. Conquest of Evil calls for Disciplined Patience.

20: 4-6
1. They were martyred but Masters of Life.
2. They were victims of evil but now are Victorious.
3. They were vanquished but are now vindicated.
4. They were Fearless and now know Christ's Fellowship.

20: 7-10
1. After Rest—Rebellion against God.
2. After Despair—Deliverance.
3. After Horror—Hallelujah.

20: 11
1. The Excellence of Personal Purity.
2. The Expulsive Power of Personal Purity.
3. The Example of Personal Purity.

20: 12-15
1. None so great as to escape the Judgement of God.
2. None so small as to be exempt from the Justice of God.
3. None so wicked as to be beyond Justice.
4. None so worthy as to be beyond Judgement.

21: 1
1. A New world for new People.
2. A New Faith for new Fellowship.
3. A New Favour for ancient Fear.

21: 2
1. The Home of Faithful Hearts.
2. The Hope of Faithful Hearts.
3. The Happiness of Faithful Hearts.

21: 3
1. The Holy Basis of our Faith.
2. The Wholesome Blessing of our Fellowship.
3. The Healing Balm of our Fellowship.

21: 5-6
1. The Divine Competence.
2. The Divine Conclusion.
3. The Divine Confession.
4. The Divine Compassion.

21: 7-8
1. The Privilege of Fellowship and the Price.
2. The Promise of Fellowship and the Possession.
3. The Poverty and the Penalty.

21: 9-10
1. The Clearer the air, the greater the Vision.
2. The Cleaner the Life, the clearer the Vision.
3. The Companions of Light, the Confirmation of the Vision.

21: 12
1. The Church of God—unique in herself.
2. The Church of God—unbroken in her story.
3. The Church of God—Universal in her appeal.

21: 13
1. The Church's Welcome to the Energy of the Young.
2. The Church's Welcome to the Enquiring Minds of men.
3. The Church's Welcome to the Enterprise of the Successful.
4. The Church's Welcome to those in the Eventide of life.

21: 14–21

1. The Kingdom—Large enough for all.
2. The Kingdom—Low enough for all.
3. The Kingdom—Lovely enough for all.

21: 22–26

1. Not now a Consecrated Place but Communion always.
2. Not Natural Light but Supernatural.
3. Not Nationalism but Supernationalism.

22: 1–2

1. Out of Communion, Cleansing for all.
2. Out of Communion, Contributions from all.
3. Out of Communion, Consolation for all.

22: 3–5

1. The Burden is lifted.
2. The Barrier is lifted.
3. The Blessing is their Legacy.

22: 10–14

1. Proclaim the news of Goodness Triumphant.
2. Proclaim the News of the Last Chance.
3. Proclaim the News of Promised Reward.
4. Proclaim the News of the all-sufficient Grace.

22: 16

1. The Personal Word.
2. The Prophetic Word.
3. The Perpetual Word.

22: 17

1. The Message of Christ.
2. The Message to Christians.
3. The Message to the unconverted.

22: 20–21

1. The Saviour's Promise.
2. The Simple Prayer.
3. The Saving Power.

PRINTED IN GREAT BRITAIN BY
LOWE AND BRYDONE (PRINTERS) LTD., THETFORD, NORFOLK

DATE DUE

251.02 Da
Dalton, Arthur C.
Brief & to the Point: Suggestions for
Preachers

DATE	ISSUED TO

251.02 Da
Dalton, Arthur C.
Brief & to the Point: Suggestions for
Preachers